Katherine Mansfield

Historicizing Modernism

Historicizing Modernism challenges traditional literary interpretations by taking an empirical approach to modernist writing: a direct response to new documentary sources made available over the last decade.

Informed by archival research, and working beyond the usual European/American avant-garde 1900–45 parameters, this series reassesses established readings of modernist writers by developing fresh views of intellectual contexts and working methods.

Series Titles

Arun Kolatkar and Literary Modernism in India, Laetitia Zecchini
British Literature and Classical Music, David Deutsch
Broadcasting in the Modernist Era, Matthew Feldman, Henry Mead and Erik Tonning
Charles Henri Ford, Alexander Howard
Chicago and the Making of American Modernism, Michelle E. Moore
Ezra Pound's Adams Cantos, David Ten Eyck
Ezra Pound's Eriugena, Mark Byron
Great War Modernisms and The New Age *Magazine*, Paul Jackson

James Joyce and Absolute Music, Michelle Witen
James Joyce and Catholicism, Chrissie van Mierlo
John Kasper and Ezra Pound, Alec Marsh
Katherine Mansfield and Literary Modernism, Edited by Janet Wilson, Gerri Kimber and Susan Reid
Late Modernism and the English Intelligencer, Alex Latter
The Life and Work of Thomas MacGreevy, Susan Schreibman
Literary Impressionism, Rebecca Bowler
Modern Manuscripts, Dirk Van Hulle
Modernism at the Microphone, Melissa Dinsman
Modernist Lives, Claire Battershill
The Politics of 1930s British Literature, Natasha Periyan
Reading Mina Loy's Autobiographies, Sandeep Parmar
Reframing Yeats, Charles Ivan Armstrong
Samuel Beckett and Arnold Geulincx, David Tucker
Samuel Beckett and the Bible, Iain Bailey
Samuel Beckett and Cinema, Anthony Paraskeva
Samuel Beckett's 'More Pricks than Kicks', John Pilling
Samuel Beckett's German Diaries 1936–1937, Mark Nixon
T. E. Hulme and the Ideological Politics of Early Modernism, Henry Mead
Virginia Woolf's Late Cultural Criticism, Alice Wood
Christian Modernism in an Age of Totalitarianism, Jonas Kurlberg
Samuel Beckett and Experimental Psychology, Joshua Powell
Samuel Beckett in Confinement, James Little

Upcoming titles
Samuel Beckett and Science, Chris Ackerley

Katherine Mansfield

New Directions

Edited by
Aimée Gasston, Gerri Kimber and Janet Wilson

BLOOMSBURY ACADEMIC
LONDON • NEW YORK • OXFORD • NEW DELHI • SYDNEY

BLOOMSBURY ACADEMIC
Bloomsbury Publishing Plc
50 Bedford Square, London, WC1B 3DP, UK
1385 Broadway, New York, NY 10018, USA

BLOOMSBURY, BLOOMSBURY ACADEMIC and the Diana logo are trademarks of
Bloomsbury Publishing Plc

First published in Great Britain 2020

Cover design: Eleanor Rose

A catalogue record for this book is available from the British Library.

Library of Congress Cataloging-in-Publication Data
Names: Gasston, Aimée, editor. | Kimber, Gerri, editor. | Wilson, Janet, 1948- editor.
Title: Katherine Mansfield: new directions / edited by Aimée Gasston,
Gerri Kimber and Janet Wilson.
Description: London; New York: Bloomsbury Academic, 2020. |
Series: Historicizing modernism | Includes bibliographical references. |
Katherine M Identifiers: LCCN 2020010880 (print) | LCCN 2020010881 (ebook) |
ISBN 9781350135505 (hardback) | ISBN 9781350135512 (ePDF) |
ISBN 9781350135529 (eBook)
Subjects: LCSH: Mansfield, Katherine, 1888-1923–Criticism and
interpretation. | Modernism (Literature)
Classification: LCC PR9639.3.M258 Z73226 2020 (print) |
LCC PR9639.3.M258 (ebook) | DDC 823/.912–dc23
LC record available at https://lccn.loc.gov/2020010880
LC ebook record available at https://lccn.loc.gov/2020010881

ISBN: HB: 978-1-3501-3550-5
ePDF: 978-1-3501-3551-2
eBook: 978-1-3501-3552-9

Series: Historicizing Modernism

Typeset by Deanta Global Publishing Services, Chennai, India

To find out more about our authors and books visit www.bloomsbury.com
and sign up for our newsletters.

Contents

Figures

Contributors

Erika Baldt is Associate Professor and Liberal Arts Division Chair at Rowan College, Burlington County, a community college in New Jersey, where she teaches composition and literature. Her research interests include Anglo-American modernism and cosmopolitanism, and she has published several essays on Katherine Mansfield and her contemporaries.

Elleke Boehmer is Professor of World Literature in English at the University of Oxford, and a Professorial Governing Body Fellow at Wolfson College. She is an acclaimed novelist and a founding figure in the field of postcolonial studies, internationally recognized for her research in colonial and postcolonial literature and theory.

Enda Duffy is Arnhold Presidential Department Chair of English at the University of California Santa Barbara. He is the author of *The Subaltern Ulysses* (1996) and *The Speed Handbook: Velocity, Pleasure, Modernism* (2009), which won the Modernist Studies Association Prize for the best book in Modernist Studies.

Aimée Gasston is Postdoctoral Research Fellow at the Institute of English Studies, School of Advanced Study, University of London. She has published on Katherine Mansfield, Virginia Woolf and Elizabeth Bowen, and was a Harry Ransom Fellow in 2018.

Nick Hocking completed a PhD on paternal figures in the work of Djuna Barnes at Birkbeck, University of London, within recent memory, following which he earns a living however he can while undergoing extensive psychotherapy.

Kathleen Jones is a poet, biographer and novelist, whose subjects include Katherine Mansfield, Norman Nicholson, Catherine Cookson, Christina Rossetti and the women of the Wordsworth and Coleridge families. Kathleen worked in broadcast journalism and is the author of two novels and four collections of poetry. She is currently the Royal Literary Fund Fellow at Teesside University, UK.

Katie L. Jones is an AHRC-funded PhD candidate at the University of Nottingham, UK, completing her thesis on Katherine Mansfield's engagements with literary culture and the literary marketplace. Her research explores the compositional and publication histories of Mansfield's texts, analysing the works in their original sites of publication. She is editor of the University of Nottingham's D. H. Lawrence Research Centre website.

Gerri Kimber, Visiting Professor at the University of Northampton, UK, is co-editor of *Katherine Mansfield Studies* and Chair of the Katherine Mansfield Society. She is the deviser and series editor of the four-volume *Edinburgh Edition of the Collected Works of Katherine Mansfield* (2012–16), and is the author or editor of a further twenty volumes on Mansfield.

William Kupinse is Professor of English at the University of Puget Sound, Tacoma, Washington, USA. He has published articles on environmental topics in texts by modernist writers from H. G. Wells to G. V. Desani. Recent work includes an article in the *James Joyce Quarterly* on discourses of sustainability in *Ulysses* and a chapter on Herbert Read's *The Green Child.*

Ann Herndon Marshall has written on Elizabeth von Arnim, Katherine Mansfield and Vita Sackville-West. One recent essay appears in *Katherine Mansfield Studies* (2019) and another in a forthcoming volume, *Modernism Revisited.* She lives in Charlottesville, Virginia, where she loves to walk and garden.

Alex Moffett is Associate Professor of English Literature at Providence College in Rhode Island, United States, where he teaches twentieth-century British and Irish fiction. He has published a number of articles on Katherine Mansfield and his book review of recent Mansfield scholarship appears in the Winter 2018 issue of *The Journal of Modern Literature.*

Chris Mourant is Lecturer in Early Twentieth-Century English Literature and Co-Director of the Centre for Modernist Cultures at the University of Birmingham, UK. He is a previous recipient of the Katherine Mansfield Society Essay Prize and is the author of *Katherine Mansfield and Periodical Culture* (2019).

Ruchi Mundeja is Associate Professor in the Department of English at Lakshmibai College, University of Delhi, India. Her research is in the areas of modernist and postcolonial literatures, with special focus on women's writing. She has published in *Katherine Mansfield and the Bloomsbury Group* (2017) and *Re-forming World Literature: Katherine Mansfield and the Modernist Short Story* (2018)

Ali Smith, CBE, is a fellow of the Royal Society of Literature, writer of novels, plays and short stories and winner of the Goldsmiths and Baileys Prize and the Costa Book Award for Best Novel.

Janet M. Wilson is Professor of English and Postcolonial Studies at the University of Northampton, UK. She recently co-edited *Re-forming World Literature: Katherine Mansfield and the Modernist Short Story* (2018) and edited *The General and the Nightingale: Dan Davin's War Stories* (2020). She is Vice-Chair of the Katherine Mansfield Society.

Editorial preface to Historicizing Modernism

This book series is devoted to the analysis of late-nineteenth- to twentieth-century literary modernism within its historical contexts. Historicizing Modernism therefore stresses empirical accuracy and the value of primary sources (such as letters, diaries, notes, drafts, marginalia or other archival materials) in developing monographs and edited collections on modernist literature. This may take a number of forms, such as manuscript study and genetic criticism, documenting interrelated historical contexts and ideas and exploring biographical information. To date, no book series has fully laid claim to this interdisciplinary, source-based territory for modern literature. While the series addresses itself to a range of key authors, it also highlights the importance of non-canonical writers with a view to establishing broader intellectual genealogies of modernism. Furthermore, while the series is weighted towards the English-speaking world, studies of non-Anglophone modernists whose writings are open to fresh historical exploration are also included.

A key aim of the series is to reach beyond the familiar rhetoric of intellectual and artistic 'autonomy' employed by many modernists and their critical commentators. Such rhetorical moves can and should themselves be historically situated and reintegrated into the complex continuum of individual literary practices. It is our intent that the series' emphasis upon the contested self-definitions of modernist writers, thinkers and critics may, in turn, prompt various reconsiderations of the boundaries delimiting the concept of 'modernism' itself. Indeed, the concept of 'historicizing' is itself debated across its volumes, and the series by no means discourages more theoretically informed approaches. On the contrary, the editors hope that the historical specificity encouraged by Historicizing Modernism may inspire a range of fundamental critiques along the way.

Matthew Feldman
Erik Tonning

Acknowledgements

Most hearty thanks must go to our authors whose role as contributors has been characterized by generosity. Special thanks also to Matthew Feldman and Erik Tonning, Series Editors of the Historicizing Modernism project, who had faith in our proposal, as well as the team at Bloomsbury Academic Publishing who have marshalled this project to fruition, especially Lucy Brown and David Avital, our index compiler, Ralph Kimber, and our diligent copy editor, M. S. Sowmya.

The editors, authors and publisher gratefully acknowledge the permission granted to reproduce the copyright material in this book. Every effort has been made to trace copyright holders and to obtain their permission for the use of copyright material. The publisher and editors would be grateful to be notified of any corrections that should be incorporated in future reprints or editions of this book. The third-party copyrighted material displayed in the pages of this book is done so on the basis of 'fair dealing for the purposes of criticism and review' or 'fair use for the purposes of teaching, criticism, scholarship or research' only in accordance with international copyright laws, and is not intended to infringe upon the ownership rights of the original owners.

Abbreviations

Unless otherwise indicated, all references to Katherine Mansfield's works are to the editions listed below and abbreviated as follows. Diaries, journals, letters and notebooks are quoted verbatim, without the use of editorial '[*sic*]'.

CW1 and CW2	*The Edinburgh Edition of the Collected Works of Katherine Mansfield*: Vols 1 and 2 – *The Collected Fiction*, eds Gerri Kimber and Vincent O'Sullivan (Edinburgh: Edinburgh University Press, 2012).
CW3	*The Edinburgh Edition of the Collected Works of Katherine Mansfield*: Vol. 3 – *The Poetry and Critical Writings*, eds Gerri Kimber and Angela Smith (Edinburgh: Edinburgh University Press, 2014).
CW4	*The Edinburgh Edition of the Collected Works of Katherine Mansfield*: Vol. 4 – *The Diaries of Katherine Mansfield, Including Miscellaneous Works*, eds Gerri Kimber and Claire Davison (Edinburgh: Edinburgh University Press, 2016).
CP	*The Collected Poems of Katherine Mansfield*, eds Gerri Kimber and Claire Davison (Edinburgh: Edinburgh University Press, 2016).
Letters 1-5	*The Collected Letters of Katherine Mansfield*, 5 vols, eds Vincent O'Sullivan and Margaret Scott (Oxford: Clarendon Press, 1984–2008).
Notebooks 1-2	*The Katherine Mansfield Notebooks*, 2 vols, ed. Margaret Scott (Minneapolis: University of Minnesota Press, 2002).

Introduction

Words in the World

Aimée Gasston

This volume is published a century on from a year in which Katherine Mansfield was consistently writing in full flow and creating some of her most funny, brutal, philosophical and moving work. Some of her stories written at this time are so finely balanced – *almost* hermetically sealed by their impeccably poised ambiguity – that it is perhaps unsurprising that they still offer up new meanings to new readers, unfurling fresh thoughts, suggesting themselves with increasing relevance and implication, inserting themselves into our world and finding themselves at home. Mansfield vehemently believed that art should be 'rooted in life', and her stories achieve this.[1] From roots come the 'signes of Spring' of which Ali Smith vivaciously writes in this volume, those which compellingly suggest the 'possible, possible, possible' (p. 14). From roots come new routes, bifurcating, splitting, flitting, perhaps forging ahead, perhaps returning and looking again.

As Lorna Sage compellingly argues, Mansfield showed such pleasure in the short story form because she felt 'at home in it, being so little at home anywhere else'.[2] Perhaps that is one explanation for the endurance of her hymns to brevity today, in increasingly unstable and disjointed times, where precarious employment is the norm, where issues of 'home' and who deserves one are at the forefront of politics, where public memory is not expected to last longer than a day, where words have come to signify next to nothing in the civic sphere, used as a tool of distraction or blame-setting, not something by which to set store or hold others accountable. Do words fail us, or do we fail words? Where words have become marketized to sell and influence, and do so by promoting fear and insecurity, have we made language costed and devalued, weaponized and subjugated, equivocal and empty rather than rich and multiplicitous?

Virginia Woolf, Mansfield's arch-ally, reminds us that words are – or should be – 'highly democratic'; they are disdainful of notions of 'purity'. They also 'hate making money'.[3] Woolf wrote, 'As we peer at them over the edge of that deep, dark and only fitfully illuminated cavern in which they live – the mind – all we can say about them is that they seem to like people to think and feel before they use them.'[4] Mansfield thought and felt a great deal before she used words, and not just words but also the spaces in between them, as chapters in this volume attest. Smith describes it in the volume's opening chapter, 'The life that words bring to things. The life, in everything, words or no words' (p. 11). Woolf's fleetingly-lit cavern of words is richly suggestive not only of Mansfield, her luminous work and her ways of working – 'Dont I live in *glimpses only*?' she once wrote to John Middleton Murry[5] – but also of Nadine Gordimer and her fireflies. As Gordimer understood it: 'Short story writers live by the flash; theirs is the art of the only thing one can be sure of – the present moment.'[6] Who is this more true of than Mansfield, who wrote: 'There's no future if youre not well, no solid substantial Xmas with £50 in the pudding. There is only TODAY.'[7] Mansfield's suggestion of new directions and of new ways forward – not only in a geographical sense but also in ways of thinking and being – becomes more audacious, more imperative, in the short-term frame of her pithy life.

There is only TODAY. Mansfield, in a review of May Sinclair's novel *Mary Olivier: A Life*, observes that 'the great writers of the past' have been 'seekers, explorers, thinkers'.[8] It is the seeking, exploring and thinking through which enables their work to inhabit successive todays – paradoxically, it's the iterative, questioning, evolving impermanence that allows access to permanence. Woolf, on words again, and the things they hate, sums up: 'In short, they hate anything that stamps them with one meaning or confines them to one attitude, for it is their nature to change.'[9] She continues: 'Perhaps that is their most striking peculiarity – their need of change. It is because the truth they try to catch is many-sided, flashing this way, then that.'[10] Multiplicity, possibility, intersectionality, complexity, phosphorescence: Mansfield recognized the capacity of language for all of this, as well as its capacity to fail, and our capacity to fail it and, if there is a secret to her innovation, that might be it. Many-sidedness – multidirectionality – is intrinsic to her aesthetic newness.

And – while in twenty-first-century modernist studies scholars are encouraged to focus on aspects other than the desire to 'make it new', to pay heed to the continuities over the difference – we must never forget Mansfield's radical newness, how she changed the structure of the short fiction form irrevocably, so that even writers who have never read Mansfield are still working within the parameters she set. In conversation with A. R. Orage, she explained that it is the artist's attitude to the world which is transmitted through their work: 'An artist communicates not his vision of the world, but the attitude which results in his vision; not his dream, but his dream-state; and as his attitude is passive, negative, or indifferent, so he reinforces in his readers the corresponding state of mind.' Mansfield responds that most writers are phlegmatically indifferent to what they see, seeking only to replicate, and by consequence induce a type of reading which is both 'passive' and 'spectatorial'. She concludes her argument by stating: 'What I am trying to say is that a new attitude to life on the part of writers would first see life different and then make it different.'[11] Mansfield is a marginal writer, always, with her side-long 'squint vision', her outsider acuity, her notice to that to which attention is not usually paid, her perpetual inbetweenness and her indefatigable ambivalence.[12] Her braveness cannot be overestimated. The prettiness of her pieces must not be allowed to disguise their underlying provocations. They cry, as did Kate Zambreno in our current century: 'Fuck the boys with their big books.'[13] She saw life differently and then made it different, shaping literary DNA in the process. This volume's chapters, in appropriately diverse and divergent ways, examine how Mansfield achieved this.

Since the publication of *Katherine Mansfield and Literary Modernism* in 2011 (this book's sister volume in the Historicizing Modernism series), there has been a significant resurgence of scholarly interest in Mansfield, much of which can be traced in some way to the work of the Katherine Mansfield Society, ten years young at the point of writing, which has fostered invaluable scholarship, sustaining research by established scholars and welcoming new arrivals to the field of Mansfield studies in an open and cross-disciplinary spirit. This volume also springs from that source, to give an updated perspective on Mansfield's literary contributions to modernism in the light of recently discovered historical documents and new critical thinking. Aiming to follow Mansfield's lead as literary innovator, this collection works to build existing scholarship out into new directions, and it does so at a fertile time in Mansfield studies. Aside from exciting critical work, the last decade has also seen the publication of two major new biographies: Kathleen Jones's *Katherine Mansfield: The Story-Teller* (2010) and Gerri Kimber's *Katherine Mansfield: The Early Years* (2016), and both authors provide further insights here.

The fourteen chapters of *Katherine Mansfield: New Directions* are organized into four sections: 'Form and force', 'Mansfield's modernisms', 'Literary spheres and influences' and 'Social and domestic transactions'. Each offers new illuminations of Mansfield's work and life, bringing together postcolonial studies, cognitive criticism, ecocriticism, manuscript studies and new auto/biographical and critical-theoretical approaches to her life and art. Together they look at growth, gaps, silence, work, relationships, laughter and literary marketplaces and influences, paying equal heed to Mansfield's texts as well as their contexts in thinking through the workings of her words in the world.

The opening section begins with a dazzling chapter by Ali Smith, another writer whose words are very much in the world: the transcript of a talk. In a wide-ranging, weighty and breathless exploration, Smith focuses on the trademarks of Mansfield's practice – time (brevity) and aesthetic ambivalence (what she calls a simultaneous 'richness and pared-back close-to-the-bone-ness' [p. 12]) – as well as thinking through the ethics of working with the 'talismanic' remains that writers leave behind them. Of course, the piece does much more than this, carrying readers in myriad directions while conveying a central passion, all the while revealing the intrinsic importance of Mansfield to Smith's personal aesthetics and practice. It would be a disservice to 'pot' it for the purposes of this introduction – much better just to read it and hold on as tight as you can.

Elleke Boehmer's chapter considers the use of ellipses and other 'gaps' in Mansfield's prose that are so well-known yet under-examined. Tasking herself with the crucial question of how meaning is shaped in fiction, Boehmer shows how Mansfield 'creates links of implication across gaps and micro-gaps within the flow of her sentences' (p. 29), drawing on the theory of under-specification from the field of cognitive linguistics. Also looking at the fiction of Ali Smith, the chapter deftly highlights the peculiar confidence inherent to Mansfield's deployment of under-emphasis, given her position as an ex-centric writer, relying on a type of 'hyper-implication'. In analysing the way Mansfield 'breaks, pauses, swerves, adjusts and withholds her meaning constantly, almost promiscuously' (p. 34), Boehmer trains the practitioner's eye upon textual machinery, without pulling the extraordinary instrument apart.

Next is Enda Duffy's contribution, which quietly guides the direction of the volume from listening to gaps to contemplating snow. Arguing that snow appears as a 'marker of a crisis point in modernist aesthetics' (p. 45), the chapter conducts an extended analysis of Mansfield's story 'Je ne parle pas français' alongside James Joyce's story 'The Dead' amid a constellation of other global and modernist reference points in building its case. Duffy suggests that snow articulates the limits of modernism, operating as a 'stand-in for the white page on which nothing is written, because nothing can be written, since the outpost of experiences which the modernist has the literary powers to express, is what has been reached' (p. 47). Macroscopic and poetic, this chapter considers the dual pull towards abstraction and humanity that might be seen at the core of modernism. The final chapter of the opening section, by Ruchi Mundeja, also contemplates the blankness of the page, what is not marked, and considers how marginalized voices are articulated in Mansfield's fiction by means other than direct speech. If women's writing can be said to be driven by one common concern, the expression of the unvoiced 'dark country' of women's lives, Mundeja asks how that silence is configured or spoken. Drawing on feminist and postcolonial theory, this chapter examines Mansfield's empathic ventriloquizing of her protagonists' silence, while also probing the ethical quandaries of such transcription, and asking how such an activity might also involve elements of 'incursion and trespass' (p. 72).

Beginning the second section on Mansfield's modernisms, William Kupinse's chapter changes course to consider themes of ecopoetics as they relate to gender and colonialism, particularly within New Zealand: he does so by examining a more tangible object – the plant that features in Mansfield's 'Prelude'. This encyclopaedic contribution poses wider questions of the medicinal in asking us to consider what healing might need to take place in the broader context of 'how gender roles and colonial power structures intertwine' (p. 88), voicing the query: 'What might be accomplished by an ecofeminism that is ecocentric, rather than anthropocentric?' (p. 88). The next chapter marks a shift in geographical focus, as Chris Mourant explores the influence of literary America upon Mansfield, using evidence of her book borrowing from the celebrated Parisian bookshop Shakespeare and Company during a stay in Paris in the autumn of 1922. Considering the work of Sherwood Anderson, Dorothy Canfield and Gertrude Stein, Mourant conducts a vital thought experiment in investigating how Mansfield's writing might have developed had she lived longer, suggesting that this reading materially influenced her decision to enter Gurdjieff's Institute – a move which is often framed in terms of a retreat from literature.

Erika Baldt similarly contemplates questions of influence, but of a very different historical texture, as she considers ancient Orphic mythologies as a likely reference point in stories such as 'An Indiscreet Journey' and 'Bliss'. In her examination of Mansfield's exposure to some of the ideas or imagery of the rites relating to burial and the afterlife as they appear in the artefacts of ancient Greece and Italy, Baldt draws on a selection of historical evidence to tease out the potential impact of the Orphic not only upon Mansfield's brand of modernism but also in her personal philosophy. Twentieth-century philosophy is a central concern for Nick Hocking, who draws on the work of Henri Bergson in his analysis of an under-examined but important element of Mansfield's work – comedy. In a dextrous piece, Hocking places Mansfield's work in dialogue with that of Samuel Beckett, Djuna Barnes, Wyndham Lewis and Conrad Aiken in examining her treatment of humour, arguing that her stories 'enact a war between two incompatible aesthetic approaches, which might retrospectively be termed "high modernist" and "late modernist"' (p. 132).

Opening the third section of the book on literary influence and autobiography, Katie L. Jones takes us to the young Mansfield's experience of the London literary marketplace between 1908 and 1909, in a chapter that argues that the influence of figures such as Orage and Beatrice Hastings on Mansfield's early literary style has been overstated. Such an approach, Jones contends, risks underplaying the active role that Mansfield took in developing her own voice and in personally ensuring the 'marketability' of her early work. In examining this intense period in Mansfield's life, characterized by her engagement in a lively verse-recitation scene, Jones maps Mansfield's attempts to forge a writing style that would appeal to her future publishers.

In examining the legacy of the publication history she would eventually leave behind, Kathleen Jones considers Mansfield's influence upon such seemingly diverse writers as Philip Larkin and Yiyun Li, showing how her writing – and especially her life writing – palpably shaped the thinking and writing of each author. Considering issues of identity, geography and the messy relationship between life and art, Jones brings the disembodied conversations between these writers, transcending time and place, to life. In her contribution, Gerri Kimber turns to a figure in Mansfield's early life whom history has often treated unkindly – her first husband, George Bowden. In a clear-sighted and often touching account, Kimber draws on a wide range of documentary evidence – primarily drawn from the Harry Ransom Center at the University of Texas – to reveal the integrity of the man, as well as his astute perceptions of Mansfield, and does valuable work to fill in gaps that are strategic absences in the personal record Mansfield left to posterity.

The final section of the volume turns to Mansfield's concerns with power structures as framed by capitalism, focusing on her treatment of labour and economy. Janet M. Wilson takes up the idea of the 'Economic Woman' in examining the ways in which the economic changes and financial forces of the early-twentieth-century shape potential opportunities for female characters in Mansfield's stories. Wilson shows how Mansfield, forever interested in destabilizing contingencies, uses bargaining strategies and transactions, both financial and sexual, to illuminate vulnerabilities and illusions of independence. Alex Moffett's examination of Mansfield's social conscience focuses on notions of the 'labouring life' to consider the BBC's recovery of her 'work' stories in the 1930s, revealing how Mansfield's final collection, *The Garden Party and*

Other Stories, might anticipate representations of the working classes in British culture of the 1920s and 1930s. Ann Herndon Marshall similarly considers the importance of labour as well as its potential for entrapment in her examination of Mansfield's complex portrayal of Miss Moss in the story 'Pictures'. Also considering the work of Jean Rhys, which complements Mansfield's so well, as well as that of W. L. George, Marshall examines these writers' engagement with the lives of female figures operating on the margins.

As a whole, this book evidences how relevant Mansfield continues to be to the world today – across social, cultural, aesthetic and political contexts – and particularly to the writers in it. There will always be more to be said about her work, as it will continue to suggest new directions of travel and thought. Indeed, to read her writing is to undertake a kind of travelling, one that is paralleled by the writing experience itself. As Mansfield wrote to Bertrand Russell on 17 December 1916:

> life never bores me. It is such strange delight to observe people and to try to understand them, to walk over the mountains and into the valleys of the world, and fields and road and to move on rivers and seas, to arrive late at night in strange cities or to come into little harbours just at pink dawn when its cold with a high wind blowing somewhere *up* in the air, to push through the heavy door into little cafés and to watch the pattern people make among tables & bottle and glasses, to watch women when they are off their guard, and to get them to talk then, to smell flowers and leaves and fruit and grass – all this – and all this is nothing – for there is so much more. [...] To air oneself among these things, to seek them, to explore them – and then to go apart and detach oneself from them – and to write [...].[14]

Words are our travelling companions, they are our vehicles, they help us to transcend borders, they place us in others' shoes (empathy, that most valuable of journeys). Mansfield reminds us of this, again and again, as do the chapters gathered here. The importance of this cannot be overstated. Here's to travelling with Mansfield without borders.

August 2019, Crystal Palace, London.

Notes

1 *Letters* 5, p. 217.

2 Lorna Sage, *Moments of Truth: Twelve Twentieth-Century Women Writers* (London: Fourth Estate, 2002), p. 53.

3 Virginia Woolf, 'Craftsmanship', in *The Death of the Moth and Other Essays* (London: Hogarth Press, 1945), pp. 126–32 (p. 131).
4 Ibid.
5 *Letters* 4, p. 236.
6 Nadine Gordimer, *Telling Times: Writing and Living 1950–2008* (London: Bloomsbury, 2011), p. 170.
7 *Letters* 4, p. 57.
8 Katherine Mansfield, 'The New Infancy', in CW3, pp. 478–80.
9 Woolf, p. 131.
10 Ibid.
11 A. R. Orage, 'Talks with Katherine Mansfield', *Century Magazine*, November 1924, pp. 36–40 (p. 39).
12 Clare Hanson, *Re-reading the Short Story* (Basingstoke: Macmillan, 1989), p. 5.
13 Kate Zambreno, *Heroines* (South Pasadena: Semiotext(e), 2012), p. 297.
14 *Letters* 1, pp. 287–8.

Form and force

1

SIGNES OF SPRING

A letter from Katherine Mansfield

Ali Smith

[What follows is the transcript of a talk given by Ali Smith on 28 June 2018 at Birkbeck, University of London, where she made her audience laugh and cry.]

But, seriously, isn't it staggering to think what may be contained in one innocent-looking little phrase? ('A Married Man's Story')

Things had a habit of coming alive like that. ('Prelude')

Tell me! Tell me! Why is it so difficult to write simply? ('A Married Man's Story')

Do you believe that every place has its hour of the day when it really does come alive? That's not exactly what I mean. It's more like this. ('Je ne parle pas français')

The work that words do. The notion of language and containment. The life that words bring to things. The life, in everything, words or no words. The difficulty of simplicity. The questions of belief about time, place. The direct address. The demand of voice; the implication, the imperative, of dialogue. The sense of heft behind something casual, off the cuff. Questions of lightness and seriousness, innocence and knowledge. The 'staggering' realisation of the knowledge that language unsuspectingly contains. The casual, demanding, vital, dialogic attempt at getting to meaning. The paradox of an announcement, in French, that someone doesn't speak French.

And that's just from a thirty-second flick through the *Collected Stories*, just the catch of the eye on a quick riffle of pages. I mean, where do you want me to start? I'm against the clock here, I've only got an hour, and there's so much to say, given *the shortness of life! The shortness of life!* ('At The Bay'), and one of the things I want to talk about, as well as all the things I've just mentioned, is the shortness of life and the allied shortness of the short story form, but I don't know if I'll have time, because I also want to talk *about* time, and about the way that richness and pared-back close-to-the-bone-ness are related in Mansfield, and also our strange attraction, as a species, to the bones, the remains of writers' lives, and I'd also like to talk a bit about the cross-border tendency in her writing, her natural internationality, and also, above all, how everything about language, and how we act with it, and how it acts on us, comes alive in Mansfield's hands whatever form Mansfield is using.

I especially want, today, to celebrate some writings in a form she particularly didn't want to have anyone else read, the letters and notebooks that she left instructions for Middleton Murry to burn, and I'm writing this looking at my *Collected Letters of Katherine Mansfield* volumes on my desk. Mansfield's friend Ida Baker, of course, did destroy a great swath of early letters; she'd brought them round one day to show Mansfield in case they were of use to her writing, and Mansfield had a look at a few, declared them dreadful rubbish and instructed Ida Baker to burn them then and there. Which, being a good loyal friend and always taking Mansfield at her word, knowing how crucial the notion of the word was for her beloved friend, she did.

And here's some of the note Mansfield wrote to give instruction to Middleton Murry after her death to destroy '[a]ll manuscripts notebooks papers letters [...] I should like him to publish as little as possible and tear up and burn as much as possible [...] I desire to leave as few traces of my camping ground as possible.'

And though I love Mansfield's determination and her instinct to clear up after herself, leave things behind her clean in the landscape, the thing I'm interested in is that the word that recurs in this instruction note is the word 'possible'. Three times in such a short space. I love Mansfield's quite self-conscious honourable decency about her presence and absence in the world, in this note, but what I come away with is the unexpected notion of possibility. Possible, possible, possible.

So I'm planning to talk a little about her letters, and to talk about what it is to be human, and make mistakes, and be mortal, and talk too about the ways in which we outlive our mortalities, and a little about what it is we ask of our writers' lives, as well as of their work, and to look a little at the gravedigging tendency, the nature of those who love their writers so much that, like Walter Scott, they'll pay a fortune to someone who promises that this skull is definitely *the* skull of Robert Burns, and that all the other skulls on the market aren't him, so the money changes hands so that the skull can sit there on the writing desk next to the collected letters volumes. Which reminds me of a couple of books by Jennifer Wallace called *Digging the Dirt*, and *Digging Up Milton*, which describe the long queues of people and the carnival atmosphere outside a church in London in August 1790, each person paying 'the price of a pot of beer' so that they could go in and not just see but also touch the skeletal remains of John Milton, dug up after 116 years (and also take a rib, a tooth, a tuft of hair, a piece of finger away with them, which quite a few of them did) which reminds me of the fact that Mansfield herself kept a skull, we don't know whose, part of the decorative accoutrement of her room, and in which she placed lit candles. Which reminds me too, this is a digression, well, this whole keynote is a digression actually – a few months ago when I went up to Edinburgh to see the exhibition in the National Library there in celebration of the centenary of Muriel Spark, an exhibition of manuscripts, first editions, letters and telegrams from writers and famous people, plus Muriel Spark's handbags, on the wall a piece of footage was looping from an old TV arts show where someone films Muriel Spark in her study talking away, and suddenly she picks up a skull off a filing cabinet or a pile of books, and she holds it up, and says, we got this in Vienna, and she presses a button and the skull goes ha-ha-ha-ha-ha, and she laughs, herself, and then, uncannily, she holds the skull up in front of her own face as if it's her own skull and leaves it there for a moment, and it really does look like the skull belongs to her body, then she presses the button that makes it laugh again, and moves its jaw, as if it's her skull laughing, then as it's still laughing, moves it to one side, here by her head and looks laughingly herself at the camera.

But that's not a digression or an aside at all, because if I look back at the twentieth century, Spark and Mansfield both, though one lived more than eighty years and one lived not much past thirty, shine out as writers who demand that we pay attention to what we're made of, that we perceive our roles in the social and historical structures that form us and which we form, and that we understand the certainty, the unseverable link, between being human, being here and being gone, while history hurtles us along, hurls us here and there. Both had known war and war's madnesses. Both had known empire across the world from an outsider perspective. Both were rigorous, disciplined artists, and Spark would have recognised and met Mansfield's dislike of 'the sort of licence that English people give themselves – to spread over and flop and roll about'. Where Mansfield put it this famous way, 'I feel as fastidious as though I wrote with acid', Spark, in *A Far Cry from Kensington*, invents the acid epithet '*pisseur de copie*' – 'it means that he pisses hack journalism, it means that he urinates frightful prose'.[1] They were both connoisseurs of precision and internationality in language, both shared qualities of exile and itinerant notions of home, both were world travellers, not just au fait with but in need of, nourished by, the natural internationality of language in the world.

Both used their knowledge to transform written form, to make possible new or renewed understanding of the relationship between fiction and life, and to make new literary structures possible, possible, possible.

I'm thinking a lot about the talismanic nature of what writers leave behind themselves, and of what their camping ground means, what shape it takes, and I'm digressing here again, but especially right now weighing up who gets to camp where, in a divided world, a world where quite blatantly, quite consciously the people in power are working to divide us, as they one more time ball up history in their fists and shake it, hurl notions like truth and lies and fiction and power around us at a rate shocking to those of us who've so far in life been fortunate enough not to be quite so at history's mercy, less shocking to those of us who have, those who are existing, themselves on small squares of camping ground under plastic makeshift tents, for now, till someone decides they're not the right kind of person, and again how the homeless are everywhere from the streets outside this lecture room to the edges of the countries which won't admit the millions of people crossing the world, in a world where the so called civilised democratic solution is to split up parents and children and put children behind bars, and I don't mean just America, there are children in indefinite detention behind G4S patrolled doors in this country right now.

And since I'm digressing . . . This might not seem at first to be connected, but it is – Mansfield can do that, reveal links between disparate-seeming things. I started out thinking about this talk with the notion that I'd maybe write, for this conference, a story Mansfield said she'd one day write, and never got to; in a letter to Ida Baker in May 1922 she tells her: 'In fact I shall one day write a cat story which will be *heart breaking*!' She's talking about Wing, the cat Ida Baker was now looking after for her, trying to persuade Ida Baker that she's not heartless for having suggested in her last letter or so that it might be best to have Wing put down. Wing, a cat who'd travelled the world, walked up and down French and Swiss railway station platforms in collar and lead, Ida Baker having brought him all the way from England to Montana-sur-Sierre in Switzerland, no easy feat. From Hampstead Heath to the mountains, Wing, there in the chalet asleep on the window sill or out chasing birds in the snow as Mansfield writes some of her best stories in the last years of her life. But then, as the year and the illness close in on Mansfield a cat becomes not possible, a weight on her conscience, a worry, so much so that she suggests to Ida Baker quite unflinchingly that it might be a good idea to have Wing destroyed, in the light of the fact that she, Mansfield, has no settled home and can't foresee one. Wing, the son of the cat called Charlie Chaplin and the brother of the one called Athenaeum. Wing, the word Mansfield uses in her letters, before the cat called Wing exists, to mean her lung, 'shot in the lung', she writes at the first signs of the onset of tuberculosis, and so when the cat comes, and is given the name Wingly, or Wing, this cat takes on a burden of meaning, the unspoken unspeakable lung plus the question of a settled home, family, affection and love, between Mansfield and Middleton Murry; the cat throughout the letters becomes an innocent-seeming messenger-symbol for the innocence they wanted to articulate to each other about their relationship, and the promise of home as something settled and steady even while Mansfield's being asked by the management to leave the continental hotel in which she's a paying guest because she's ill and making the other guests uneasy.

Wing. Destroyed. Yes, I could write a pretty heart breaking story in her honour about that.

But then I found I wasn't able to sleep, because it kept waking me up, the weight of the story of Wing, even the word Wing – the fact that I couldn't find out what happened to Wing in the end meant I actually couldn't sleep. I sat up in bed and thought, Mansfield's done it again, I can't sleep because I'm worrying about the fate of a cat in 1922 or 3. I'm still worrying about it. Right now. Did her friend Koteliansky take him? (She wrote to ask him to.) Did Wing live to the end with Ida? *Was* he destroyed? And then I searched the internet in the middle of the night to see if I could find any photographs of Wing. And finally I began to get annoyed with myself, and annoyed with the level of nerve-end involvement that reading her letters had once more visited on me.

Because I'm not really a person much drawn to what I've long believed the rather dilettante trappings, the aftermath luxury of graverobbing, the skulls and the fingerbones and the handwritten pages of the not-really-relevant real lives of the gone writers.

But then again, I've surprised myself recently by doing something that's become a ritual for me for my own work in this time. I'll explain. I'm in the middle of a kind of fictional experiment, writing four short novels each named after the seasons, with any luck to make in the end one single four-part novel. They're about time, the place where synchronic time meets cyclical and diachronic time, but the idea is to write them as close to their publication as possible so that when they're published and available to readers they'll be as contemporary as it's possible to be, as well as about the structure of time regardless of the surface we're living on.

Before I started these books – I was starting with *Autumn*, and it was published in 2016, and this was late 2015 – I went with my publisher, Simon, to the British Library. I had an idea that seeing the handwritten manuscript they hold there of Keats's poem 'To Autumn' might be inspiring for a book called *Autumn*. So we went, as a kind of *jeu d'esprit*, a gesture. It was a wonderful thing to do. The kind librarian in charge of literary manuscripts, Rachel Foss, laid out the notebook for us and let us spend time with it, it's kept in a room whose air temperature is tightly controlled, a room which locks on a timer then removes its own oxygen so no fire will ever destroy the things kept in it. And as if it wasn't special enough to get to see the straight neat lines, the places where the pen thickens the letters with ink then watch the ink lessen and lessen until the pen is dipped again, the elegant slope of the fs and the ts and the ys, she brought us a manuscript of the unfinished long poem 'Hyperion' too, with its crossings out, its mistakes, its changes of mind, its added lines in the margin. And then, when we left that special room the librarian had laid out Angela Carter's manuscript of *Wise Children*, and a box of J.G. Ballard correspondence and manuscript, just in case they were of interest, well, I'd thought I wasn't interested in the pen and ink leavings, the literary litter of writers I love, but it was like a portal, it opened to a connecting force, one that moved from actual hand to actual hand down through time and up through time simultaneously.

Simon and I thought we'd repeat the gesture for the book called *Winter*, and for *Winter* I wanted to visit, early last year, the pages of manuscript that the British Library hold in what they're now 99.9% certain is Shakespeare's handwriting, from *The Book of Sir Thomas More*, including a stunning speech against racism set in the middle of the bullying anti-foreign riots in More's contemporary London, a furious brilliant speech about the treatment of immigrants, I mean, talk about contemporary, talk about opening a portal from there to here. A Shakespeare specialist explained to me, while we looked at the pages, the reasons the writing was pretty definitely the work of the man they think was Shakespeare, from the vocabulary, the innocent-seeming phrases, the particular traits in the handwriting, even down to the fold of the page.

And for spring? Where are the songs of Spring? Ay, where are they? Well, I've always associated Mansfield with spring. I've had in my head for years now a line from one of her letters where she declares 'What a name for a book – April!' and all those beautiful letters she writes about how she wishes spring would never end. To Ottoline Morrell especially, she bursts forth all blossom about spring. 'Why are human beings the only ones who do not put forth fresh buds – exquisite flowers and leaves. [...] We have been wintry far too long.' And 'I wonder if you feel too, this year more than any other year, a longing for Spring to *stay* Spring. The flowers have fallen from the pear tree outside my window – just a few little silver petals are still spinning down – & the green is darker. I grudge it so. My Lotus Land would be an eternal first spring day.'

Affectation? Performance? Her letters are theatrical masterworks, it's true. This is because they're gifts for the person to whom she's writing. They're kinds of inverse character study. She makes herself in the recipient's mould. She writes to the task, the meeting of the needs of the recipient. This doesn't mean she loses herself. It means she becomes the right self for that particular person.

The letter I particularly wanted to see, as a talisman for this next novel, was one of the last, thought to be the actual last, in her life, the one found tucked into her letter case at the end unsent, to Ida Baker, the one written up against the frightful odds of her own illness, up against all the odds, written in the freezing cold of the early January week that she'll die in, the one in which she writes 'I am looking for signs of spring already'.

This staggering, innocent-looking phrase, holds all Mansfield's nature. It is itself life force. And that particular letter, the last in the last of the collected letters volumes, has haunted me from the moment I read it. It stands, in its way, for all the letters she wrote from Gurdjieff's commune, letters liberated from herself and her deteriorated physical state, and yet also so concentratedly herself, properly attentive to both the freeing of the self and the responsibility of leaving the camping ground resolved and clean and clear.

I think in general these late letters are a kind of heroism enacted up against worst odds. This one is, even just on the glittering surface, witty, seductive, frank, generous, by turns grave, unflinching and funny. But it's more than its surface, as so many of her letters are. It is an astonishing literary work in itself.

Here's a part of the letter, in the version in the *Collected Letters*.[2]

Le Prieuré / Fontainebleau-Avon / Seine-et-Marne

My dear Ida
I have purposely not written to you before because I felt you wanted me to disappear . . . for a little. I was right, wasn't I? But you have been in my mind today. How are you? How are the cows? [...].

Very much is happening here. We are in the throes of theatre building which ought to be ready by the New Year (Russian style) on January 13th. Its going to be a most marvellous place. Mr Gurdjieff has bought 63 carpets for it & the same number of fur rugs. The carpets which were displayed one by one in the salon last night are like living things – worlds of beauty. And what a joy to learn which is a garden, which a cafe, which a prayer mat, which l'histoire de ses troupeaux [...]. My thoughts are full of carpets and Persia and Samarkand and the little rugs of Baluchistan. [...] I am looking for signs of spring already. Under the espalier pear trees there are wonderful Xmas roses which I saw for the first time this year. They reminded me of Switzerland, and somebody found four primroses the other day. I have moods when I simply pine for the S. of France or somewhere like Majorka. When this time is over I shall make for the South or the East & never go North again.

My blue wool dress is in large holes. Those cashmir cardigans look as if rats have gnawed them. As to my fur coat – its like a wet London cat. The last time I was in the stable I caught one of the goats nibbling it. How are you off for clothes? Would you like brown corduroys? That big woman Miss Marston whom you took such a fancy to, wore them. She got them from Barkers – outsize – 35/- – They are breeks and a smock & long plain coat. Very practical.

Write and tell me how you are will you? Dear Ida?

Our calf is still allowed to be with its Mother. I can't understand it. Its a huge creature now. We had great trouble with the mother who had to be massaged daily. Do you massage your cows? Will you tell me how your stable is kept? What is the condition of the floor. I'll tell you about ours in my next letter. It worries me.

With love from
K.M.

Consider a last letter which begins by taking as its subject the act of her own disappearing. Consider its seduction of Ida Baker into what it promises, what it has to say, via the subtle sensing of the shifting terms of the friendship. It follows this with offers, generosity, and a comic moment of self-critique, instinctual and practical, with a tenderness, in all senses of the word, sensitive, painful and gentle, the feeling for the slightest moodshifts followed by a frankness of declaration. *But you have been in my mind today.*

Then the subject shifts to performance, to the making of a place for a performance to take place, and a showcase moment of Mansfield's ability to make a theatre of things come alive, to make even carpets *living things – worlds of beauty*. The worlds of beauty open to domestic death, the farm deaths of the pigs, a brutal *frightful* description, and a description whose factualness, because it has been properly attended to with determined, unflinching precision, can lend it a final paradoxical determined note of comfort. *But we kill them outright*. Comfort uncompromised.

Immediately up against this everyday bloody death Mansfield places her determination to find *signs of spring*, to which she adds the proof of spring she has already found, and the hearsay too about even more signs of spring, and she follows this with a set of reminders of the places that she and her friend have been and survived together, then a place they haven't yet, and in the space of a single paragraph after that description of blood and slaughter she holds in balance what's been and what will be, holds in balance for her friend a steady past then an underlined when, which becomes a compass swerve into an emphatic attitude-full future, attached but independent, with which she's keeping herself and her friend, both, warm.

So naturally, the next paragraph is about clothes, and since clothes are also a kind of performance accoutrement for Mansfield, this paragraph is full of laughs, things to make her friend laugh, as well as the signalling that something is eating away at her, quite bestially, rats, goats, and fur coat *like a wet London cat*, because all sophistication is laughable from where she now is.

Then, a further ambiguous kindness, where she acknowledges, rather annoyedly, with a double-edged put-down, a woman who's caught Ida Baker's attention, *That big woman Miss Marston* – to remind Ida Baker to whom she really belongs and at the same time to signal a couple of very practical things, one being good practical clothing, the other being Ida Baker's ability to look elsewhere.

Then a triple supplication. *Write and tell me how you are, will you. Dear Ida?* And a final paragraph, whose subject is a weaning-off, about how to manage it, then some lines about what they have in common, *will you tell me how your stable is kept? What is the condition of the floor*: about the ground under their feet, and finally a promise of more, a declaration of worry, and love.

This letter. Absence. Presence. The bringing of things to life. Frankness about the mundanity of death. The promise of continuance. The comedy of being human. Common good. Love.

The thing is, I think you can do exactly that with much of Mansfield's everyday correspondence. She writes by force of habit at a level of complex psychological construction, performance, and resonance, while the surface glitters with seduction, trivia, innocent-looking phrases. *I am looking for signs of Spring already.*

So I wrote to Rachel at the British Library and asked could we come and visit this letter and off we went to the library, and when we got in there downstairs in the archive Rachel put down four large binders in front of us, and told me these were viewable in the Rare Books room and I could come any time and spend time with them. The slimmest one was the manuscript of the story called 'A Suburban Fairy Tale'. Rachel opened the fairy tale and turned the pages of Mansfield's famously difficult to read handwriting, I was actually too amazed to touch the pages, and what I saw was Mansfield, in handwriting terms, starting out steady and finishing at force, at speed, the shift from steady to urgent in her can be experienced physically just by turning the pages of this manuscript.

Then Rachel opened a binder and put that last letter to Ida Baker down in front of me. But it was typewritten.

I read it, for a moment wondering whether Mansfield had typed her last letter – and I got to the line that I love in the letter, I am looking for signs of spring already, and it didn't say signs, it said SIGNES, the French for signs. I am looking for signes of spring. It struck me because it was such a typical Mansfield slippage, her letters are full of slippage between English, French and German, right from her very first letters to her last. And into my head comes Saussure, sign and signifier, and everything a word means when it makes a jump into the defamiliarised, so that sign becomes *signe* suggesting a step closer to the French verb to sign your name, *signer*. Anyway, suffice to say I saw it as a sign in itself, though I wasn't sure what of. Then something was beginning to dawn on me, this wasn't *the* letter, was it? Surely it was a copy, and then I read the little note at the top of its page and I realised, ah, this is Ida Baker, not Mansfield. It's Ida Baker who's made the slippage from sign to *signe*.

Sure enough the binder was full of Ida Baker's transcripts of the handwritten letters to her which Mansfield had sent her since 1918.

The handwritten originals were there too, in an accompanying binder. I came back to the library a week or two later and spent the day with the final letter in several forms, in its handwritten actuality, in its transcript by Ida, in its transcript by the mighty Margaret Scott, the brave decipherer of her handwriting, what could be 'almost a new hand for every day', and first let me just note that on the last page of the handwritten letters binder, a binder whose letters start in 1918 and come all the way to this last, January 1923, at the bottom right hand corner of the last page, there's this aged envelope, spotted, browned, see-through with age, unposted, no stamp, addressed in Mansfield's hand to Ida Baker at the farm she was staying at in Lisieux, and the envelope, this detail of it, this throwaway scrap, in its unsentness, its thinness, its near transparence, is very, very physically moving, as if still waiting to be delivered, as if time has stilled – and then the whole binder of handwritten letters, its fragility, the thinness and lightness of the different papers, the way the pages are cut so that they hold the letters rising above and shifting below each other, cut into, fixed into blank thicker sheets of paper much larger than they are, which somehow heightens their fragility.

A careful peruse of the letters in this handwritten binder, which begins at a terrible and tough time in her life, at the time when she was first diagnosed with TB and is writing to her friends to break it to them, and she's berating Ida Baker for not getting the RIGHT thermos flask for Jack, and I catch drifts of phrase, 'now aren't you thankful you're not going to have dinner with "me in this mood"', the word harmony drawn out with dashes to read 'har – mo – ny', as if singing, the phrase 'see MORE CORRUPTION every day', furious capitals, and I see a postcard of the River in Looe, Cornwall, on which she's written to Ida Baker instructing her to buy her some cigarettes called Grenade, and I imagine what that must've been like, the thing that killed her own brother as the name of a cigarette make, her brother Leslie had died in 1915 in a grenade exercise mistake, a terrible accident, and this is the brand she prefers, and I wonder, again, at her unflinchingness, and what I write down in my notebook is: 'you can actually feel the thought and machination come weirdly off the paper, as it arrives, and it's as if whatever answer there'd be to this letter or card is still to come, hasn't happened yet, is still waiting to happen, even though I'm sitting in the British Library literally a hundred years later to the day 12 June 1918'.

There's a lot I can't read, then suddenly I can read, clear as day, 'I am a very MODERN woman. I like life in my clothes.' Capitals on modern. Yes you are, I think, and I think of the extraordinary act of complex life in that paragraph on clothes in the last letter to Ida Baker again. I note how the writing from 1918 looks as if she's losing her mind. It swings about, small, spidery, then huge and scrawled; it is staggering to turn several pages, cross years, and see it regulate itself again, as if her mind is back, she's in control, neat, small, perfectly held, when she's in Switzerland in the mountains for the air and writing some of her finest fiction. I spend a lot of time, too, over a little strip of foolscap with the rusty print of where two paperclips once were, holding a cheque in place on it, fascinated by the ghosts of Mansfield's paperclips, that's how sad I am, no let's rephrase that, that's how I'm interested in the metal of time. And I see she underlines, on 28 October 1922, the words I am happy.

Anyway that's some of the fruit of my single day so far with the artefacts, the handwritten letters.

But what I found when I compared the handwritten original of the final letter with the transcript by Ida Baker and the one in the *Collected Letters* was that neither of the transcripts were exact. And this fact filled me with another unexpected surge of pleasure and another unexpected leap of joy at the ways in which Mansfield, always slippery, escapes us. I mean there are lots of little punctuation slips between the three, and you'd expect those, because she was an unsteady slippery punctuator. And spring, which has a lower case letter in the *Collected Letters*, has, I think, an upper case, a capital, in the handwritten original.

But I'm more excited by the fact that whole words have slippage between the *Collected Letters* version and the original handwritten. How are your cows? she writes. *Collected Letters* changes your to the, how are the cows. That's sort of interesting. But more exciting, to me anyway, tenses change a couple of times between the original and the version in the *Collected Letters*. The original has 'Under the espalier pear tree there were wonderful Xmas roses which I saw for the first time this year'. Collected letters makes 'were' into 'are'. Under the espalier pear tree there are wonderful Xmas roses. And when we get to Miss Marston whom you took such a fancy to, and her corduroys, the original says 'That big woman Miss Marston whom you took such a fancy to wears them'. *Collected Letters* has 'wore them'. Why does this pedantry, or lack of it, fill me with such pleasure? Well, it's a sign. Or, as Ida Baker wrote, a signe. A signe of life. One of the things I love most about Mansfield, who liked to sign herself off in her letters as differently each time as multiplicity would allow, in pseudonym after pseudonym, version after version of herself, sometimes himself, is how she gives all pinning down the slip from the start of her writing life all the way to its end, writing to Middleton Murry, 'your wife won't have a tomb – she'll have at most a butterfly fanning its wings on her grave and then off'. None of Eliot's 'unspeakably dreary' Prufrockian formulating, 'sprawling on a pin, when I am pinned and wriggling on the wall' here.

Here's Mansfield writing to Violet Schiff in August 1922. She's just come back to London from time in the mountains.

> Its strange to be here again. London is empty, cool, rather shadowy – extraordinarily unlike Paris. I feel sentimental about it. Only the people Ive seen so far seem fatigué fatigué beyond words! One feels that they have come to an agreement not to grow any more, to stay just so – all clipped and pruned and

> tight. As for taking risks, making mistakes, changing their opinions, being in the wrong, committing themselves, losing themselves, being human beings in fact – no, a thousand times! 'Let us sit down and have a nice chat about minor eighteenth century poetry' – I never want to sit down & have that chat as long as I live.

Taking risks. Making mistakes. Being human beings. These are at the heart of her literary project. They're at the heart of her form. At least, I like to tell myself this because I once made a Mansfield mistake myself, listen to this. Someone at Penguin Classics wrote to me in 2003 or 2004 and said would I like to write the introduction to their reprinted *Collected Stories*, and up to this point in my life I'd read almost no Mansfield, I'd only read *In a German Pension* and an edited version of the journal, I'd read them only glancingly, once, though I'd liked them both immensely, and I gamely thought to myself, well, there aren't many collections, and they're all slim, and I looked at the deadline, four months, and I thought, yeah, why not, it's not going to take me long.

Then I read her, and I was shocked, I was staggered beyond belief, left inarticulate on the innocent-seeming surface of the phrasery, unable to get to what I knew was dimensional beyond my understanding, and it took a trip to Brazil and serious jetlag and me reading her in the middle of the night as a foreigner on the other side of the world to shift my clock, as it were, to Mansfield's timing, and then it took three, nearly four years, for me to write the intro, and so all the years later, with an apology letter for taking so long, I sent it off, and got a nice email back saying they liked it a lot, and off it went into the presses and the proofs came back and I corrected them, and sent them back, and then I was standing in King's Cross station one day looking up at the departures board – and I realised – I mean, it literally struck me – ouch – I'd not proof corrected a schoolgirl error, I'd called her the wrong birthname, I'd written Katherine Beauchamp instead of Kathleen and hadn't corrected it – and when I say it struck me I mean my back actually jarred, in pain, at my own stupidity. So I got home and emailed Penguin and asked them to change it and got an email back saying it was too late, and they'd change it for the next edition. So I limped about, literally, in my stupid mistake, for months. And the next edition came out and they still hadn't changed it. I was mortified. I was still limping, it had done for my ankle. They didn't change it till a mountain of irate letters, plus an absolute beauty of a complaint from my agent did it, and the fourth edition finally had her real birth name. But I had to have cranio-sacral stuff, and actual psychotherapy after that mistake, I'm not kidding, and one of the things the therapist said to me was, describe Katherine Mansfield to me, so I did, and she said, but she sounds like someone who liked to slip from name to name, from personality to personality, what's it you wrote, 'she changed her names as if changing her hair', and she sounds very skilfully persuasive, well, there you go, she did it again, through you, it's very likely, even subconsciously, you did what you thought she wanted you to.

Well, yeah, right.

Who am I performing here, careless Jack, enslaved Ida or stupid me? Only the last. I'm no fool and I'm a rubbish academic, and I know from Ida Baker's *Memories of LM* that 'she never allowed anyone to alter her work by so much as a comma', and I know from reading Mansfield's letters how furious she was about the mistakes, for instance, the typist made who typed out her stories for *The Garden Party*, how 'greatly troubled' she was to find the word 'bath' substituted for 'basin' and 'sole' for 'sour'. But one way or another, that dialogue, and the very notion that I was in some kind of live dialogue, even a mistake-making one, with Mansfield's spirit, as it were, sorted my back, sorted my mountain back into a molehill. All the same, I wonder if anyone else in this room has been given the slip or the slippage by Mansfield, or if it's just my own fantasy that that's what she does.

And let me say I take great pleasure in the news story I read online from *The Dominion Post* which tells me that she also managed to give her own primary school in Wellington the slip – her name was misspelt on a memorial plaque near a memorial birdbath there for decades, only just righted last year.

A browse of *The Dominion Post* also alerted me to the recent interest in digging Mansfield's actual bones up, and returning them to New Zealand to celebrate Wellington as a city of culture, which made me laugh, given that everybody who's read Mansfield knows that her bones aren't bones at all but liquid light ('supposing ones bones were not bone but liquid light', she wrote in her journal at the start of her writing life). It made me think, too, sorrowfully, of the doctor who said to her once, 'well, dear, of course you won't make old bones'.

What do we make of the world, the people, that reduce our lit up selves to bones? What did she make of it?

Comedy, social acuity: *We are such a happy family since my dear man died* ('Frau Fischer'). An anatomy of longing: *Can one do nothing for the dead?* ('Six Years After'). Realism: *Query: Why am I so bitter against Life? And why do I see her as a rag-picker on the American cinema, shuffling along wrapped in a filthy shawl with her old claws crooked over a stick?* ('Je ne parle pas français'). Release: *We whirl along like leaves, and nobody knows – nobody cares where we fall, in what black river we float away* ('Revelations'). Sensory social observation: *Miss Anderson rustled, rustled about the house like a dead leaf* ('The Doves' Nest'). Acuity of modern understanding: *As soon as a person was dead their photograph died too* ('The Daughters of the Late Colonel'). Ancient story: *I've only one night or one day, and there's this vast dangerous garden, waiting out there, undiscovered, unexplored* ('At the Bay'). Articulation of the inarticulable: *What did garden-parties and baskets and lace frocks matter to him? He was far from all those things* ('The Garden Party').

She made an art of it all, time, bones, mistakes, comedy, tragedy, homelessness, homefulness, modernity, urgency, realism, metaphysicality. Bones, light – it makes me think of the sittings, or seances in Paris, where she went for x-ray treatment, which was thought to be good for her ailments, 'the old rays are working hard in my joints and bones', she wrote to her sisters in spring 1922. But, then when it was clear the x-ray treatment was not working, 'I gave up everything and decided to try a new life altogether' she writes to Elizabeth, her cousin, on the last day of 1922. Relinquishment. Followed by the declaration of rejuvenation, even when there's none possible. I am looking for signs of Spring. Possible, possible, possible.

Experiencing the courage of the late letters, and the sense in them of her liberation from everything she's been even as she sends people the money she owes them, tidies her camping ground, readies herself to leave the life; the sense in these letters of new possibility even up against the literal impossibility of such a thing; this adds a whole new level of lit-up-ness to Mansfield's bones and Mansfield's spirit. 'Do send Lit Sups. They are so good for lighting fires', she writes from Fontainebleau to Middleton Murry.

Thank God nobody burned the late letters. Thank God we have what we have of the letters all across her life, these extraordinary, vital, literary / psychological / theatrical / intimate artefacts in her handwriting, in transcription, translation, in their comparable forms, all over the world. We can even, if we want, sing the two-note musical sequence she hears a bird at the window sing and transcribes in a tiny stave into a letter to Sylvia Payne more than a hundred years ago, December 1903, and here's that live moment, and that bird still singing. She knows even from the earliest of her letters, that voice, in dialogue, even with itself and its own thought process, is a source of life, and that voice and performance are never that far apart, and that through performance, or mask, a truth can be reached. She looks constantly to be matched, in these earlier letters, with her reader. She woos each reader. She is asking reciprocity on a layered scale, light and social and deep and soulful.

But us reading her letters? She'd have abhorred it. She'd have hated it. In her notebook she slips into another language to try to talk up freedom from the world of autobiography and its accoutrements of the actual life:

> Der Mensch muss frei sein – free, disentangled, single. Is it not possible that the rage for confession, autobiography, especially for memories of earliest childhood is explained by our persistent yet mysterious belief in a self which is continuous and permanent, which untouched by all we acquire and all we shed, pushes a green spear through the leaves and through the mould, thrusts a sealed bud through years of darkness until, one day, the light discovers it and shakes the flower free and – we are alive – we are flowering for our moment upon the earth. This is the moment which, after all, we live for, the moment of direct feeling when we are most ourselves and least personal.

So it's not surprising she bought, burnt, chased up and worried about letters she'd sent to people over the years. I'm not surprised. Her letters are astonishing personal gifts. They're all about the act of giving. They're literal signs of life. And she lived viscerally from postal delivery to postal delivery, went into regular letter-fret when letters meant to arrive didn't arrive, descended into a sort of end-of-the-world despair.

She knew the life of letters herself, the way they embody the writer, the risk they run, the sign and performance of self they are and the constantly erotic intimacy and energy they fuse.

And yet she knows too how little of the life the literary letter represents. 'Let us be honest. How much do we know of Tchekhov from his letters. Was that all? Of course not. Don't you suppose he had a whole longing life of which there is hardly a word?' Then read the final letters. He has given up hope. If you desentimentalize those final letters they are terrible. There is no more Tchekhov. Illness has swallowed him.' Notebooks 1922.

How much do we know of Mansfield from her letters? Well, we know her generosity, we know her seductiveness, we know her charm, we know her social and psychological imperatives. We know her courage. We know the life in the life of her: 'A storm rages while I write this dull letter. It sounds so splendid, I wish I were out in it.' She's writing this, remember, in the chalet in the mountains, writing at a pitch she is hoping is faster than illness, she couldn't much talk for coughing, so the writing of letters becomes even more acute on the one hand as a form of performance, as a form of uniting the impossible with the vision of its opposite, the possible, because there she is, out in the storm, even though she's not, and on the other hand a crucial literal form of contact, as she sits writing, with the existential very real mountains at the back of everything. 'Also, the least postcard or letter penned in view of these mountains,' she writes from Switzerland in May 1921, 'is like presenting ones true account to ones Maker.'

(And this is an aside, since we're talking mountains – I've been thinking too about Mansfield's recourse to the Swiss mountains and her nickname for Ida Baker, The Mountain, and the way she disparages her, 'under the shadow of the Rhodesian Mountain', and makes her, to coin a phrase from just a little bit later in time, the Margaret Dumont to Mansfield's Groucho.

'She's about the nearest thing to eternal that I could ever imagine', she says in a letter to Murry in May 1915. But is this disparaging? Or something more, from the person who had no stability, who moved house more times than, as Lorna Sage says, she had hot dinners. She goes to the mountains to try to lose her consumption, as she wrote to William Gerhardi. She goes to the mountains to survive. She grants Ida Baker height, stature, and then, in the poem she wrote for her, depth too, 'In the profoundest Ocean / There is a rainbow shell, / It is always there, shining most stilly / Under the greatest storm waves / And under the happy little waves / That the old Greeks called "ripples of laughter". / And you listen, the rainbow shell / Sings – in the profoundest ocean. / It is always there, singing most silently!')

My aside's over.

Well, this whole talk has been an aside. It's nearly over.

Mansfield always does this to me. Lost and found, both. 'The important thing is to write, to find yourself in losing yourself.' She lit the candle in the skull. In midwinter? She was looking for signs of spring.

Here's a letter from 1920. 'I am dead certain that there is no separating Art & Life. And no artist can afford to leave out Life. If we mean to work we must go straight to Life for our nourishment. There's no substitute. But I am violent on this subjeck. I must leave it.'

The short story form, in its shortness, is a constant reminder, that that's the thing about the subjeck of life, and being subjeck to life. We must all leave it.

The short story by Mansfield is one of those gifts of art by which we know this inarticulable truth.

But the truth was – Oh, better not inquire what the truth was. Better not ask what it was that kept them going. ('Father and the Girls')

The whole room broke into pieces. ('Carnation')

The morning whisked away as foreign mornings do. ('Mr and Mrs Dove')

Home! To sit around doing nothing, listening to the clock, counting up the years, thinking back . . . thinking! To stay fixed in one place as if waiting for something or somebody. No! no! Better far to be blown over the earth like the husk, like the withered pod that the wind carries and drops and bears aloft again. ('Father and the Girls')

Yes, everything had come alive down to the minutest, tiniest particle. ('Prelude')

A bend in the road, and the whole place disappeared. ('The Woman at the Store')

The rigorous keeping going. The brokenness of living. The speed of time. The belonging and not belonging. The act of liberation from a notion of home, and the notion of uproot as seminal, as itself a kind of home. The aliveness of all things. The journey, the going, and after them both the lasting story of both.

I sat in a library and I looked at a piece of old yellowed thinned written-on paper, a 'semi-transparent envelope', to borrow an innocent-seeming phrase from Virginia Woolf, at the end of the binder of Mansfield's handwritten letters to The Mountain, and I thought of the life *down to the minutest tiniest particle* that everything she wrote, whether it was meant for us to read or not, makes possible, possible, possible, there all along in that last midwinter, another spring.

Notes

1 Muriel Spark, *A Far Cry from Kensington* (London: Constable, 1988).

2 A new 4-vol. edition of Mansfield's letters is currently being edited by Gerri Kimber and Claire Davison for Edinburgh University Press (2020–23), with entirely updated transcriptions.

2

Reflecting (upon) ellipsis

Katherine Mansfield as case study

Elleke Boehmer

This chapter reflects on ellipsis in selected short stories by Katherine Mansfield. Adapting critical procedures from relevance theory, I try to illuminate some of the ways in which the New Zealand–born writer makes and shapes meaning in her work, and look in particular at how she creates links of implication across gaps and micro-gaps within the flow of her sentences. My sense is that Mansfield is especially receptive to reading for relevance because of the extent to which her writing works suggestively (some might say impressionistically); or, differently put, because of how her work relies on the device of what relevance theory terms under-specification. In her writing, under-specification operates in tandem with ellipsis, or is bound up in it. We might even say that the effect is constitutive of her style, running like a watermark through her writing. This is to the extent that a close reading of ellipsis in Mansfield can operate as a case in point for under-specification; in effect, her work encourages, supports *and* exemplifies reading for relevance.

Ellipsis for our purposes here refers to various forms of incompletion and not saying, signalled by sentence breaks, turns and shifts, and usually marked in a text by dots and dashes. On occasion, the effects of ellipsis may be heightened by evocative forms of repetition. As Anne Toner observes in *Ellipsis in English Literature*, elliptical effects have allowed writers over time to reflect the interruptions of spoken utterance; Virginia Woolf, for example, used these breaks and pauses to give an impression of the 'indeterminacies of thought', if not the 'fragmented nature of experience' itself.[1] Like Woolf, Mansfield is particularly attuned to these as-if-uttered reflections or renderings of experience. Few lines in Mansfield are not concerned with guiding, shaping and even animating readers' responses to plot and character precisely through such breaks and incompletions. She draws upon the hints and suggestions – or 'implicatures' – set off by ellipsis to spark and then direct and channel the reader's experience of the thought-worlds of her stories.

The understanding of reader reception that informs this chapter builds upon various cognitive and so-called post-critical moves in literary studies that have characterized the past decade or so. Linking these is the idea that reading or interpretation is not necessarily something *done to* a poem or other text. A critical act does not need to be (and need not be conceived as) invasive or aggressive; a dismantling, unmasking or unpicking; a decoding set on 'untying the text' and unscrambling its secrets. Such deconstructive activities make up a critical mode that commentators on texts have taken almost as second nature for about thirty and more years. Here, instead, as Rita Felski, for example, begins to suggest in the conclusion to her study *The Limits of Critique*, comprehension and interpretation might rather be seen as what happens *within* the course of reading the text, in this case the short story; it concerns the flow of meaning that emerges through the story's play of inferences.[2] In this alternative reading scenario, the reader is constantly tuning and retuning into the meanings of the words on the page as they unfold in relation to each other and in relation to the 'horizon of expectations' the text lays down.[3] Or, as Felski further writes, here in a *New Literary History* essay, interpretation or reading 'is fundamentally a matter of mediation', a process of 'transduction' that manifests between the text and the reader.[4]

According to this inferential approach, a reading does not set about attempting to winkle out some secret or latent meaning in a text, like a mussel from its shell. It does not probe for a deeper interpretative code or repressed message that allegedly lies behind the linguistic codes operating at the text's surface. Significance is not something that lies behind the lines. Relatedly, a reading also avoids plastering meaning or themes over a text like so many post-its (for instance, 'identity', 'the city', 'cosmopolitanism', etc.). As relevance theory has it, meaning rather comes through the reader linearly processing the words and sentences they read. Encountering and working through a text we effectively set different trains of implication running, or (to try a different metaphor), we constantly plait and re-plait the threads of meaning that words, as they are read, generate. As the reader engages with these, his or her responses repeatedly modify and adjust in relation to one another, in an ongoing temporally bound process. With that accent on the temporal, the text might thus be seen as a kind of choreography or a musical score, as I've said elsewhere, where the reading brain is the instrument that sets the dance in motion or that plays the tune.[5]

Many of these ideas of reception as flow, and of the text's constant micro-momentary (re-)calibration and adjustment of meaning, are activated and in some sense anticipated in Mansfield's elliptical, always strongly 'imagiste' and expressionist writing. Even her early stories, and certainly those of her fruitful 1914–22 period, invite her readers to think about how they read. Their often fragmentary and broken-off utterances, sentences and paragraphs constantly ask us to reflect on how we construe their meaning – not least those that trail away into silence. They do this in large part, I would venture to say, by drawing us into the very thinking process that makes them up, turning us into active, self-aware reader-participants, in ways that the linguistic theory of under-specification can help to illuminate. In my own case, my attraction to reader-centred interpretation has always been encouraged and supported by Mansfield's writing. I have been interested to observe how her craft – the particular shapes of her sentences, their stop-start rhythms and scattered patterns – moulds our imaginative responses as we read, and how these patterns then cast light on the intricate, thoughtful ways she builds up implication in her writing.

Reading inferentially

Before going on to consider Mansfield's implicatures in more detail, I will first expand on what reading for relevance entails and on the critical cognitive tools the approach supplies. Key questions here include how the reading mind takes up and processes emergent, current and on-flowing meanings within a text. How are implications weighed against each other, with some retained and others set aside? To answer these and related questions, technical terms drawn from relevance theory can be fruitful for moving our understanding of interpretation away from those now almost habitual and restrictive assumptions of decoding, and towards more fluid concepts of cascading and unspooling. What we are talking about here in essence involves slowing, channelling and even pooling (in order to reflect upon) the always inventive flow of our thought as we read.

For relevance theory, the comprehension process that is involved in the reception of any utterance entails a continuous adjustment of hypotheses as to the meanings being made.[6] As we read or hear a stream of words, we are constantly making micro-decisions on what will come next, and on how we understand the words we hear now (their emergent meanings) in the light of what has just gone before. Throughout, as in any communicative act, considerations of content and context are balanced in relation to each other, as the listener or reader makes their inferences concerning the communicator's intentions to convey a certain meaning. So, as the utterance or text proceeds, meaning at once spreads out and is funnelled by the reader. At every moment we are processing new elements (references, implications, assumptions) that are provided as part of the same communicative flow, even while at the same time steadily discarding others.

As this might suggest, in any given Mansfield story, indeed in any text, each sentence, each paragraph, each section creates a space, however momentary, within which the reader's perceptions are activated. The space opens an affordance or area of possibility wherein our concern to interpret can be exercised. It is in this way that the story becomes part of and shapes our imagination, even as our imagination reacts to it. This dual flow of perception and interpretation can be compared to how on a train journey, say, we are at one and the same time aware of the wider landscape sliding by outside the train, and of our emotional reactions to these passing scenes, yet also of the flow in our thoughts of other memories, anticipations and retrospections that inform that first skim of meaning. The 'mind's eye' combs through different strands of internal perception, even while taking in perceptions from the outside world. At least two sets of moving pictures, often more, run in our thoughts at once. As we will soon see in relation to Mansfield, relevance theory's framework for this loose sifting of both literal and more figurative meanings, as Deirdre Wilson writes, allows us to become more attentive to these two concurrent processes.[7] It provides us with the tools to slow them down in order to reflect upon them.

Another way of thinking about this process is to consider how the interrelated responses of looking, recognition and identification can work in visual art. For example, when a painting or a piece of sculpture particularly stimulates us, we look more closely at it; our initial look is repeated, but more intensely, with quickened recognition. The painting, having caught our attention, invites us to look again, to check that with which we first identified, or to which we related, informed as it now is by what we have perceived and thought since, however momentary that 'since' might be. This response of looking and looking again is often stimulated by gaps, breaks and incompletions – unexpected, often surprise effects that require us to weigh and interpret different inferences, and focus back in. So a haystack by Claude Monet, or 'Lattice' by Lubaina Himid, for example, might show us first an abstract pattern, a dome and a rectangle shape, or diamonds of different blue hues, and then, at our second look, even if just seconds later, it might show us glimmering straw, or sunlight on water, and then, as we look even closer, or as we step back, to check again on that perception, we see those shapes in another light: we see a haystack under morning snow, or at midday (in the case of Monet), or we see bright Zanzibar sunshine filtered through a lattice screen carved in stone (for Himid).

Importantly, in both these accounts of inference, that of the loose, self-aware sifting of a text's meanings and that of looking and looking again at visual art, we notice how we are in effect released from the drag of re-presentation upon us, from the locked-in dualism of signifier and signified. We move away from the idea that art and literature always in some sense point outwards and stand for something in the 'real world'. Instead, we are freed to consider interpretation as something lighter and more fluid, as well as reciprocal and internalized. Reading, we respond to the call of the work upon us. No matter how other or exotic its subject may be, we move towards it and it draws us in, just as we also draw its meanings and perceptions into our imaginative worlds.

Ellipsis and the short story

It is probably uncontroversial to say that modernist short stories rely upon elliptical techniques. More interesting is to consider how ellipsis actually works within the short story form, how it becomes dynamic not because of the often-assumed compression of the story, but in relation to its sense of limit and outline or what Clare Hanson calls its 'frame'.[8] In fact, by implying comparison with longer narrative forms, compression may not be a very helpful description for our reflections on how the autonomous short story makes meaning across its breaks and gaps.

In Mansfield, intentional omission and subtraction often powerfully direct or advance the suggestiveness of the writing in relation to its enclosing frame – which is how her writing always provides such rich occasion for thinking about ellipsis. She uses versions of the device frequently and dextrously, along different vectors, both denotative and connotative. As already implied, these usages make up a kind of writerly genetic code, one that is repeated and recognizable in the writers who have trained themselves in part by following her technique, not least the contemporary British writer Ali Smith. In Smith's work, too, we observe how the narration sometimes falters, wanders off, dwindles away and then resumes, or loses and retrieves its thread, as spoken language might, as if the narrative were tracking the stops and starts of a conversation, or mimicking the halts and hesitations of a character's thought.

Of the structural requirements of the short story, Hanson observes that 'the frame acts as an aesthetic device, permitting ellipses (gaps and absences) to remain in a story, which retains a necessary air of completeness and order because of the very existence of the frame'.[9] Its frame in place, it is then a particular paradox of the short story that it lends 'itself to the presentation of the partial, the incomplete'.[10] As Hanson agrees, Mansfield is especially deft at working (with and within) these limits. She creates her concentrated effects always with reference to them. How ellipsis and frame work in relation to each other then becomes a fundamental aspect of her style, underlying and making possible its characteristic quicksilver qualities, its velocity and impressionistic shimmer effects. She creates maximal tension through maximal omission, often extending or stretching her ellipses to their very limits. Under these conditions, ellipsis can be made to carry a wide range of emotional signification – agitation, dismissal, defiance, exasperation – all depending on the contextual markers in relation to which it is used. Above all, Mansfield's gaps are used to invite and sometimes compel the reader to make that double manoeuvre I traced earlier, of looking, and then looking again, informed by the new meanings that even in that micro-instant of moving on and then looking back, the text or image has accrued.

Out-of-country and peripatetic, the New Zealander Mansfield was always in some sense a writer in translation; therefore, the necessary fragmentariness of the short story form suited her especially well. It allowed her to deploy the central paradox of ellipsis, subtracting on one level to add imaginative effect on another, encouraging her reader regardless of their position or context to fill in her narrative frames by supplying their own personal and emotional details and colours. In Mansfield's hands, under-specification could generate richer meaning and fuller resonance regardless of her own and her characters' relative rootlessness.

However, precisely because of her cosmopolitan ex-centricity, ellipsis was at the same time an audacious, high-risk approach for Mansfield – and hence represents of course the greater achievement. As writers on the edge cannot assume that they will be immediately understood by those at the centre, their natural tendency is often to overstatement and explicitness, not implication. Deemed not to speak the dominant language with authority, the ex-centric writer uses it with overcorrection and over-emphasis. Yet this was quite the opposite in the case of Mansfield, who was always if anything profligate with understatement. So confident is she as a short story practitioner that she breaks, pauses, swerves, adjusts and withholds her meaning constantly, almost promiscuously, in spite or perhaps because of working within this most disciplined of narrative forms. Indeed, she uses not just ellipsis, but strong, daring, ostentatious ellipsis, what we might call hyper-implication – implying the more in order to pique or stimulate the more. Significantly but not surprisingly, this strong ellipsis emerges in especially haunting ways in her wartime writing, as in my main example below. Though this is not war writing as it might conventionally be described, it uses ellipses in powerful ways to suggest the unsaid and unsayable of war, its experiences of loss, breakage and absence.

'The Wind Blows', twists and turns

I move now to showing how strong ellipsis amplifies meaning in Mansfield by considering some evocative if inevitably selective examples from her work, the first very well-known and dramatic. I want to look at these passages through the cognitive framework supplied by relevance theory in order to explore in more detail how allusive narrative prose operates in the hands of this arch-practitioner. How do Mansfield's elliptical devices, far from restricting meaning, allow it to cascade copiously through a text? These insights will also shed interesting light on the workings of literary language more broadly; on how it often carries and shapes meaning through understatement rather than ostensive meaning; how it supports, expands, clarifies and even enables our thought processes, as I was beginning to say. As Terence Cave has pointed out in *Thinking with Literature*, adapting the insights of Deirdre Wilson, a defining feature of what we call literary writing may in fact be that it underspecifies, not the opposite. In my own creative practice, certainly, I can vouch that at those moments when the teacher or explainer in me wishes to intrude upon a scene I am writing, the momentum or *flow* of the writing can help to override these efforts to point out and direct.

My first case in point is of course 'The Wind Blows' (1915), a story that bears perhaps one of the most thrilling instances of ellipsis in Mansfield's work, an instance so mobile and disruptive that it creates a dramatic torsion or time-twist at the story's end. Based on childhood memories of a windy day in Wellington, and narrated from the point of view of Matilda, the Mansfield surrogate, 'The Wind Blows' is famously full of wind energy, registered through both longer and shorter breaks, starts and gaps. The story comes in two parts: the first concerned with a music lesson on a windy morning and the second set later that day, as Matilda evades chores by going out walking with Bogey her brother.

Most of the short, dashing paragraphs in 'The Wind Blows' carry at least one ellipsis and together these work to suggest, variously, the rush and disruption of the wind, the hither-and-thither movements of windswept trees, other plants and waves, and the feelings of restlessness and jumps in attention that these stimulate. Throughout, the running if inevitably broken line of ellipses that the story effectively traces, reinforces the onrushing effect of the present-tense narration, insisting that it is read at speed. The overall effect is powerfully kinesic – both the words and the gaps between words coming together to suggest something of the pounding and gusting of the wind – effects that then build to the dramatic break in time and focus that forms the climax towards the end of the story.

However, the ellipses in 'The Wind Blows' do not work only to heighten the effects of the wind. Many of the breaks and shifts also trigger a countervailing impulse to check back rather than to rush on, prompting that impulse that I described earlier, of looking and looking again – an effect that is particularly resonant in a story about reminiscence and loss. The quality is further enhanced by some of the story's other repetitive effects, in particular by the many instances of repeating words and phrases, such as 'revolting [...] revolting', 'Goodbye, goodbye', and, in particular, 'The wind, the wind'. This last becomes a kind of refrain or running motif in the story, the thrice-repeated phrase first appearing separated by a comma and, then, moments later and at the story's close, by a stronger ellipsis, a rushing dash.

Turning to consider salient examples of these effects from the story, notice in particular those instances where a hyphen or ellipsis – such as '. . .' – breaks an utterance off, leaving its meaning implicit, and/or those where the gusting of the wind or the emotion it generates seems to rush into the gap, as it were sweeping the words away. Notice also the differing lengths of the ellipses, which range from the relatively short pause of hyphens to longer triple-dot and four-dot ellipses.[11]

> 'How hideous life is – revolting, simply revolting . . . . And now her hat-elastic's snapped'.
>
> 'Her fingers tremble so that she can't undo the knot in the music satchel. It's the wind. . . . And her heart beats so fast she feels it must lift her blouse up and down'.
>
> 'She doesn't believe he even hears . . . and then suddenly his fresh hand with the ring on it reaches over and opens Beethoven'.
>
> 'Why is he so . . . She will not cry – she has nothing to cry about . . .'
>
> 'Hasn't anyone written poems to the wind? . . . "I bring fresh flowers to the leaves and showers." . . . What nonsense'.[12]

As this column of quoted lines immediately demonstrates, so many of the story's lines are paused and fragmented that they seem themselves battered by the force of the wind that they at the same time evoke. The cumulative effects thus become not only atmospheric but also performative. True, the gaps are nonetheless conducive to interpretation, and various implications might be construed to fill them, such as: 'It's the wind [that makes her feel so on edge]'; 'She doesn't believe he even hears [her speak]'. But the overall impression is that in the circumstances, buffeted by the wind, such completions are needless, even excessive. The wind has created feelings of agitation so pervasive as to fray and shred the story's sentences themselves – just as the 'Teneriffe-work teacloth' on the line is torn into ribbons.[13]

At the same time, interspersed with these breaks, the contrasting effect of the many repeated words and phrases – 'It is dusky – just getting dusky'[14] – appears to still the run of the sentences momentarily. Yet this potential is set aside almost as soon as posited. With the overriding accent on onward rushing, the dominant verbal effect of the repetitive phrases is instead of a series of fretful, involuntary cries and exclamations produced by and accentuating the general mood. Balancing brief halts against momentary havering, Mansfield puts maximal pressure on these various forms of under-specification to give the reader a world awry, blown out of kilter. At which point we remember that an earlier version of the story first appeared in *The Signature* in 1915 (under the title 'Autumns: II'), the year of her brother Leslie's death in the war.[15]

These countervailing effects of interruption and repetition – not forgetting also the break or breath taken between the repeated phrases – then build to the paragraph in 'The Wind Blows' in which the sister and brother, Matilda and Bogey (his voice breaking), who have been walking in the wind on the breakwater, look at the steamer with 'lights everywhere' leaving Wellington harbour and 'putting out to sea'.[16] In a remarkable instance of switchback, of twisting or turning to look and look again, the two see their future selves on the deck of the departing boat, looking back at their past selves, in fact their present selves, windswept, standing on the shore. The effect here is accentuated by the emphasis on *They*, the brother and sister standing together, at one and the same time here and there, now and in the future: 'It's the light that makes her look so awfully beautiful and mysterious. . . . *They* are on board leaning over the rail arm in arm.' They (in the future) recall the music lesson on that windy day years ago (in the narrative present), and both now and in the future the chant of goodbye begins: 'Goodbye, little island, goodbye. . .'. This is the second-last or third-last ellipsis depending how we count: the point of view returns to the shore as the dark stretches a 'wing' over the tumbling water, and we think once again of

Bogey's death. At which point the last ellipsis comes, 'Don't forget. . . .'; and then, closing, the refrain 'The wind – the wind'.[17]

The final jump-cut of the ship departing now and in the future creates an unsettling effect of a double valediction, a repeated farewell – 'goodbye [...] goodbye' – sharpened by way of that strange device of anticipated hindsight. This proleptic imagining of the war's losses is reminiscent of some of Edward Thomas's poetry of this same period, in particular 'The New House', but also the suggestion of the 'would have been different' of 'The team's head-brass', for example. In 'The New House', a wind is again blowing, again creating a sense of restlessness and foreboding. The sounds of the wind bring memories of 'old griefs' but also feelings of dread that come to pivot around the unbalancing, out-of-kilter pause in the first line of the last stanza. For the wind that blows now will also blow in the future, long after 'the griefs not yet begun' that haunt the soldier-speaker will themselves have passed away:

> All was foretold me; naught
> Could I foresee;
> But I learnt how the wind would sound
> After these things should be.[18]

As in Thomas, so in Mansfield, the elliptical effects that spark these abrupt shifts into an anticipated yet unimaginable future can be amplified through an inferential model of reading. Similarly, the juxtaposition of the two writers can help reciprocally to illuminate the powers of inference-making in both, as here. In both, but perhaps especially in Mansfield, the use of ellipsis brings an aesthetic looseness that is nonetheless highly disciplined: it provides an object lesson in literary under-specification. Mansfield shows us how ellipsis might pause a reader's involvement, yet paradoxically drive it on; how it now constrains and now opens out our interpretation. Her ellipses signal that various possibilities might unfold from this point, yet the preceding flow of the language at the same time tells us that one possibility in particular is strongly suggested, which is why the rest can be understated or left implicit. This returns us to the paradoxical aspects of ellipsis: how the seeming gaps in meaning are in fact full of meaning, the breaks in direction charged with directedness. Mansfield's characteristic sudden pauses and re-statements repeatedly jolt the reader into thinking about where we stand in relation to the story. We find ourselves self-reflexively suspended in the flow of a character's consciousness at the very moment that these elliptical effects jump us out of it.

'Miss Brill', among other stories, offers another clear example of how sudden pauses and repetitions can expose what can't be openly admitted, yet is hidden in plain sight. The eponymous Miss Brill will not let on to herself about the poverty, isolation and unfashionability of her situation, which is epitomized in the stark reality of the tiny 'cupboard' room that she inhabits. A sense of her determined self-deception comes through the evasive starts and pauses that begin to build from the first paragraph of the story, leading up to the first oblique mention of her room: 'They looked like they'd just come from dark little rooms or even – even cupboards!'[19] The subterfuge on which Miss Brill's entire mode of being depends is mimicked in the sidestepping movement of the words, the delaying repetition of 'even' balanced on either side of the hyphen's further pause, before the almost-unsayable 'cupboard' is finally uttered. It is a case not so much of looking and looking again to confirm a recognition, as looking to look away and then obsessively back again, repeatedly to deny recognition: '[She] went into the little dark room – her room like a cupboard – and sat down on the red eiderdown.'[20] The tiny switchback manoeuvres follow the micro-movements of Miss Brill's consciousness, noting the things she observes but cannot fully acknowledge. As Mansfield herself described it, she put effort into getting the 'rise and fall of every paragraph [right] to fit [Miss Brill] – and to fit her on that day at that very moment'. The replay in Mansfield's own sentence is indicative and arresting, as is the description of the process of tuning into Miss Brill as akin to playing over a musical composition: 'After Id written it I read it aloud – numbers of times – just as one would *play over* a musical composition, trying to get it nearer and nearer to the expression of Miss Brill – until it fitted her'.[21]

There are so many other instances in Mansfield of delicate yet unmistakeable inference – instances where under-specification heightens ellipsis, even as the ellipsis at the same time informs how the implications are processed. So, again, 'A Cup of Tea' unfolds as an answer to the opening question as to whether rich Rosemary Fell is pretty, accentuated by the ellipsis in the second line: 'No you couldn't have called her beautiful. Pretty? Well, if you took her to pieces. . . . But why be so cruel as to take anyone to pieces?'[22] The story of Rosemary's awkward pickup of the 'shadowy' Miss Smith, whom her husband finds 'so astonishingly pretty',[23] rushes into the break after the word 'pieces'. 'The Fly' for its part is syncopated throughout by ellipses indicating realities that the characters – Old Woodifield, the boss – once again cannot quite name or accept. These culminate in the dull thud of the final pause and break, confirming the boss's vapidity, his inability to acknowledge the enormity of the loss that has befallen him: 'He fell to wondering what it was he had been thinking about before. What was it? It was. . . . He took out his handkerchief and passed it inside his collar. For the life of him he could not remember.'[24] A vicious counterpoint is at work in that final four-dot ellipsis: the enormity of the loss is too great to process, but the implication is also that he is too limited to do so.

In closing I want to look briefly at that contemporary master of inference, Ali Smith, who has so palpably learnt from Mansfield how to 'fit' her narrative to the movements of narrative consciousness especially, as in my example, of a *moved* consciousness. (Her debt is now as it were fully acknowledged with Mansfield's appearance as part of an important backstory in *Spring* [2018].[25]) Smith, too, provides clear object lessons in under-specification, concertedly using repeat-phrases, doublings-back and other stop-start effects to evoke, even to re-enact, moments charged with memory and emotion. To illustrate, I take just one example from an early Smith short story 'The world with love', which stands out for the way in which the moment of recognition it records opens the rest of the story.[26] Filled with echoes and counter-echoes, the story flows from that point in the narrative present when the narrator Sam's memory is sparked by a chance encounter with a former classmate and crush in an unfamiliar city. Her friend's parting remark, a reference to the time their French teacher went 'mad', takes Sam back to the day when various thrills and sympathies – including for this other girl, and for the French language – simultaneously came into focus, encapsulated in the sentence the 'maddened' teacher wrote on the board: 'Look Upon the World With Love', "Then *it comes, of course it comes*, God yes, you say, what a day, eh? and as you're walking along the road, late for your appointment, *it all comes, it all comes* flooding back".[27] The twice double-repeats of this remarkable sentence, highlighted above, follow the folding-back and then release of Sam's memory as 'it comes [...] it comes [...] it all comes, it all comes'.

We think at once of many similar doublings and returns in Mansfield, sometimes for dramatic or performative effect, memorably in 'The Wind Blows', sometimes marking or arresting the flow of time, sometimes signalling a lack, absence or falling short. The closing conversation between Constantia and Josephine in 'The Daughters of the Late Colonel', perforated with no less than five ellipses of different kinds, is a powerful example of this last effect. The death of their father the Colonel has further hollowed out the purposelessness of the daughters' lives, yet they lack a means of expressing this in words. Instead their pauses, breaks and inability to say give a repeating echo of this all-consuming vacuity. Their utterances in this sense know more about their situation than they.

For Terence Cave, an 'intentional calculus' is involved in any act of reading: the reader continually weighs and reconsiders the implications that the writer offers and opens out to us.[28] Ellipsis plays a key role in that calculus. In all the instances we have explored, ellipsis here and there aided by repetition has insisted upon a second look or re-consideration, and that reflection back has in turn required that one set of those implications is preferred over others. Close reading the inferential patterns of Mansfield's writing in this sense clarifies some of the cognitive moves that we make as we read, even as those patterns simultaneously heighten our sense of reading's evanescent yet strongly determinative processes.

Notes

1 Anne Toner, *Ellipsis in English Literature* (Cambridge: Cambridge University Press, 2015), p. i.

2 Rita Felski, *The Limits of Critique* (Chicago: University of Chicago Press, 2015), pp. 186–93.

3 I draw on the phenomenologist Hans Robert Jauss's term, in *Toward an Aesthetic of Reception*, trans. Timothy Bahti (Minneapolis: University of Minnesota Press, 1982).

4 Rita Felski, 'Introduction', *New Literary History*, 45, no. 2 (2014): v–xi.

5 Elleke Boehmer, *Postcolonial Poetics: 21st-Century Critical Readings* (Basingstoke: Palgrave Macmillan, 2018), pp. 1–6.

6 This account is indebted to Dan Sperber and Deirdre Wilson, *Relevance: Communication and Cognition*, 2nd edn (Oxford: Blackwell, 1995). For literary critical applications of relevance, see Terence Cave, *Thinking with Literature: Towards a Cognitive Criticism* (Oxford: Oxford University Press, 2016); Adrian Pilkington, *Poetic Effects* (Amsterdam: John Benjamins, 2000).

7 See Kathryn Banks, '"Look Again", "Listen, Listen", "Keep Looking": Emergent Properties and Sensorimotor Imagining in Mary Oliver's Poetry', and Deirdre Wilson, 'Relevance Theory and Literary Interpretation', in *Reading Beyond the Code: Literature and Relevance Theory*, eds Terence Cave and Deirdre Wilson (Oxford: Oxford University Press, 2018), pp. 129–48, 185–204.

8 Clare Hanson, 'Things Out of Words: Towards a Poetics of Short Fiction', in *Re-reading the Short Story*, ed. Clare Hanson (Basingstoke: Macmillan, 1989), p. 25.

9 Ibid. She continues: 'We accept this degree of mystery, elision, uncertainty in the short story as we would not in the novel'.

10 Hanson, 'Introduction', in *Re-reading the Short Story*, p. 2.

11 Note that Mansfield's, '. . .' and, '. . . .' ellipses are usually double-spaced out of respect for her typography.

12 CW2, pp. 226–9.
13 CW2, p. 226.
14 CW2, p. 229.
15 'Autumns: II', *Signature*, 1, 4 October 1915, pp. 18–23. Signed 'Matilda Berry'. Mansfield would revise the story as 'The Wind Blows', transcribed into the third person, for the *Athenaeum*, 4713, 27 August 1920, pp. 262–3.
16 CW2, p. 229.
17 CW2, pp. 228, 229.
18 Edward Thomas, 'The New House' and 'As the Team's Head-Brass', in *Collected Poems*, ed. Edna Longley (Highgreen: Bloodaxe, 2004), pp. 68, 123–4.
19 CW2, p. 252.
20 CW2, p. 254.
21 Letter to Richard Murry, 17 January 1921. *Letters* 4, p. 165.
22 CW2, p. 461.
23 CW2, p. 466.
24 CW2, p. 480.
25 Ali Smith, *Spring* (London: Faber, 2019).
26 Ali Smith, 'The world with love', in *Free Love and Other Stories* (London: Virago, 2015), pp. 141–9.
27 Ibid., p. 142.
28 Cave, p. 34.

3

Dirty snow

Mansfield, Joyce and the modernist snow globe

Enda Duffy

This began as a chapter on 'Mansfield's Energy' but has morphed into a document I've code-named 'Youki'. 'Youki' is the Japanese word for snow. It was also the name that the modernist Japanese painter Foujita gave to his first French partner – as her skin, to him, was as white as snow. Foujita, modernist painter[1] with an idiosyncratic style, newly arrived in Paris from Japan, and Katherine Mansfield, modernist writer, newly arrived in London from New Zealand, had much in common: both found themselves very quickly at the fulcrums of the London and Paris art and literary avant-gardes. Foujita and Mansfield became central actors in their respective 'smart sets'. Both, in part because of their very different Pacific coast origins, went on to produce art that was perversely at an angle to, and offered an always perverse glance upon, the various avant-garde conventions of their times. Each was celebrated as central but each was also – sometimes subtly, more often overtly – condemned as marginal, tiresome, and not quite 'sound' by the local arbiters of taste. Both, thereby, managed all the more effectively to bring to the surface in their works much that is most interesting in the Eurocentric modernisms. Each in their own way strove for what, using a conventional shorthand for literary or painterly 'depth,' one might call 'profundity'. Both seemed to work to grasp a crucial modernist dialectic: how to be both 'smart' and 'deep' at once. In this chapter, we focus on how this worked itself out in Mansfield's reading, as a 'smart' London-based writer, of the au courant literary scene in Paris. This is the subject of her short story 'Je ne parle pas français'.

The world of bohemian literary and artistic ambition described in 'Je ne parle pas français', a milieu which Mansfield knew on occasion first hand, was the very world over which Foujita, along with Kiki de Montparnasse, Man Ray, Chaim

Soutine, Moïse Kisling, Pablo Picasso, Gertrude Stein, Tristan Tzara and the rest, presided in Paris. The Montparnasse café, nightclub and artist-studio culture described, for example, in the memoirs of Kiki de Montparnasse[2] – the artist's model and artist in her own right Alice Prin[3] – gets recast in Mansfield's 'Je ne parle pas français' as a less glamorous milieu of frustrated youthful ambition, pretentiousness and pervasive ennui. At the same time, both Kiki's memoirs, with their celebration of a flashy, vaguely louche, glamour, and 'Je ne parle pas français', with its limning of a more threadbare loucheness, are each centrally concerned with the question of whether what might be termed 'superficiality', that is, the lacquer-hard surface gloss characteristic of modernist 'smartness', can ever be reconciled with a 'depth model' of art's value, the implication of profound significance offered by the Western critical tradition of aesthetic critique.[4] Consider how, on the one hand, the critical-aesthetic background of the various modernisms consists of a long-running defence of high art's value which stretches from Walter Pater's *Studies in the History of the Renaissance* (1873)[5] to Theodor Adorno's *Aesthetic Theory*, while, on the other, it is marked by interventions that consider its strange newness, from Mikhail Bakhtin's *The Dialogic Imagination*[6] to the final chapter of Eric Auerbach's *Mimesis* ('The Brown Stocking, on Woolf and Proust') first published in 1946.[7] Considering the work of the short story writer and British modernist coterie star Katherine Mansfield, in relation to the work of the painter and Parisian modernist coterie provocateur Foujita, this chapter will attend to moments when the modernist dialectic of smartness and depth reaches a crisis. For both – as for a good number of other Western modernists who were slightly off-kilter in relation to their contemporaries, ranging from such high literature figures as D. H. Lawrence and James Joyce to the prolific French detective-novelist Simenon – these moments, strangely, involve snow. For Foujita, for a start, there is Mouki. For Mansfield, we will focus here on the key, wondrous paragraph in 'Je ne parle pas français' that describes a snowfall.

Snow is not what one associates with this story's milieu. Yet snow turns out to be at the heart of modernism. From Claude Monet's *Wheatstacks, Snow Effect, Morning* and numerous impressionist snowscapes by Camille Pissarro, Claude Monet and Alfred Sisley to the snow-white *Suprematist Composition: White on White* (1918) of Kazimir Malevich and the post-Second World War *White Painting* of Robert Rauschenberg (1951), the white-canvas works of Cy Twombly, Agnes Martin and Lucio Fontana, a snow-effect, pioneered, appropriately, in post-enlightenment Western painting by the German romantic Caspar David Friedrich, has been a signature of the dialectic of significance and depth, and meaningless and nothingness, in modern Western art. Similarly, the snow sublime pervades post-enlightenment Western literature at crucial moments. As with Friedrich in painting, Wordsworth in English poetry launched the modern poetic association of snow, profundity, sorrow and indecipherable nothingness in 'Lucy Gray' (1799): 'Her feet disperse the powdery snow,/That rises up like smoke'.[8] It is the modernists, however – Joyce in the famous ending of 'The Dead', Lawrence in the scene of the death of Gerald among the wastes of white snow in *Women in Love*, or even the depiction of post-partum madness in Emily Holmes Coleman's searing novel *The Shutter of Snow* (1930),[9] or George Simenon's account of criminal life in a Nazi-occupied brothel, *La neige était sale* (*Dirty Snow*)[10] – who render snowscapes as the indices of blank intensity. Snow appears in the text as a marker of a crisis point in modernist aesthetics.

In Mansfield's 'Je ne parle pas français', written in 1918, a young writer, whose gender is not revealed for some pages, enters an unexceptional Paris café, sits in a corner and orders coffee. He observes the *patronne* and the waiter, the one gazing out the window, the other shuffling about, as he cradles a glass of coffee in his hands. It is the moment between dusk and dark; it is quiet. Then comes the snow scene:

> Outside, one could just see through the dusk that it had begun to snow. One could just see the shapes of horses and carts and people, soft and white, moving through the feathery air. The waiter disappeared and reappeared with an armful of straw. He strewed it over the floor from the door to the counter and round about the stove with humble, almost adoring gestures. One would not have been surprised if the door had opened and the Virgin Mary had come in, riding upon an ass, her meek hands folded over her big belly. . . .[11]

This scene cannot but remind the reader of the other great short story snow scene in early-twentieth-century writing, another moment when the hero is intensely touched by the sight, through a window, of the snow beginning to fall. Here is the ending to James Joyce's final *Dubliners* story, 'The Dead':

> A few light taps upon the pane made him turn to the window. It had begun to snow again. He watched sleepily the flakes, silver and dark, falling obliquely against the lamplight. The time had come for him to set out on his journey westward. Yes, the newspapers were right: snow was general all over Ireland. It was falling on every part of the dark central plain, on the treeless hills, falling softly upon the Bog of Allen and, farther westward, softly falling into the dark mutinous Shannon waves. It was falling, too, upon every part of the lonely churchyard on the hill where Michael Furey lay buried. It lay thickly drifted on the crooked crosses and headstones, on the spears of the little gate, on the barren

> thorns. His soul swooned slowly as he heard the snow falling faintly through the universe and faintly falling, like the descent of their last end, upon all the living and the dead.[12]

Following Joyce's own critical register, the standard reading might see it as the account of a supreme epiphany, that is, of a moment in which a stimulus, unexceptional in itself, for some inexplicable reason triggers the hero-viewer's response. This stimulus engenders something akin to insight, a new level, perhaps, of what Georg Lukács, in a famous essay, would term 'consciousness', or merely what the critic Paul de Man would subsequently term 'insight'. Yet this register, it seems clear, is wholly inadequate to describe what is happening in these snow epiphanies. Or rather, the snow scene, the use of snow as emblem of unreadable nothingness, in putting the trope of the pathetic fallacy to the test, brings the epiphanic logic to the brink, and leaves it open to inspection. Moreover, Mansfield's snow-globe moment, published at the end of the First World War (Joyce's work was written in 1907 and published in 1914),[13] may be said to offer a more complex exegesis than does Joyce's. Joyce's caressing, repetitive lines, with 'The snow [...] falling faintly [...] and faintly falling', still hugs the shores of the French *symboliste* tradition, as well as that of fin-de-siècle decadence in the wake of Walter Pater and J. K. Huysmans, even if it also satirizes it. Mansfield's narrative turn, after the waiter pulls the blinds and the snow-show is over, suggests that in her writing she is more self-consciously negotiating within and around a range of subsequent modernist-isms and, in doing so, acting altogether more playfully as she explores the possible symbolic possibilities of snow.

The modernist snow aesthetic in general encompasses expected elements. It signals, in the first place, a concern with illness, with traumatic crisis and with death. One of the great moments in this regard in English modernism is the scene of Gerald Crich's death among the snows in Chapter 30, 'Snowed Up', of D. H. Lawrence's *Women in Love*. (Since the Lawrence-Middleton-Murry and Mansfield circle – they had first met in 1913 – may be a model for the Dick-Raoul-Mouse triangle in 'Je ne parle pas français', and that *Women in Love* was mostly written in Cornwall in 1916–17, a case might be made for direct influence.) Next, consider the white Alpine snow-world of Thomas Mann's *The Magic Mountain*, in which the excursions, debates, intrigues and medical examinations of the tuberculosis-afflicted patients, the whole *danse macabre* of slow death from TB's death-sentence, is orchestrated against a background of incessant snowfalls and snowy days. After the Second World War, Giorgio de Rezori wrote one of the most distinguished memoirs of fading European aristocratic life under the title *The Snows of Yesteryear*, while one of the most perfect post-war novels of Nazi occupation and bleak existential ennui is George Simenon's *Dirty Snow*. In all these works, snow is associated with death, and specifically with death as blank oblivion. It is also in each associated with the past, with remembrance. In Joyce's 'The Dead', likewise, the snow-revelation follows Greta's report on Michael Furey, the boy from the gasworks who she says died young; in 'Je ne parle pas français' there is no dying as such, except that the story is cast as an evoked memory of a dead or discarded friendship. Mansfield, in giving us the snow scene without the death, and then analysing it, lets us see how this scene is not a resurgence of the fear of dying, nor is it a modernist, secular version of that old, sub-religious narrative form, the ghost story (even if the snow scene in modernism often reads as a soft alibi for the gothic). Rather, what we are given in Mansfield is the snow scene as sign of a fear of death in life, of a life unlived. Snow in 'Je ne parle pas français' refers to a fading-out, a *petit mort*, a life-limit.

Note that the snow paragraphs from 'Je ne parle pas français' and 'The Dead' both invoke religious imagery, only to undercut it. Joyce's Gabriel, it appears, has a soul: 'His soul swooned slowly'; this swooning soul is cited as the prerequisite of his communion with the dead. Raoul, in Mansfield's story, also waxes religious: 'One would not have been surprised if the door had opened and the Virgin Mary had come in, riding upon her ass, her meek hands folded over her belly.'[14] Yet both invocations counter religion with parody. This implies at least three levels of knowingness. First, we sense a tragic awareness that here are attitudes and images ('her meek hands', 'His soul swooned slowly'), in which smart modernisms no longer believe. Second, there is a defiant celebration of the distance that makes such parody possible. Third, there is a hint of wistfulness that there might be some alternative way of intensely or deeply experiencing, that would substitute for the former one, which the familiar religious iconography had been adequate to evoke. There might, the jokey religious imagery implies, be something more to experience beyond the white blankness of the snow.

Snow, therefore, might be a stand-in for the white page on which nothing is written, because nothing can be written, since the outpost of experiences which the modernist has the literary powers to express, is what has been reached. The arrival of snow signals modernism's test-case, its limit. What is being tested, therefore, might be restated as follows: not simply meaning versus meaninglessness, but rather – since the snow itself is a blank page, a layer of abstraction scattered over everything in the observable world – intensities of being-in-the-world versus the incapacity to experience one's existence. On the one hand, modernism is cast as the literature of alienation, of anomie, of ennui – literally, of the capacity to be cool, not to have feelings. In most Mansfield short stories, and in virtually every short story in *Dubliners*, in Eliot's 'The Love Song of J. Alfred Prufrock' or in the character of Gregor Samsa in Franz Kafka's 'Metamorphosis' and very literally, even in the title, of Robert Musil's *The Man Without Qualities*, what we are shown is the anomie of 'stunted' lives. We are presented with characters – Miss Brill or Gabriel Conroy or J. Alfred Prufrock – who are not simply bored, or lonely, or philistines in Matthew Arnold's Victorian sense of the term. Neither is it the point of these texts that these characters are unable to 'succeed in life'. Rather, their tragedy (and it is limned as a tragedy to varying degrees in each literary instance) is that each is experiencing the slow death of affect. They do not really or fully live, which is to say, none of them deeply or profoundly feel. This is presented as the governing condition of Western urban modernity. Snow, simply a kind of white weather, is the image wheeled into place when this realization reaches a crisis.

Nevertheless, Raoul and Gabriel, and also Prufrock and Samsa, are each presented implicitly as pathetic, even tragic figures. We are made privy to Gabriel's host of regrets, his feeble self-loathing. We are shown Raoul's pallid regrets also, at missing out on some human connection with this brittle, grasping and finally uninteresting British couple in whom he had hoped to find, foolishly he now realizes, some version of authentic value. All end up alone, and this aloneness is rendered as an index of their pathos. At the same time, the fact that the text presents us with an awareness of this tragedy implies that there is someone – the author – hovering in the background, 'like God paring his fingernails', as Joyce put it, who can judge these lives as tragic because he or she knows of a better, fuller mode of experiencing. There must be an awareness of an alternative, more valid, life form, if these figures' lives, when presented, are found wanting. The epiphanic moment, then, when an unexpected, casual event manages to arouse the character into a new insight or feeling, should be the trip-switch that ends the downward cycle of unfelt, somehow under-lived life. The epiphany involving snow, however, turns out to be a special modernist case: the call to the observing character by this falling snow is not from the vantage point of a richer life – it is not what Eliot in 'The Waste Land' termed 'the music from a further room' – but rather, it is from the point of total blankness, of the total impossibility to live life not 'deeply', but at all. The epiphany, in other words, relies, as its condition to occur out of the blue, on a kind of last-stage awareness, a species of physiological memory, that there is a 'more full' life to be lived than the one that the modern Western subject is currently living. The epiphany, encountered by the person who has almost forgotten about the possibility of intense feelings and opened perceptions, suddenly jolts her into remembrance and realization. The snow epiphany, however, presents that subject with a more daunting truth: that the dormant memory, forgotten, can still be recalled, but that there is no store of past intensities there to be dragged into the open of consciousness. For the modern subject, this is a shocking denouement.

It is this realization, then, that 'Je ne parle pas français' places at the very start of its story. This is exactly the opposite to Joyce, who places it at the very end: 'The Dead', thereby, mimics Gabriel's cowardly need to defer the truth. It means, however, that while 'The Dead' can leave the reader ambivalent about the precise meaning of the snowfall witnessed by Gabriel through the window of the Gresham Hotel, 'Je ne parle pas français', in its very structure, sets itself the responsibility of analysing the meaning of the limit-epiphany. Indeed, the story is set up very consciously in this way: there is no need to begin with a long vignette of the narrator in his favourite café and certainly not to see a snowfall through its window. The tale, we are often told, is subsequently narrated through a series of flashbacks. The very term 'flashback' is a fascinating one in this regard: it refers to a visual memory, a memory recorded and retrieved as an image and, specifically, as a moving image, as in a film. The term has a specific resonance in film editing and the construction of filmic temporal narratives. The *Oxford English Dictionary*, therefore, records its first usage in a film review of 1916, while its first quasi-literary usage is attributed to H. G. Wells in his *Experiment in Autobiography*[15] of 1934. It is thus a quintessentially modernist word, derived from film editing and the speeded-up possibilities of film narrative enabled by the splicing of film shots. This new speed of memory-retrieval as moving image, enabled by analogy because of the technological advance in representation that was the movies, is taken on by Mansfield as the fast-flashbacks logic by which she constructs her short story (and the movies are referenced in the 'Je ne parle pas', when Raoul, incongruously, and, again, 'out of the blue', speaks of 'a rag-picker on the American cinema').[16] At the same time, it is as if the literary-textual form of the short story is not quite ready, in 1917, for the speedy jerkiness of the filmic flashback, so that, after the snow-moment occurs, we get two pages of the narrator Raoul's attempt to understand and embroider it. Or rather, the filmic mode floods into what might have been an analytic, measured narrative: what we get in fact is a modernist, even surrealist montage of clashing, unlike elements, each popped before us in an excited piling-up. It is as if Raoul, even though he wants to be a writer, has had an education of his mind's eye through those American movies he confesses, by the way, to having seen as a matter of course. In fact, in a rare moment of direct self-judgement, Raoul blames the cinema: considering why he is 'so bitter against life', he provides an unexpected and unexpectedly succinct answer: 'The direct result of the American cinema acting upon a weak mind.'[17]

Thus this analysis becomes a filmic moving-image montage, a collection of modernist fragments, in which images crowd in, and we are shown the Raoul, the would-be author of poetry, determined to physically write them down as a way to turn them into text that, literally, he will not need to remember. First, the narrator Raoul tells us he wants to write down his religious image (and its 'dying fall', with its Miltonic resonance, which will soon be taken up (1922, probably written early 1921) by Eliot in 'The Waste Land'). This coming to consciousness, therefore, is presented as the writer's avariciousness, his greedy banking of not only his own images, but those he admires from past writers. This merely breaks 'the spell'. Despite this, the snow scene seems to set up the condition for a cascade of others. As Raoul reaches for paper, he finds 'only a morsel of pink blotting paper, incredibly soft and limp and almost moist, like the tongue of a little dead kitten, which I've never felt.'[18] The simile of the tongue of the dead kitten, soft, moist and limp, is surreal: it introduces animals (pets), death (of a small animal), tactility (the thought of touching a dead cat's tongue), clichés of femininity (pink, cat-like) and, via the tongue, notions of orality which are another register of telling memories, as opposed both to the image from the movies and the written text, which Raoul wants to compose. It turns from white snow to pink skin. It is smart, self-referential about writing, and it is mordantly funny, both in its perverse excessiveness and in its open admission that here is an experience which the narrator has not had: 'which I've never felt'. In other words, its surreal resonances are legion: it generates an imaginative fusillade of associations. And then, 'rolling the little dead kitten's tongue around my finger', Raoul reads the writing on the paper: 'My eyes took in the girls' names and dirty jokes [...] They are always the same.'[19] The snow, which had morphed into a pink tongue, has now become a page, inscribed with names and slogans from the blasé, feeling-deprived life. 'But then' – what's this, the real epiphany behind the snow scene? – 'Quite suddenly, at the bottom of the page my eyes fell on that stupid stale phrase, "*Je ne parle pas français*"'. What follows is a full analysis by Raoul of that moment:

> There! it had come – the moment [...], it tumbled me over; I was simply overwhelmed. And the physical feeling was so curious, so particular. It was as

> if all of me, except my head and arms, all of me that was under the table, had simply dissolved, melted, turned into water. Just my head remained and two sticks of arms pressing on to the table. But, ah! the agony of that moment! How can I describe it? I didn't think of anything. I didn't even cry out to myself. Just for one moment I was not. I was Agony, Agony, Agony.[20]

What follows is a quick joke showpiece on how, on the one hand, self-consciousness can kill the spontaneity which the romantics deemed necessary for feeling, and, on the other, how any assumed spontaneous overflow of powerful feeling will invariably be enacted as a display for the self: 'Am I capable of feeling as strongly as that? No second-rate mind could have experienced such an intensity of feeling … so purely'.[21] Then, at last, comes the 'reveal': after deeming that a sense of history and of the past is mere regret, and claiming, rather ruefully, that 'I have made it a rule of my life never to regret and never to look back', he compares himself to a dog (after the cat, another animal, another pet) who 'thinks at last, at last, he hears the familiar step again' and cries out to Mouse 'Where are you?'[22] Mouse, as we discover in the rest of the story, is a silent young Englishwoman whom he had once met.

The epiphany which becomes the story's title, therefore, results from an awakened memory. Joyce's 'The Dead' and Mansfield's 'Je ne parle pas français' have that in common: behind the epiphanies in each is a superficially intriguing, in fact highly dubious, backstory. The first is told by Greta about her first love, Michael Furey, who died. The second is now told to us by Raoul about an Englishman he had befriended, who brought a young woman, 'Mouse' to Paris, where Raoul found her rooms at an hotel. In each case, the backstories have two parts, and each of them provides numerous possibilities for speculation, all of them false clues as to the meaning of what appears to really matter, the epiphanies. Each in a real sense is noticeably over-conventional, even clichéd, as it tells of a love triangle: Greta-Michael-Gabriel and Raoul-Dick-Mouse. Each leaves us as the overhearers of the tales, with gossipy questions: Did Michael really die of thwarted love, and was Raoul in love with Dick and jealous of Mouse? This reaction of curiosity is then trumped by the much more illegible (and possibly 'authentic') reaction of the main characters in each story – that is, the epiphanic moment experienced by both Gabriel at the end of 'The Dead' and Raoul in the café early in 'Je ne parle pas français'. Each of the backstories wobbles uneasily, in their conventionality, between a certain timelessness (the vicissitudes of love) and a modern smartness (note, for example, in the case of both Greta and Dick, the smart modern, almost P. G. Woodhouse-like, names).

Crucially, however, these two modern figures, Greta and Dick, are each shown to have experienced a timeless tug of passion that in each case the central figures in each story – Gabriel and Raoul – decide that they themselves have never felt. The 'function' of Greta and Dick in their respective stories, therefore, is to signify the impossibility, in modernity, of finding a deep meaning in life by following the currents of physical desire.

Greta and Dick loved the dead Michael and the living, if enigmatic, 'Mouse'. These latter two – Michael and Mouse – have a dubious existence: the question of 'did they really exist at all, or did they exist more strongly as projected fantasies than as real people?' attaches itself to each of them. This patina of unreality is reinforced by the fact that, for the hearer of Michael's story – Gabriel – and for the witness – Raoul – in Mansfield's tale, the final fate of both Michael and Mouse is in the last instance signified, as it were, by scenes of falling snow. Michael and Mouse are shadow figures, and their shadows – their shades, their ghostly presences – fade into the oblivion of falling whiteness. Thus these two characters – placed before us as potentially the most 'interesting' in each tale – are shown in each story to fade into oblivion, the oblivion of snow. The fact that in each story the snow, which it is implied carries the shades of both Greta and Michael, is seen through a window further enhances its movie-like, spectacular and ethereal, quality. This snow itself is very noticeably kitsch. It's the snow seen on a Christmas card or in a snow globe. (In 1941, at a very late modernist moment, Orson Welles would take up this snow-globe logic literally, making it a motif in the film *Citizen Kane*. Snow globes were invented by accident in Vienna in 1900 by Erwin Perzy,[23] a mechanic of surgical instruments who was experimenting with how to improve the brightness of the newly invented electric light bulb. Thus the snow globe is a quintessentially modernist invention and art-form, a kitsch souvenir object that supposedly makes us dream of a place, invented as part of an experiment to enhance vision.)[24]

The snow globe is both a quintessential modern kitsch object – a tchotchke that spun off from the newly invented electric lightbulb, a bright-spot intensifier of enlightenment – and a reminder of the fortune-teller's crystal ball, and thus an atavistic talisman of fate. Its glass surface, its watery centre and, above all, its fake snow obscuring the diorama within turn out to be a means by which the new mass-consumer culture of the souvenir secretes old atavisms at the heart of its modern inventions, and, conversely, the proof that an apparently harmless kitsch object is thoroughly in league with the latest technological realities of modernity. It might tell fortunes or it might make us rethink the role of significant spaces in modernity. The snow scenes in 'The Dead' and in 'Je ne parle pas français' work in the same way. Each has us look at a snowfall through glass and find it extraordinarily portentous – without naming this significance. This is pathetic fallacy in the age of film: nature, signified by the weather itself, is shown to be both reassuringly fake and uncannily false, and this mixture of the reassuring and the uncanny catches the modern subject up in the recognition of his own artificiality and lack of access to the reality of the cold snow. Both Gabriel and Raoul know that something has died – which is to say that they recognize, while they each look at their snow-globe scenes, that the past has died. In these modernist texts, this implies that they still want to live, yet what eludes them both is the sense that they are fully alive. The snow seen through the glass is both a requiem for the past that is dead and an incitement, however low wattage, to a dream of a life lived intensely.

Let us return, to understand the low charge of this incitement, to Raoul's analysis of how he felt in 'that moment'. What was the 'Agony', repeated three times, like a mantra?[25] (This triple invocation would be echoed four years later by Eliot in the famous ending of 'The Waste Land': 'Datta. Dayadhvam. Damyata./ Shantih shantih shantih'.)[26] It was, Raoul avers, a 'physical feeling so curious [...] as if [...] all of me that was under the table, had simply dissolved, melted, turned into water'.[27] Considered within a conventional poetic register, this is simply standard-issue Keatsian romanticism: 'Fade far away, dissolve, and quite forget/ What thou among the leaves hast never known,/ The weariness, the fever, and the fret' of 'Ode to a Nightingale'. Or, again, it's the dream of being like the animal, like the simile-invoked dog that appears to be Raoul's only model for historical, embodied and instinctive memory, or even the dead kitten, with the blotting-paper tongue (an image of the fearful animalistic secreted in the written record), or Mouse herself, shadow human with the name of the most harmless, most elusive animal. What matters, however, is that in Raoul's analysis – and in Mansfield's story – this is registered as a 'physical feeling'. It exists as what can be registered by Raoul upon his own body, as opposed to the mental calculation of Raoul the ambitious minor author, whose self-consciousness and self-regard threatens to demolish the sensation. What he and we are left with, therefore, is a registration of the physical sensation of actual aliveness. Reading back to the beginning of the story, we see that the author-narrator has been preparing us for this by continually bringing up the topic and the word: 'Life'. He speaks of 'the most thrilling instants in life' and of how 'every place has an hour of the day when it really does come alive', of how 'Life seems to be opposed to granting you these entrances'.[28] He asks: 'Why am I so bitter against life?' and finally decides: 'Now at last I was coming to life'.[29] There is a life-mania at work in the first portion of this story, an almost frenzied effort to grasp what it means to be alive. The snow epiphany marks the end of this mania in Mansfield's story, and in that of Joyce also. What it achieves is to bring Joyce's meandering story, at last, to silence. In Mansfield's story, what it achieves is to show Raoul that all that is actually allowable in defining life is the registration of the variable sensations of being alive upon one's own body. It is not the snow, but Raoul's own body that, while the snow falls, he perceives is ready to melt.

'Now at last I was coming to life,' says Raoul. Of what does this 'coming to life' consist? The search for an answer resembles the sensation itself: it dissolves. In the repetition of the word 'Agony', which invokes Christ's final agony, in contrast to the Christmas-card Christ's birth scene of the Virgin Mary on the ass, the life-sensation is cast as a dissolution because the narrator is fearful of it. He senses that it is a vital moment, and he marks it as such in a hyperbolic, highly wrought mode. But he does so only for a paragraph, and then he passes on, or rather, retrieves the memories, the past and the regrets, all of which, he has professed, he had resolved not to do. The narrative out of the (dead) past is retrieved and recycled as a kind of cover-up for the possible analysis of what living intensely in the present and the future involves. As the narrator attempts to record his epiphany and its accompanying imagery on paper, he encounters the admonition 'Je ne parle pas français'. This, before all else, is the acknowledgement that life is something he – or any other of the anonymous scribblers on blotting paper – cannot speak. The search for what 'Agony' signifies comes up against a blankness, the blankness of the snow.

This snow signifies a number of kinds of nothingness, which we shall now briefly consider, in its uniform whiteness. In the first place, reading the iconography of the café setting, we see that it too is cast in black and white. This reminds us that the new technologies of representation in the modernist era – principally photography and film – had both cast visualization as a matter of black, white, and, most commonly, grey. Photographs had from early on often been 'colourized', but in pastel shades; while there were many early attempts to colourize movies, and the first colour film was made in 1902, it was only with 'Technicolor' in 1922, improved in 1932, that colour films on a large commercial scale became possible. 'The Wizard of Oz', released in 1939, with its first scene in black and white followed by a burst of Technicolor, while by no means the first film in colour, vividly announced the possibilities of colour in film. Modernism's up-to-date technologies, then, asked its viewers to see in black and white.

'Je ne parle pas français', from its opening, adheres to this monochrome limitation of the visual. Consider the café setting: The workmen who patronized it are 'all powdered over with white flour, lime or something', the *patronne* is dressed in black, but has 'white cheeks and white hands'.[30] The waiter, who stands as if 'waiting to be photographed in connection with some wretched murder' for a photograph (no doubt in black and white) to be entitled 'Interior of Café where Body was Found', is himself described as 'grey'.[31] Photography, black-and-whitenesss, modernity: there is no question that the world of modernist anomie was often imagined in monochrome.

The predominance of cinematic black and white as *the* modernist colour scheme might even help explain why so many modernist texts are nocturnes – set at night. Examples include 'The Love Song of J. Alfred Prufrock', the climactic 'Circe' and subsequent episodes of *Ulysses*, and such Mansfield stories as 'Bliss'. In each of the snow scenes in 'The Dead' and 'Je ne parle pas français' the snow is seen through the night's darkness. The analogy to the movies – a medium whose materiality is light manipulated in a darkened room – is inescapable. This reminds us that while modernism's pervasive black-and-whiteness was the perfect colourless counterpoint to modernity's anomie, it also reflected a glossy and up-to-the minute sheen of glamour. Le Corbusier's very chic modernist architecture, for example, was focused on the 'white wall' (an analogy not just for 'purity,' but also for the blank cinema screen), and the modernist fashion for lacquer, as in the screens designed by the Irish-Parisian designer-architect Eileen Grey,[32] as well as the rage for Bakelite jewellery, often involved the colour black. The snow's whiteness in the two snow scenes, in other words, partakes not just of snow-globe kitsch nostalgia and an appeal to various atavisms (the cosy hearth, Christmas), but also to modernist glamour. It partakes of a modernist glamour-referencing that implies coolness – the ability not to feel, but the freedom, as in Raoul's 'Agony' and Gabriel's soft soul-swooning, to be sensate.

There is a final horizon in the modernist whiteness craze, of course, that is inescapable. That is the horizon of race. What is at stake is all that is summed up in the title of J. M. Coetzee's study of Anglophone fiction in South Africa, *White Writing*,[33] and it merits at least a whole essay of its own. In this sense, both Joyce and Mansfield belong to a phase of modernism for which the matter of empire in politics and the matter of race in global human relations was what Fredric Jameson would call its political unconscious. This was the period that may be said to have been finally brought to an end with the publication of Frantz Fanon's *Black Skin, White Masks* (in French Martinique, as *Peau noire, masques blancs*) in 1952, four years before the Suez Crisis that forcefully marked the waning power and reach of the British Empire.[34] Given Joyce's Irishness, born a subject in Britain's oldest colony, and his interest in Irish politics, and

Mansfield's origin in the settler world of New Zealand and her interest in Māori life and culture, the particularly anomalous and off-centre relation of the work of both writers to empire and to its race ideology has long been discussed.[35] In the case of 'The Dead', its place within the Irish gothic tradition, and thus the sense that the ghosts being evoked in the snow scene are those, for example, of the Great Famine (1845–9) and other imperial atrocities and crimes, is tangible.[36] In the case of 'Je ne parle pas français', Mansfield almost demands that we read the whiteness of the crucial snow scene in racial terms, as, at the key moment of Raoul's ruminations on his writerly identity later in the story, she has him tell us of the incident in his childhood when his black African nurse one day 'tore open her bodice and put me to her'.[37] Urmila Seshagiri rightly reads this as 'the encrypted origins of the modernist writer', and points out its uncanny echo of the invocation by F. T. Marinetti in *The Futurist Manifesto* of 'the black breast of my Sudanese nurse'. She reads it as the crucial admission of 'the racial oppositions, sexual perversion and racial indecision that have characterized Raoul's modernism'.[38] The truth of this is underlined by the fact that when the British publisher of the first public edition of the story, in 1922, demanded that the passage about Raoul's boyhood encounters with the African nurse, and his admission that he later was happy to offer his own body for a price when he needed money, both be censored, Mansfield, upset, wrote to Middleton Murry that she did not want to 'pick the eyes out of the story'. Seshagiri connects Raoul's childhood sexual encounter with the black breast of the African nurse to his apparent hatred or fear of women, and his final vision of Mouse disappearing into the 'feathery snow'.[39]

To what extent, given all of this, can we read the very whiteness of this snow, the appearance of which launches Raoul into his reminiscences, as the unconscious invocation of a bulwark of utter whiteness against the racial blackness represented by the African woman's breast? After Fanon, such a reading is inescapable: Western modernism's assumption of whiteness as a totalizing effect can never be read innocently, just as the scene of the African nurse can never be read, in the first instance, other than symptomatically. Mansfield's snow, for Raoul, for the story and for us the readers, wants to cover – and perhaps smother – all power relations in an assumption of unspoken whiteness. Whiteness is 'purity', it is 'nothingness', it is, in its totality, 'abstraction'. But it is also the colour code for an assumed, unspoken declaration of Western power. In this sense, in the final instance, the snow, in Mansfield and in Joyce, represents the reality of Western hegemony as unspeakable and even unquestionable. At this limit image in modernism, each text reaches the point where it will say no more on political or actual power realities. Instead, each retreats into the personal, in Joyce's case to Gabriel's 'soul'; in Mansfield's, to Raoul's Freudian search for his own significance in the story of his sexual awakening, which he attempts to make 'interesting' by rendering it perverse.

Yet, perhaps we can turn this apparent failure to go beyond the snow-line inside out and ask if this refusal to overcome the snow-globe effect, at the climactic moments in these thoroughly hard-bitten stories, is not a taunt to the reader to take that step herself? When the feathery snow begins, in these stories, to descend, the writers are anticipating the moment in literature and the other arts, after modernism, of full-bore abstraction – and they are putting us on our guard to not fail to discern in the blankness of that abstraction ideological imperatives regarding the art's attitude to power. When Cy Twombly, for example, painted his enigmatic squiggles on a slightly muddied white background, he was remaking without knowing it the 'Je ne parle pas français' blotting paper, marking graffiti in the snow. Likewise with the pure white canvases, interspersed with sharp, callous paper-cuts, of Lucio Fontana. Even Franz Klein, with black force-fields cutting across expansive whitish backgrounds, is giving us dirty snow. The vast expanses of roughened grey in the canvases of such post-war German artists as Anselm Keifer and Rosemarie Trockel are still within this 'dirty snow' tradition. The 'dirty snow' effect is generally read as evidence of the post-Second World War arrival at existential horror, a step beyond the registration of post-Munch and post-Ibsen *anomie* that concerned Joyce and Mansfield. However, the uneasiness generated by the refusal to see the full meaning of snow in the modernist stories might alert us to the fact that the reach for abstraction in the post-war artists can also cover a vast refusal of global critique in late modernity.

This brings us back to Foujita, who, laying down the chalk-white background to so many of his works, was the modernist avatar of the post-war Abstract-Expressionist urge to paint white. (The other avatar was Malevich, whose *Suprematist Composition: White on White* of 1918 commemorates the political revolution rather than elides it.) Foujita, arriving in Paris from Japan,[40] returning to Japan in dubious circumstances for the duration of the Second World War, had his own anomalous relation to mainstream modernism and its politics. Like Raoul, in typical modernist fashion, he subsumed this in an overt concern for sexuality, and for animals – especially his pet cats, which often feature in his self-portraits. In Foujita's portraits of women, including Youki ('snow-woman'), and in his many self-portraits, he first laid down lead paint to create a white surface, with the bodies and faces he drew remaining white also. In his 'Grande Composition' of 1928, for example, he drew a bizarre, Michaelangelo-esque assortment of muscled white male and female bodies in combat, against a grey-white ground, interspersed with pet animals, tigers and lions. In his portraits of Youki, as in the large *Reclining Nude, Youki*, of 1927, the whole canvas, with the exception of her gold-auburn hair, is white: against a white background, her body appears almost to radiate an even more intense whiteness. This fascination with whiteness in general draws its inspiration from Japanese art, with its washes on white paper; however, in its evident yearning for the totally white canvas, and its obsession with the whiteness of the white Western body, it is impossible to look at this work without seeing it as a meditation on whiteness in the context of a rising global consciousness regarding race. It begs us to ask what happens when gender relations, inextricably bound up with registers of race-obsession, eventuate in abstraction – the moment when the sensing, recumbent (as in Foujita) or agonized (as in Raoul's case, in Mansfield) fades into the blankness of snow. This image of the Western female body fading into the feathery snow is, after all, the last vision of Mouse that we have. For Mansfield, as for Foujita, the apparent knowledge of the knowing, characteristically modernist 'smartness' of each artist works towards achieving an end to physical presence, a dissolving of not merely the feelings which nurture human connections, but the sensations through which one is aware one is alive, into the abstraction of white lead paint or of snow. Yet, as Raoul avers, 'The physical feeling was curious'; that is, once we reach a consciousness of what is covered by this total snow, behind the scrim of the snow-screen, some new rhythm of life (free of the ambivalence engendered by regret) might emerge.

Notes

1 On Foujita, see Phyllis Birnbaum, *Glory in a Line: A Life of Foujita – The Artist Caught between East and West* (New York: Farrar, Straus and Giroux, 2006).

2 Among the many books on the Parisian scene around the time of the First World War, see Billy Klüver and Julie Martin, *Ki Ki's Paris: Artists and Lovers 1900–1930* (New York: Abrams, 1989).

3 See Kiki de Montparnasse in Billy Klüver and Julie Martin, eds, *Kiki's Memoirs* (New York: Ecco Press, 1996). The book was first published in English in 1929 as *Kiki's Memoirs* by Black Manakin Press in New York with an introduction by Ernest Hemingway, where it was banned as pornographic, reprinted by Samuel Roth in the 1950s as *The Education of a French Model.*

4 Nowhere is this more evident than in the work of Theodor Adorno and Max Horkheimer. See, for example, Theodor W. Adorno, *Aesthetic Theory*, eds

Gretel Adorno and Rolf Tiedemann, trans. Robert Hullot-Kentor (Minneapolis: University of Minnesota Press 1997).

5 See Walter Pater, 'Conclusion', in *The Renaissance: Studies in Art and Poetry* (Oxford: Oxford World Classics, 1998 [1873]), pp. 118–21.

6 M. M. Bakhtin, 'Discourse in the Novel', in *The Dialogic Imagination: Four Essays*, eds and trans. Michael Holquist and Caryl Emerson (Austin: University of Texas Press Slavic Series, 1983), pp. 259–422.

7 Erich Auerbach, 'The Brown Stocking, on Woolf and Proust', in *Mimesis: The Representation of Reality in Western Literature*, trans. Willard R. Trask (Princeton: Princeton University Press, 1953), pp. 525–3.

8 William Wordsworth, 'Lucy Gray', in *Selected Poems*, ed. Stephen Gill (London: Penguin, 2004 [1800]), p. 73.

9 Emily Holmes Coleman, *The Shutter of Snow* (Nornal: Dalkey Archive Press 1997 [1930]): 'An avalanche of snow gathered and fell and buried the sub beneath', p. 3.

10 'Part 3: The Woman at the Window', in George Simenon, *Dirty Snow*, trans. Marco Romano and Louise Varese (New York: New York Review of Books Classics, 2003), pp. 177–244 (published in French as *La Neige était sale*, 1948).

11 CW2, p. 114.

12 James Joyce, 'The Dead', in *The Dead*, ed. Daniel Schwarz (New York: Bedford Books, 1994), p. 59.

13 Richard Ellmann, *James Joyce* (Oxford: Oxford University Press, 1982 [1959]), p. 353.

14 CW2, p. 114.

15 H. G. Wells, *Experiment in Autobiography: Discoveries and Conclusions of a Very Ordinary Brain – since 1866*, vol. 2 (London: Victor Gollancz, 1934), p. 487. The full sentence reads: 'When goddesses and Sea Ladies vanish and a flash back to the ancestral chimpanzee abolishes the magic caverns of Venus, human beings arrive.'

16 CW2, p. 113.

17 Ibid.

18 CW2, p. 114.

19 Ibid. (both quotes).

20 CW2, pp. 114–15.

21 CW2, p. 115.

22 Ibid. (all three quotes).

23 In Kristi McKim's extremely interesting book, *Cinema as Weather: Stylistic Screens and Atmospheric Change* (New York: Routledge, 2013), she claims (p. 135) in passing that snow globes first appeared in Paris in 1878, before Perzy's subsequent mass production. See in particular McKim's chapter 'Cinematic Snow', pp. 134–62.

24 In the opening scene of the film *Citizen Kane* (1941), at the close of the modernist era, the dying Kane is shown letting a snow globe, which shatters, drop from his hands. Later in the film we realize that it had belonged to Susan, and reminds Kane

of his childhood. In the dialectic of nostalgia for past 'authenticity' and ambition for future 'progress', the snow globe may be a locus classicus of modernism.

25 CW2, p. 115.
26 T. S. Eliot, 'The Waste Land', in *The Waste Land and Other Writings* (New York: Random House, 2001), p. 57.
27 CW2, pp. 114–15.
28 CW2, pp. 112, 113.
29 CW2, pp. 113, 114.
30 CW2, p. 112 (both quotes).
31 CW2, p. 113.
32 For a very interesting study of gender, sexuality and the matter of modernist designer bakelite, see Jasmine Rault, *Eileen Gray and the Design of Sapphic Modernity: Staying In* (Abingdon: Routledge, 2016). There is now an extensive literature on Gray. See Peter Adam, *Eileen Gray, Architect, Designer: A Biography*, revised edn (New York: Harry A. Abrams, 2000).
33 J. M. Coetzee, 'Prospects', in *White Writing: On the Culture of Letters in South Africa* (New Haven: Yale University Press, 1988), pp. 188–201.
34 Frantz Fanon, *Black Skin, White Masks*, revised edn, trans. Richard Philcox (New York: Grove Press, 2008).
35 For one of the first and path-breaking interventions in these terms, see Vincent Cheng, *Joyce, Race and Empire* (Cambridge: Cambridge University Press, 1995). For an excellent analysis of 'Je ne parle pas français' in terms of race, see Urmila Seshagiri, *Race and the Modernist Imagination* (Cornell: Cornell University Press, 2010), pp. 127–39.
36 Luke Gibbons, *Joyce's Ghosts: Ireland, Modernism and Memory* (Chicago: University of Chicago Press, 2015).
37 CW2, p. 116.
38 Seshagiri, p. 139.
39 CW2, p. 116.
40 There was a comprehensive exhibition of Foujita's work in 'Foujita: Painting in the Roaring Twenties', at the Musée Malliol, Paris, in May–July 2018.

4

In-scribing silence

Reading how the silences speak in Mansfield's stories

Ruchi Mundeja

The same peal, the same low, slow ha! ha! which [...] thrilled me.
Charlotte Brontë, *Jane Eyre* [1]

Between articulating and invading silences

Writing to Richard Murry in 1921, Mansfield uses a strange word – 'terror' – when speaking of the writerly act of bringing an entire '*living mind*' alive 'with nothing left out', which of course would include the mind's recesses, its silences (emphasis in original).[2] For a writer so frequently associated with a fascination for inhabiting multiple selves, the word 'terror' seems to nevertheless bode a self-consciousness about bringing to voice the 'unknown', silent spaces of the other.[3] Mansfield has often been discussed as endowed with the theatrical deftness to role-play and authenticate diverse lives; for example, Ali Smith unforgettably describes her as 'merrily dextrous'.[4] This chapter aims to redirect scholarship from an ongoing interest in Mansfield's experiments in voice to an exploration of silences in her fiction, with a focus on the writer's awareness – or otherwise – of crossing class borders in her ventriloquizing of characters' silences. It will analyse those stories in which Mansfield enters into the lives and silences of underclass characters, and also those that evoke the affective intensities that inhere in (women's) silences, while simultaneously raising questions related to the ethics of representation.

Inscribing the silences of the disempowered is a concern prominently shared by women's writing and postcolonial literature. Read and interpreted through both theoretical frameworks, Mansfield's work is engaged in bringing into visibility those who, to borrow a phrase from Chiara Briganti, have traditionally had 'walk-on parts' in literature.[5] But I am equally interested in who speaks the silences in Mansfield's stories and how they do so. This enquiry probes Mansfield's stories with a view to discovering how, and whether, that self-reflexivity appears in her work. The three stories discussed here, 'Revelations' (1920), 'Life of Ma Parker' (1921) and 'A Cup of Tea' (1922), have been chosen for these reasons. 'Revelations' opens with the protagonist, Monica Tyrell, as a performer of silence, while in the latter half of the story she finds herself reading another's silence. 'Life of Ma Parker' and 'A Cup of Tea' are especially pertinent, since I argue that Mansfield inserts what might be termed 'literary doubles' in these two stories. In my subsequent discussion of these stories, I will suggest a reading of the 'literary gentleman' in 'Life of Ma Parker' and of Rosemary Fell in 'A Cup of Tea' as surrogates, albeit 'unsuccessful' ones, of the writer figure. The unnamed writer, Ma Parker's employer in 'Life of Ma Parker', and Rosemary Fell can be seen as readers of the silence of the other. Their desire for narrative inscription, narrative expansion in Rosemary's case, implies that they move between a curious probing and a forthright invasion of that silence, so that the 'recording' of these silences often borders on the appropriative.

In her seminal study *Silences*, Tillie Olsen speaks of 'the silences where the lives never came to writing [...] the barely educated, the illiterate, women, their silence, the silence of centuries'.[6] In writing silence into speech, however, the question of whether there are dangers of over-reading the silence arises. There is a fine line here between under-representation and over-inscription, as my epigraph from *Jane Eyre* illustrates, which presents, in the figure of Bertha Mason, the most written about silence in feminist criticism. Bertha Mason stands poised at the crossroads of speech and speechlessness. If Brontë links her non-verbal utterance – the 'thrill' of the 'goblin laughter' resonating with the 'mutinous' in Jane's psyche – to Jane's emancipatory trajectory, then it acts in counterpoint to Jane's poised outbursts of feminist rebellion.[7] This paradox lingers troublingly in recuperative feminist work on Brontë's text that has deployed Bertha's *speechlessness* as speech. In the landmark troping of the figure of Bertha Mason as the 'madwoman in the attic', the line between representation and effacement in the act of 'voicing' the voiceless blurs in the conflation of Jane's 'voice' and Bertha's 'voicelessness'. Laura E. Donaldson notes that Sandra Gilbert and Susan Guhar's memorable feminist reading of *Jane Eyre* evokes a decidedly female 'tapestry', yet one 'which bleaches women of color into an asocial invisibility'.[8]

Silence is of course an important site in women's writing, unfolding at the cusp of oppression (that produces it) and self-expression (within it). Hence, it is not unusual that silences of women are read for traces of the oppositional. There is an identifiable strain in women's writing, especially during the modernist period with its interest in interior narration, where silence seems to be delicately poised between signifying oppression and being a repository of counter-speech. One can think of Charlotte Perkins Gilman's 'The Yellow Wallpaper' or Virginia Woolf's *Mrs. Dalloway* and the silent yet resonant space of the attic. Whether in the irreverence of the counter-talk that constantly buzzes in the interior consciousness of Jean Rhys's women or the 'unhomely' that resides in the silences of Mansfield's housebound women – women's silences are indicative of the effects of gender-based oppression, yet also a repository of asides that speak truth to power. This chapter takes cognizance of what might strike some as a paradox, but if so, a necessary one: that women's writing unfolds at the borderlines of breaking silences and yet also seeing women's silence as a resource in itself – where a counter-discourse of disobedience, unquiet thoughts, unassuaged yearnings or rage lies brooding. This attributes a certain presence to the blankness of silence. One is compelled to ask: Is silence absence or presence? Or are we brought up short against the interchangeability of the two registers? Recent work on speech and silence would suggest this. Aimee Carrillo Rowe and Sheena Malhotra argue against assuming 'an equation between voice and agency, and its inverse equation – silence and oppression'.[9] One wonders if there is even a performative aspect to silence, where silence in the case of women may signify a sly or stubborn recalcitrance to authoritative discourse. When is silence a performance, a ritualized obtuseness of response, and when is it a banal indicator of powerlessness?

In exploring and representing these facets of silence, Mansfield was to ponder on the importance of finding the 'fit' between the voice of the writer and the character, such as when speaking of 'Miss Brill', she says in a letter: 'In Miss Brill I chose not only the length of every sentence, but even the sound of every sentence – I chose the rise and fall of every paragraph to fit her'.[10] But this chapter also debates whether perhaps too snug a fit between writer and character implies presumption, an occupation of subject positions not known. This is of particular interest in the case of a writer like Mansfield, whose experiments with voices are noteworthy. It might be argued that writers by their very nature are interlopers and eavesdroppers. Their senses are primed to feed on narratable material from other lives. That Mansfield was aware of this is evident in how she magnifies that temptation to disturbing proportions in Raoul Duquette from 'Je ne parle pas français' (1918), one of the 'literary gentleman' in her fictional corpus. One recalls Duquette's expansive embrace of 'greediness', and then of course that unapologetic curiosity towards other lives as adding to the hoard of riches of the writer voiced in that compelling line: 'Art can't and won't stand poverty.'[11] In that exposition of writerly hunger, the ethics of 'regret', which in my argument figures as self-critique, is completely jettisoned by Duquette: 'I have made it a rule of my life never to regret and never to look back. [...] Looking back, of course, is equally fatal to art. It's keeping yourself poor.'[12] As I will argue, Mansfield implicates herself in that writerly hunger as battening onto unexplored silent realms while simultaneously being aware of the ethics and politics of it.

Speaking from the silence

I will now move to analyse one of Mansfield's 'domestic' stories, as these often pulsate with the force of the unvocalized. In 'Revelations', there are two types of silence because the female protagonist, Monica Tyrell, is both the bearer of a restless silence and the decoder of (another's) silence. In the first section, the narrative voice positions itself inside Monica's recalcitrant silences, writing from inside the intimate texture of women's insubordinate silences. However, in shifting focus to Monica's own reading of the broken silence of her hairdresser after the loss of his child, the story ponders the limits of 'inhabiting' another mind.

One is left with an uneasy feeling, after a reading of an ostensibly unthreatening, domestic Mansfield story, of the 'unsaid' that haunts it as subtext. In a letter to Anne Drey, Mansfield says: 'I try and make family life so gorgeous – not hatred and linoleum – but warmth and hydrangeas.'[13] There is, however, a dark underbelly to that 'warmth and hydrangeas'. In 'Revelations', it is Monica Tyrrell's angry silence that ferments below the surface of 'family life'. Monica and her husband are a well-off couple; he is a doting spouse by all accounts, and yet readers are encouraged to see his indulgent infantilizing of his wife as part of her malaise. However, it is characteristic of Mansfield that while Monica's marital discontent appears through the bile in her silence – her husband's intrusion into her bedroom evokes 'anger [...] close, close, violent, half-strangling her' – the second half of the narrative shows her as closed off from other, less advantaged, lives, however much she tries to be a part of them.[14] The beginning of the story, in making us privy to Monica's interior world, focuses on the violations she feels she endures at the hands of her spouse, and her embitterment resulting from his invasion or undermining of her solitude, though the strain of self-indulgent dramatization born of Monica's bourgeois sense of entitlement is emphasized. But in Monica's later encounter with her hairdresser who we learn has just lost his daughter, Monica herself comes close to violating his privacy and reading into his silence.

Through Monica Tyrell's acidic asides in 'Revelations', the writer introduces the 'unsaid' into the sacralized structures of family and marriage. The narrative voice in the story situates Monica within the cocooned world of middle-class marriage, while also creating space for a critique of the stasis that marital routines can entail. The narrator's ironic tone certainly suggests an acutely self-conscious performativity in Monica's distress, as here: 'Monica fell back into her bed, and then "ring-ting-a-ping-ping [...]." It was the telephone. The limit of her suffering was reached.'[15] But the story's title is equally suggestive of all that remains unspoken in marital contracts, that trembles as women's 'hysteria' at the edges of these arrangements, and is figured as eruption by the writer: 'She could not stand this silent, flat, noiseless Marie, this ghostly, quiet, feminine interior. She must be out.'[16] Earlier in the story, when there is a suggestion that Marie, the housemaid, should guard her door, Monica thinks, only half-jestingly, of 'Marie as a kind of cross between a wardress and a nurse for mental cases!'[17] Thus, both the jealous guarding of her solitude – her 'feminine folly' even – and the desire to 'be out', 'anywhere, anywhere' are for Monica Tyrell a way of breaking the stranglehold of paternalism.[18] In her complex portrayal of Monica, Mansfield 'reveals' her protagonist's self-involvement, but underlines also the 'revelatory' that might become the by-product of her performative silences. Indeed, the silence that Monica builds in the solitude of her chamber is a direct counterpoint to the restlessness of the story's atmosphere. Monica's room is marked conspicuously by discord and turbulence, conveyed in the narrative through a deliberate heightening of physical phenomena – the blinds flying in 'a sharp tearing rip', the curtains 'flapping, jerking', and 'the tassel of the blind knocked-knocked against the window'.[19] Noise and silence play off against each other; this inner chamber where she harnesses solitude is far from restful. It is where all that cannot be vocalized in marital structures throbs inside her head.

In an article entitled 'On the Family as a Realized Category', Pierre Bourdieu suggests that the domestic sanctum functions within a certain lexical economy, and is 'founded on a set of cognitive presuppositions and normative prescriptions about the proper way to conduct domestic relationships'.[20] The rage-filled silence of Monica Tyrell works to interrogate these accepted grammars of intimacy and knowability. A narrative overwritten by self-sustaining fictions such as the husband's insistence that intimacy entails knowing his wife inside out is a claim that her silent ripostes proceed to tear apart: 'Understand her? He had understood nothing [...]. She could almost have laughed.'[21] Her silence becomes the bearer of a concealed restiveness that her spouse with his idealized view of domestic togetherness fails to fathom.

Sylvia Berkman has read 'Revelations' as an uncharitable study of neurotic women, an interpretation that points to the self-involvement of the secure bourgoisie.[22] I contend, however, that the balance of sympathies in the story is more delicate than that, because the story examines the politics of silence from the other side too, moving from questions of gender to those of class; from the restive silence of a middle-class woman to the numb silence of a lower-class working man, the story exemplifies my initial suggestion that there are silences that speak and silences that are blank. Some silences are oppositional, and possess the power to destabilize bourgeois institutions like marriage, while others emanate from a void of mundane, everyday suffering. Both are in different ways a comment on unequal power structures. The second half of the story revolves around Monica's visit to the hair salon, where she has always been served by the same hairdresser. Overwhelmed by a tragedy of his own, the death of his young daughter, the hairdresser George on this particular visit is unable to communicate with Monica Tyrell on the level of genteel small talk she has come to expect. By showing the breakdown of exchange, the story underlines Monica's previous presumption of familiarity with the man who styles her hair. She has never wondered what lies beyond his good manners, and only at the point of breakdown, when speech is replaced by silence, is she forced to confront his separate humanity, beyond the function he performs.

If, in Monica's case, silence in the domestic sphere may be read as at least in part a staged recalcitrance, in the latter half of the story she confronts a silence that she simultaneously wishes to penetrate yet leave in the realm of the unspoken. Monica notices George's signs of disarray and uncharacteristic unkemptness but it is his silence that haunts her: 'Something awful had happened here. The silence, really, the silence seemed to come drifting down like flakes of snow.'[23] As Monica attempts to read the hairdresser's 'wooden' silence, she evades its empty finality by extracting from it lessons on the nature of human life: 'Oh, how terrifying Life was, thought Monica. How dreadful. It is the loneliness which is so appalling. We whirl along like leaves, and nobody knows – nobody cares where we fall, in what black river we float away.'[24] Monica's attempt to decipher and transcribe George's internal world becomes abstracted to the universal. Charles Ferrall's argument that the very 'unrepresentability [of the silenced working classes] enables the dissection of middle-class prejudice',[25] is relevant to Mansfield's delineation of Monica's maudlin interpretations here.

Monica's acute self-consciousness, even self-specularity – 'She looked at him; she saw herself looking at him in the white kimono like a nun' – brings the story to a point where the performative in her now imperils any genuine contact with him.[26]

Monica is both a performer and a reader of silence in the story, and as an unsuccessful reader she avoids the implied truth of the silence. Her earlier visits to the salon have relied on the niceties of speech. When confronted with the unnerving silence of this visit, she shrinks from the abyss she senses lies behind it. From investing in the realm of silence as a 'feminine site', the story opens itself out to the problematics of class and thus preserves the difference between one kind of marginality and another when inscribing silence.[27] Mansfield moves within the story from the potentialities of silence to its terrible emptiness, from gendered affect to questions of class, and its inequalities; these lie at the centre of the next story I look at.

Speaking without speech

The body can become a potentially crucial factor in the cusp between speech and speechlessness. In 'Revelations', Monica Tyrell's body, as her nerves are jangled by surrounding sounds, becomes the site of rupture. 'Life of Ma Parker' brings out the idea of 'speaking' the body in another way. As Ma Parker, in silence, carries out the chores allotted to her by the 'literary gentleman' in whose house she works, two categories of sound stand directly, strategically, counterpointed to Ma Parker's silence – the sounds of labour and those of the body. Ma Parker's erasure as subject is marked in the story by how her body is only a functional instrument of labour for her middle-class employer. By constructing the ambient universe of Ma Parker's silent world with the exterior sounds of the body, hers and those of her loved ones, Mansfield uses the body's vocabulary of pain as an emblem of protest against social inequality.

The first sentence of the story, as Ma Parker, plunged in a blank sadness following the death of her grandchild, enters her employer's house, suggests that Mansfield is pitting words against wordlessness. Designated the 'literary gentleman' in the story and hence belonging to the world of words, her employer is eager to offer comfort and penetrate Ma Parker's inner world by saying 'something – something more'.[28] Mansfield introduces, in this reading, her own stand-in, the literary gentleman, but the narrative also creates satirical distance. It is as if Mansfield juxtaposes her own writerly inscription of Ma Parker's silence against his 'inscribing' of the other, which is exposed as inadequate, making the narrator's voice appear more reliable.

As Ma Parker quietly informs her employer, on his enquiring after her grandchild, of the death of her young grandson, he is discomforted by her spare response:

> But he felt awkward. He could hardly go back to the warm sitting-room without saying something – something more. Then because these people set such store by funerals he said kindly, 'I hope the funeral went off all right.'
>
> 'Beg parding, sir?' said old Ma Parker huskily.
>
> Poor old bird! She did look dashed. 'I hope the funeral was a – a – success,' said he. Ma Parker gave no answer.[29]

As he falters in the face of her inwardness and indeed blankness, and struggles to fill the silence, he turns fatuously to the idioms of his literary world, blundering into Ma Parker's inner world through such (insensitively) inappropriate comments such as hoping that the funeral was a success. Mansfield, in implying a certain intellectual presumption in the way the 'untranslatability' of the other's experience is made visible by the writer-intellectual, casts a glance back at the writerly function. In his interpretation of Ma Parker's reticence, the literary gentleman in fact presumptively negates her otherness. He voices assumptions about 'these people'.[30] In bringing the speechless subaltern into the enunciative field – 'For occasionally he laid aside his tomes and lent an ear [...] to this product called Life' – the writer in Mansfield's story glibly claims access to knowability.[31] And in doing so, he erases, indeed dishonours, the affective value of the silence. As readers, I suggest that we are to understand the narrative voice setting itself up as a counterpoint and speaking that silence from a more empathetic position. The narrative voice sets up a kinship with the sufferer, Ma Parker, whereas the literary gentleman in the story shrinks back from that visceral communion.

When Ma Parker tells her employer that her deceased husband was a baker, his subsequent attempts at summoning up quaint images of a 'clean trade' are belied by her admission of having lost seven out of her thirteen children, leading him to withdraw, 'shuddering, and taking up his pen again'.[32] While writing becomes social withdrawal for him, the narrator of the story shows a more direct writerly engagement with the abandoned other (Ma Parker). Voicing silence is to enter the abyss of dispossession and marginality to which certain lives are consigned, and Mansfield's 'double' in the story proves unequal to the task. In a review of a Louis Couperus novel, Mansfield wrote: 'What is it that differentiates these living characters from the book-bound creatures [...]? Is it not that the former are seen ever, and always in relation to life [...] and the other are seen in relation to an intellectual idea of life?'[33] The literary gentleman remains 'book-bound' in more ways than one, while Mansfield's narrator surrogate is presumably redeemed from that charge in the inscription of Ma Parker's life. The writer character in the story may be said to cling to his fictional conception of a sanitized world of hard work and labour, whereas the story itself purports to uncover the harsh conditions under which those like Ma Parker live. Both are equally interpretations and voicings of the silent world of the disadvantaged, but one can argue that the reader is guided towards deciding which is the more 'authentic' record, or at least one that suggests a greater engagement with the 'other'.

Simon During has argued that Mansfield's fiction does not announce its fictionality, or 'bare the device' as he puts it.[34] But in 'Life of Ma Parker', Mansfield seems to be nodding towards good and bad ventriloquizing of silences. In the present reading at least, there is a suggestion of a greater interest in the processes of inscription. Mansfield's use of the body in the story is directly combative of the social oblivion that surrounds lower-class figures such as Ma Parker. Notably, as Mansfield moves to convert absence into presence, 'Life of Ma Parker' is sometimes perceived as carrying signs of the writer's excess. Susan Lohafer feels that the story in its 'exaggerated affect' and 'oversimplified message' seems an 'embarrassing lapse' in Mansfield's oeuvre.[35] That juxtaposition between lack and excess needs to be reckoned with, especially since it indicates slippages between under-inscription: the character's erasure, and over-inscription: the story's own overstatement. Ma Parker 'speaks out' rarely, keeping 'herself to herself'.[36] The third-person voice however introduces both interior speech and the sounds of her labouring body, as well as the afflicted bodies of her loved ones, to counterpoint Ma Parker's reticence. How then does one balance the idea of circumspection in voicing the other's silence with Lohafer's suggestion of the story's none-too-subtle appeal to the reader's sensibilities? Bill Ashcroft's broader formulations on the idea of postcolonial excess might act as frame. Speaking about excess as too insistent, too repetitive, too verbose, Ashcroft reads its overstatement as an essential strategy in foregrounding disempowerment.[37] The story's use of symbolism operates in that realm – the bubbling sound in the grandson's chest counterpointed by the water bubbling in the tea kettle at the gentleman's house, or the nature of Ma Parker's work, associating her with the detritus of her employer's daily existence, underscores her social abjection:

> As he explained to his friends, his 'system' was quite simple [...].
>
> 'You simply dirty everything you've got, get a hag in once a week to clean up, and the thing's done.'
>
> The result looked like a gigantic dustbin. Even the floor was littered with toast crusts, envelopes, cigarette ends.[38]

Mansfield's recourse to excess is her chosen mode to denote the lack and tedious emptiness of Ma Parker's life. Through insistent mention of her body, its aches, pains, creaks and stoops, the writer brings Ma Parker's life out of the silence of obscured suffering. In a story where Mansfield undertakes to render forgotten lives into visceral materialities, she moves from the challenges and aesthetics of impersonation to the politics of representation. What happens to silences that are intractable – that in their blankness resist incorporation into any vocabulary of protest? The author shows her own implication in the process as she bares the silence in all its unrelieved everyday tedium.

Self-worlding through the other

As women write women, narcissistic self-expansion on the part of the aspiring or would-be author can stand delicately poised against emphatic fusion with the character or subject group. In the story 'A Cup of Tea', these dynamics are transposed onto the interaction between the idle, rich Rosemary Fell and the vagrant Miss Smith in a chance encounter between the two women from very different backgrounds. This accidental meeting, poised as it is at a telling juncture in the story – Rosemary's failed desire to acquire an antique item producing a lack in her and the vagrant young woman appearing out of nowhere in answer to that – catalyses Rosemary's desire to re-narrativize her staid bourgeois existence through a fervid re-scripting of her life, as she ventures into underworlds of poverty and distress through her meeting with Miss Smith. With a single-mindedness she seeks to possess the strange woman's silence and 'mystery'. Rosemary's imaginings, framed by the dusk and her sudden evocation of the dark world of Dostoevsky, furthers our impression of her gushing eagerness to build an enigma around the girl's poverty, quite different from its mundane realities. From the first moment of the encounter, Rosemary is already authoring a certain script in her mind: 'Supposing she took the girl home? [...] It would be thrilling. And she heard herself saying afterwards to the amazement of her friends: "I simply took her home with me", as she stepped forward and said to that dim person beside her: "Come home to tea with me."'[39]

The idea of women as sisters is repeatedly voiced in the story, so bears closer examination. Almost the first thing that Rosemary says to Miss Smith by way of reassurance, and which seems to assume an implicit 'connection' is: 'Don't be frightened. After all, why shouldn't you come back with me? We're both women.'[40] Rosemary seeks to establish a sisterhood by making inroads into the stranger's silence. Is Mansfield implying a divisiveness even as one woman seeks to interpret the silence of another? Carla Kaplan has argued that recuperative readings that set out to redress women's silencing, literary or otherwise, mark 'feminism's heroics', yet (citing Susan Lanser) she cautions that 'a reading politics of identification turns women's texts into self-indulgent mirrors'.[41] In my discussion of the gendered affect in 'Revelations', I implied an affective kinship between woman writer and female character. In 'A Cup of Tea', on the other hand, Mansfield explores the limits of that assumed sisterhood between women divided by the gulf of class. Meghan Marie Hammond discusses empathy as involving an 'experience of foreign consciousness'.[42] Mansfield's 'A Cup of Tea' highlights the ironies of that proposed empathic communion as Mansfield's narrator attributes it to Rosemary's craving for the foreign element.

In this context Mansfield's extensive use of tropes of hunger and food in the story are important. In the very first moments of their meeting, as the girl warily responds to Rosemary's almost immediate decision to take her home, the narrator uses a somewhat strange word to signify her reaction: 'The girl put her finger to her lips and her eyes *devoured* Rosemary.'[43] It might be contended that the story does not let us lose sight of different manifestations of the appetitive. Rosemary's 'appetite' for the exotic has already been established at the start of the story, such as the intensity of her response when her craving to purchase an expensive antique box remains unsatiated.

The young woman's rudimentary, bodily hunger is set against Rosemary's hunger for narrative largesse: 'And really the effect of the slight meal was marvellous. When the tea-table was carried away a new being [...] lay back in the big chair [...]. Rosemary lit a fresh cigarette; it was time to begin.'[44] Mary Addyman observes that eating implies a willed abdication of boundaries between self and world, an ingestion of alterity, of foreign matter.[45] The girl's hunger satiated, Rosemary sets out to satisfy her own expansive desire. As I have argued elsewhere, the young woman becomes another 'collectible' in Rosemary's appetite for the exotic as a way of escaping 'marital anonymity'.[46] In her portrait of middle-class marriage, Mansfield often maintains a difficult balance between a desire for self-definition and a desire for self-indulgence in her women. Rosemary swoops down, ready to feed off the other's silence.

Quite clearly, then, the desire to world the history of the downtrodden is in the ultimate analysis a self-worlding for Rosemary. The story describes her desire for proximity with the stranger as part of an attempt to script a tale where 'rich people had hearts and [...] women *were* sisters' (italics in original).[47] Charles Ferrall's observation that the girl in the story is given no interiority, thereby remaining 'opaque', is certainly pertinent.[48] If this be read as deliberate, it works to exacerbate the gap between the girl's separateness and Rosemary's attempts to fit her within a pre-written narrative. Mansfield keeps the girl a non-presence in the story. Even her occasional displays of obvious emotion, such as when she bursts into tears, are brought to us through Rosemary's consciousness: 'She really was touched beyond words [...]. Now at last the other forgot everything except that they were both women.'[49] As Rosemary's desire for connection and sisterly communities is articulated in increasingly florid terms, the opacity of the woman's silence forms a deliberate contrast.

'My business is circumference', Emily Dickinson famously stated in a letter,[50] and indeed impersonation, performativity and the protean are integral to Mansfield's writing. It underscores Mansfield's attempts to widen the circumference of women's writing – clearly implied in the following letter to her cousin about writers' voracity for narratives, as related to the desire for amplitude: 'Would you not like to try *all* sorts of lives – one is so very small – but that is the satisfaction of writing – one can impersonate so many people' (emphasis in original).[51] In my reading of stories that plumb the processes of both reading and inscribing silences, I have attempted to show how Mansfield negotiates between the importance of voicing certain silences and the representational presumptuousness, or to use Chris Bongie's recent term 'scribal politics',[52] that might be involved in doing so, between expanding the circumference to include the unvoiced and yet remaining aware of the possibility of incursion and trespass.

Notes

1 Charlotte Brontë, *Jane Eyre* (London: Penguin, 2006), p. 130.
2 *Letters* 4, p. 165.
3 Ibid.
4 Ali Smith, 'Introduction', in *Katherine Mansfield: The Collected Stories* (London: Penguin, 2007), p. viii.
5 Chiara Briganti, 'Giving the Mundane Its Due: One (Fine) Day in the Life of the Everyday', *ESC: English Studies in Canada*, 39, no. 2–3 (June/September 2013): 161–80 (p. 169).

6 Tillie Olsen, *Silences* (London: Virago, 1980), p. 10.
7 Brontë, pp. 173, 15.
8 Laura E. Donaldson, *Decolonizing Feminisms: Race, Gender and Empire-Building* (Chapel Hill: University of North Carolina Press, 1992), p. 16.
9 Aimee Carrillo Rowe and Sheena Malhotra, eds, *Silence, Feminism, Power: Reflections at the Edges of Sound* (London: Palgrave Macmillan, 2013), p. 1.
10 *Letters* 4, p. 165.
11 CW2, p. 115.
12 Ibid.
13 *Letters* 4, p. 168.
14 CW2, p. 214.
15 CW2, pp. 213–14.
16 CW2, p. 215.
17 CW2, p. 213.
18 CW2, pp. 214, 215.
19 CW2, p. 213.
20 Pierre Bourdieu, 'On the Family as a Realized Category', *Theory Culture Society*, 13, no. 19 (1996): 19–26.
21 CW2, p. 214.
22 Quoted in Dan Shen, *Style and Rhetoric of Short Narrative Fiction: Covert Progressions Behind Overt Plots* (New York: Routledge, 2014), p. 95.
23 CW2, p. 217.
24 Ibid.
25 Charles Ferrall, 'Katherine Mansfield and the Working Classes', *Journal of New Zealand Literature*, 32, no. 3 (2014): 106–20 (p. 117).
26 CW2, p. 216.
27 Cheryl Glenn, *Unspoken: A Rhetoric of Silence* (Carbondale: Southern Illinois University Press, 2004), p. 2.
28 CW2, p. 292.
29 Ibid.
30 Ibid.
31 CW2, p. 294.
32 Ibid.
33 CW3, p. 546.
34 Simon During, 'Katherine Mansfield's World', *Journal of New Zealand Literature*, 33 (2015): 33–66 (p. 46). During's essay argues for Mansfield's place in the field of 'world literature', by suggesting that Mansfield, in constructing 'monads', coherent and complete fictional worlds, exemplifies a more particularized and in-turned definition of 'world literature' than the sweeping catholicism of the David Damrosch school of thought. That is a provocative argument from my point of view, since this chapter inclines towards moments where Mansfield *does* rupture the 'coherence' of her fictional worlds.

35 Susan Lohafer, *Reading for Storyness: Preclosure Theory, Empirical Poetics and Culture in the Short Story* (Baltimore: Johns Hopkins University Press, 2003), pp. 73, 72.
36 CW2, p. 295.
37 Bill Ashcroft, 'Excess: Post-colonialism and the Verandahs of Meaning', in *De-Scribing Empire: Post-Colonialism and Textuality*, eds Chris Tiffin and Alan Lawson (London: Routledge, 1994), p. 33.
38 CW2, p. 293.
39 CW2, p. 463.
40 CW2, p. 464.
41 Carla Kaplan, 'Reading Feminist Readings: Recuperative Reading and the Silent Heroine of Feminist Criticism', in *Listening to Silences: New Essays in Feminist Criticism*, eds Elaine Hodges and Shelley Fisher Fishkin (Oxford: Oxford University Press, 1994), p. 176.
42 Meghan Marie Hammond, *Empathy and the Psychology of Literary Modernism* (Edinburgh: Edinburgh University Press, 2014), p. 9.
43 CW2, p. 463 (emphasis mine).
44 CW2, p. 465.
45 Mary Addyman, '"All else is vain, but eating is real": Gustatory Bodies', in *Food, Drink and the Written Word in Britain, 1820–1945*, eds Mary Addyman, Laura Wood and Christopher Yiannitsaros (London: Routledge, 2017), pp. 207–20 (p. 208).
46 See Ruchi Mundeja, 'Space of Debate, Debating Space', in *Katherine Mansfield and the Bloomsbury Group*, ed. Todd Martin (London: Bloomsbury Academic, 2017), pp. 181–99 (pp. 190–1).
47 CW2, pp. 463–4.
48 Ferrall, p. 115.
49 CW2, p. 465.
50 Letter to T. W. Higginson dated July 1862 in Thomas Wentworth Higginson, 'Emily Dickinson's Letters', theatlantic.com, October 1891. https//www.theatlantic.com/magazine/archive/1891/.../emilydickinson-letters/30652 (accessed August 2018).
51 *Letters* 1, p. 19.
52 Chris Bongie, *Friends and Enemies: The Scribal Politics of Post/ Colonial Literature* (Liverpool: Liverpool University Press, 2008), p. 32.

Mansfield's modernisms

5

What plant's in 'Prelude'? Colonialism, gender and speculative botany

William Kupinse

In an earlier incarnation, the plant gave its name to Katherine Mansfield's 'The Aloe', the realist predecessor to her modernist masterwork 'Prelude'. Ousted from the title of the latter, and not appearing until halfway through the story, the aloe haunts 'Prelude', as an integral but enigmatic presence. Kezia finds herself mesmerized when she stumbles upon the solitary plant with its 'tall stout stem' and welter of vigorous and grotesquely withered leaves. The plant is entirely outside her experience, leaving her to wonder 'Whatever could it be?' Her mother supplies an answer, identifying it as an aloe. Like her daughter, Linda Burnell sees the plant for its remarkable duality: it floats above them yet grasps the ground with claw-like roots. Even its natural processes are extraordinary. In response to Kezia's question, 'Does it ever have any flowers?', her mother punctuates her answer with half-closed eyes and a cryptic smile. 'Yes, Kezia', she tells her, 'once every hundred years'.[1]

The problem with Linda's answer is that aloes *don't* bloom every hundred years, a fact that debate on the aloe's figurative and aesthetic role has largely disregarded. Linda may simply be mistaken, but as Andrew Gurr observed back in 1984, it is likely that she's thinking of another spiky succulent, *Agave americana*.[2] Commonly called an aloe despite being only distant kin, the agave is more closely related to asparagus. The agave's other alias, century plant, is inspired by – though exaggerates by at least a factor of three – the length of time it takes the plant to bloom. Alas, Gurr's identification of the mismatch between plant name and flowering cycle does not grow into a correspondingly illuminating reading of the plant's role in Mansfield's story. Deeming the depiction in 'Prelude' of an impossible hybrid of agave leaves and aloe stem, Gurr wonders 'whether Mansfield was simply ignorant of the plants which grew in the various gardens of her childhood, or whether she deliberately created a symbolic monstrosity'.[3]

I disagree with Gurr's claim that a botanically realist account of the plant species is impossible, or that such an account would betray the modernist innovation of 'Prelude'. More is at stake here than nitpicking at an earlier generation's scholarship. Far from being incidental to what we might take to be the proper concerns of the story – its portrayal of characters' interiority, its critique of gender roles, its impressionist technique – the botanical species at the centre of Mansfield's story is deeply entwined with these psychological, social and aesthetic foci. The aloe is so much at the heart of 'Prelude', in fact, that it is difficult to imagine a critical focus unaffected by its biological and historical facticity. In the first half of this chapter, I present the evidence for understanding the plant to be an *Agave americana* versus a species of true aloe, and I discuss the respective interpretations that these two possibilities entail. Significant differences in emphasis and sociohistorical implication emerge from the two readings, but there is crucial consensus on what I propose as the central concern of Mansfield's story: the connection between gender and colonialism. I conclude by suggesting that this botanical conundrum invokes issues that extend beyond Mansfield's story, contributing to ongoing debates within ecocriticism about the interplay between ecological mimesis and aesthetic innovation, as well as to ongoing discussions in narratology about the relation of actual and virtual worlds.

The strongest evidence that what Linda calls an aloe is an agave is that she's far from alone in her mistake. People have been confusing the various species of true aloe with *Agave americana* for many years. Despite disparate geographies, agave and aloe reached European greenhouses within a relatively short time span, with agave arriving in the mid-sixteenth century and true aloe appearing a century later. Based on their spiky succulent leaves, the two plants were grouped together under the name 'aloe', the ancient Greek word which Dioscorides used to describe the medical uses of true aloe in his first century AD *De Materia Medica*. It wasn't until 1753 that Carl Linnaeus assigned each plant its own genus, though this hardly cleared up the matter in popular usage.[4] The confusion was still present in 1840, notes Anne Pratt in *Flowers and their Associations*, as she attempts to correct the record: 'It was to a plant properly called agave, though usually termed aloe (the Agáve Americana) that our forefathers attributed the remarkable faculty of flowering once in a hundred years. This was for many years commonly asserted, but that great teacher – Time, has proved the assertion fabulous.'[5] Pratt rightly describes the *Agave americana*'s hundred-year flowering cycle as more fable than fact; a century plant will bloom on average ten to thirty years from the time it germinates. Having its once-a-century claim debunked did not diminish the awe the plant inspired among the early Victorians. The blossoming of *Agave americana* was such a rare event that the public would be invited to witness the floral spectacle.[6]

Whether under the name of aloe, century plant or maguey, agaves retained their celebrity in New Zealand well into the twentieth century. 'BAND TO GREET A FLOWER', the *Mataura Ensign* announced in 1912, noting that the Kingsdyke Prize Silver Band had been hired to play at the flowering of an 'aloe' in Whittleby.[7] Reporting that same year on a soon-to-bloom century plant at the Brighton Beach Hotel, the Nelson *Colonist* observed that when such flowerings occurred in years past, 'people came from all parts of the country to see them'.[8] As with the *Otago Witness* photo, the *Colonist* article emphasized the dimensions of the flowering stalk: 'about twenty-five feet in height, with twelve branches, thirty blooms on each branch'.[9] This botanically accurate description coincides with Kezia's vision of a 'tall stout stem' and her mother's impression of the 'blind stem cut[ting] into the air', offering further support to the claim that the 'aloe' of 'Prelude' is an *Agave americana*. If anything, Kezia's and Linda's experience understates the stalk's immensity, though that might be explained if the soon-to-bloom stalk has yet to reach full height. And while the flower stalk dominates media coverage of the agave, news accounts also mention the plant's 'thick, pulpy, spine-tipped leaves' and tenacious roots – also consistent with the description in 'Prelude'.[10]

The agave's celebrity in New Zealand was due in no small part to the American mystique it carried with it; newspapers often called it the 'American aloe'. In 1903 the Christchurch *Star* published 'The Sheriff of Aloe', a cowboy-western short story by the American screenwriter Emmett Campbell Hall. With a cast of characters including Gentleman Dan, Rawhide Pete and Snaggletooth Sam, 'The Sheriff of Aloe' could easily be mistaken for satire. The story's titular town of Aloe almost certainly references the fierce *Agave americana* – whose role in the production of the intoxicating liquor mescal was emphasized in New Zealand reportage – rather than the true aloe of lotions and potions.[11] Often this mystique drew upon the agave-aloe's connection to Native American culture. Comparing Native American 'wizards' to the fakirs of India, the *Wanganui Chronicle* claimed in 1904 that tribes of American Indians such as the Chippewas

> have acquired the art of sorcery to a very high degree, [that] Catholic missionaries, and other equally reliable witnesses, say they have seen century plants, two or three feet high, produced on bare Western prairies, within a few minutes – simply, it seemed, by a few incantations and a little hocus-pocus.[12]

Like so much of the turn-of-the-nineteenth-century pākehā culture, the indigenous resonances of the aloe-agave were in part a British inheritance, as the epigraph to Anne Pratt's chapter on aloe-agave reveals: 'But high, in amphitheatre above, / His arms the everlasting aloes threw'.[13] The lines come from Thomas Campbell's *Gertrude of Wyoming; a Pennsylvanian Tale*,[14] a narrative poem set amid the 1787 Battle of Wyoming, in which a troop of American Revolutionaries was routed by a coalition of British Loyalists and Seneca warriors. In the poem, the Scottish-born Campbell mounts a defence of settler colonialism based on racist stereotypes of Native Americans as either bloodthirsty warriors or vanishing Americans whose extinction is inevitable. Campbell connects the latter myth to the pastoral bounty of the New World via the symbol of the 'everlasting aloes', by which he presumably means agaves, though neither plant is native to Pennsylvania.

If Mansfield's 'aloe' is an *Agave americana* living under an assumed name, its presence in 'Prelude' operates metonymically to register the simultaneous exoticization and erasure of the indigenous cultures of the United States, a settler nation like New Zealand. As with 'The Sheriff of Aloe' (with which it shares nothing else), 'Prelude' is silent as to the native history of the land in which it is set. This silence takes on added import when we consider that – though resisting association with a Māoriland literary movement of pāhekā authors appropriating Māori elements in service of romantic cultural nationalism – Mansfield does attend to Māori culture in her sketch 'A True Tale' (1903), *The Urewera Notebook* (1907), and 'How Pearl Button was Kidnapped' (1912).[15] In place of the myth of the vanishing American used to justify US colonialism – a trope that Mansfield would have encountered in the poetry of her early and enduring literary influence, Walt Whitman – 'Prelude' instead registers only by omission an indigene who has disappeared seemingly without a trace.[16]

Even as it evokes the myth of the vanishing American as counterpart to its own silence on matters of Māori history, viewing the plant in 'Prelude' as an agave insinuates another kind of death – maternal mortality. A monocarpic plant, the agave reproduces once in its lifetime, then dies.[17] New Zealand papers made much of this fact, while also purveying the fiction that blooming agaves were necessarily female; in reality, each agave plant bears both male and female flowers. This feminizing of the agave evokes the image of a mother who gives her own life for that of her children. 'This century plant is a female,' the *Colonist* article wrongly asserts: 'At its blossoming period it gives birth to numerous progeny, but dies in giving them birth.'[18] A dramatic *Timaru Herald* report of an agave bloom has the 'mother plant dying at its close'.[19] These tragic accounts of dying mother agaves anticipate the threat of maternal mortality that Linda herself voices as she attempts to discourage Stanley's amorous attentions. 'You know I'm very delicate', Linda recalls telling him upon her second visit to the aloe. 'You know as well as I do that my heart is affected, and the doctor has told you I may die any moment. I have had three great lumps of children already. . . .'.[20] Haunting the ellipses is the threat that a fourth pregnancy could kill Linda, that in bringing new life into the world, she might meet the same end as the agave. For if the 'aloe' is an agave and what Mrs Fairfield sees are buds, Kezia's focus on the plant's withered leaves is prescient: the central figure of 'Prelude' is soon to die.

If the case for the 'aloe' in 'Prelude' being an *Agave americana* has in its favour the widespread misnomer and botanical description, its weakness is that it requires us to accept an improbable coincidence. Given how rarely an *Agave americana* flowers, what are the chances that a lone aloe should be beginning its once-in-its lifetime flowering at precisely the moment the Burnell family move in, so that Linda, fearful of a fourth pregnancy, can envy its reproductive agency? Fiction traffics in coincidences, of course, but modernist fiction is wary of such alignments, lest coincidence seem contrivance.[21] Should the plant indeed be beginning to blossom, the more likely explanation is that Linda is mistaken in her identification of its flowering cycle, but correct in its name. That is, Linda has accurately identified the plant as an aloe, but has mistakenly applied to it the well-publicized accounts of the agave's glacial pace of reproduction – an easy mistake to make, given how often the century plant was called an aloe. If this is the case, how do we reconcile the imposing description in 'Prelude' with our image of a windowsill houseplant? The answer is that the aloe vera grown in potted miniature is but one of aloe's many faces. Linda's impression of the plant's claw-like roots, menacing leaves and formidable stem suggests a number of species as possibilities: *Aloe marlothii*, or mountain aloe; *Aloe ferox*, known as Cape aloe or bitter aloe; and *Aloe arborescens*, whose common names include torch aloe. All three species may reach a height of ten feet, retain a strata of dead leaves below live leaves, and bloom from a single stalk – just what Kezia observes. The three aloes may also develop treelike trunks so short as to barely lift the plant off the ground, making the aloe seem to levitate – precisely Linda's vision.[22]

Another common name for *Aloe arborescens*, krantz aloe – krantz being the Afrikaner word for cliff – points to its origin, which it shares with *Aloe marlothii* and *Aloe ferox*. Like *Agave americana*, all three aloes are settler colony transplants. Unlike the agave, they are Old World plants, imported by European colonizers from southern Africa as ornamentals and as medicine. This southern African connection would have held special meaning for New Zealanders during the

1890s in which 'Prelude' is set, given that the South African War (also known as the second Boer War, 1899–1902) was the first time the colony sent troops to serve the British Empire. These troops trained in Karori, the rural Wellington suburbs where 'Prelude' is set and where Mansfield's family lived from 1893 to 1898. During the South African War, the aloe became a multivalent symbol of the conflict, sometimes associated with the Dutch-descended Boers, at other times associated with Britain's colonies. One New Zealand newspaper account described ridges dotted with aloes resembling men, and a business arose marketing the seeds of aloes and other South African plants to the families of soldiers who died there.[23] Surveying the aftermath of the Battle of Spion Kop, an Australian war correspondent remarked upon the intertwining of natural beauty and mechanized violence, describing 'the hillside covered with aloes with their large fleshy leaves and their exquisite candelabra-shaped crimson and yellow blossoms', but noting ominously that 'Barbed wire was strung from aloe to aloe right to the top'.[24] This description suggests krantz aloe, whose other common name, candelabra aloe, reflects its vivid, branching inflorescences. The juxtaposition of krantz aloe and barbed wire is significant. The Boers had long planted lines of spiky-leaved krantz aloe at the edges of paddocks as a kind of natural barbed wire to pen in cattle. The British brought actual barbed wire to South Africa, where they pioneered its use in the Boer War, both as frontline defence and in concentration camps where they imprisoned the wives and children of Boer soldiers.[25] The correspondent's description thus juxtaposes a tool of settler colonialism alongside an analogous technology of global imperialism, the latter used to subjugate the practitioners of former. Absent are accounts associating the aloe with the region's original inhabitants, such as the Zulu people, who had themselves at times fought both the Boers and the British. When we consider the aloe in 'Prelude' – assuming that it is a krantz aloe – we encounter a symbol evoking conflicting colonial histories and effacements.

The Zulu, Xhosa and other southern African peoples had long made use of the anti-inflammatory properties of *Aloe arborescens* and other aloe species for both external and internal applications.[26] These dual uses became well-established in England by the nineteenth century, often drawing upon traditional knowledge of plant medicines developed in Britain's colonies. Aloe was used topically to treat inflammation of all kinds, from swollen lymph glands to haemorrhoids to ophthalmia. Internally, aloe extracts were taken as a purgative to treat everything from constipation to an enlarged spleen. Whether external or internal, aloe's disparate medical applications depend upon a common principle: aloe reduces swelling.

These purgative and anti-inflammatory qualities bear directly on Linda's experience of the aloe. During her first encounter, she sees it as a 'fat swelling plant', her phrasing recalling the doctrine of signatures, the medical theory of Dioscorides' day that reasoned that a plant resembling a particular part of the human body must be good for treating that body part. This phrase further recalls her earlier dream, in which a baby bird 'swell[s]' via a grotesque phallic transformation into a hungry baby. Given the revulsion Linda feels towards swelling dream-birds, swelling penises and what we may deduce is her own swelling belly, there is a certain logic behind Linda's selection of the aloe as her guardian plant.

But aloe reduces swelling in organs beyond skin and eyes, and it clears more than bowels, liver and spleen. Among its internal applications, aloe has a long history of use as a birth control agent and abortifacient.[27] Like the curving leaves that for Linda symbolize strategic concealment, the aloe's 'fat swelling body' is not the sign of fertility it might suggest. Linda's admiration for the long reproductive cycle of the century plant suggests that she is well aware that she is in the early stages of an undesired pregnancy.[28] If the plant is a true aloe and thus the source of a medicine that can prevent or terminate pregnancy, different but no less powerful possibilities for female reproductive agency emerge.

Significantly, in both readings, Linda can imagine the possibility of autonomous female sexual agency only through the figure of a non-human entity. In her interpretation of the 'aloe', whatever species it may be, that sexual agency is exercised as a reproductive control that she envies but cannot herself practice within the strictures of Victorian settler colonial culture. The aloe serves a crucial function for Linda in that its non-human status provides a neutral imaginative locus from which to consider her own situation. From that reflection, a series of insights about the interrelations of gender, sexuality, national identity and colonialism emerge. While that imaginative space depends upon the aloe's relative alienness, that separation contains within itself possibilities for two forms of connection: between women and, more surprisingly, across species.

We see both potentials revealed in the second of the story's two scenes involving the aloe, when Linda excuses herself to look for her mother. She finds her out in the garden:

> The moon that Lottie and Kezia had seen from the storeman's wagon was full, and the house, the garden, the old woman and Linda – all were bathed in dazzling light. [...]
>
> As they stood on the steps, the high grassy bank on which the aloe rested rose up like a wave, and the aloe seemed to ride upon it like a ship with the oars

> lifted. Bright moonlight hung upon the lifted oars like water, and on the green wave glittered the dew.
>
> 'Do you feel it, too,' said Linda, and she spoke to her mother with the special voice that women use at night to each other as though they spoke in their sleep or from some hollow cave – 'Don't you feel that it is coming towards us?'
>
> She dreamed that she was caught up out of the cold water into the ship with the lifted oars and the budding mast. Now the oars fell striking quickly, quickly. They rowed far away over the top of the garden trees, the paddocks and the dark bush beyond. Ah, she heard herself cry: 'Faster! Faster!' to those who were rowing.[29]

An ideal of female solidarity suffuses the passage, as moonlight joins aloe, grandmother and mother to absent daughters Lottie and Kezia. This visual cue finds its aural counterpart in Linda's 'special voice' of night-time female affiliation. The 'hollow cave' from which it emerges seems less the uterine image Cherry Hankin proposes than a version of Plato's allegorical cave, in which female characters see only the shadows of gendered expectations, not the colonial ideology driving them.[30] When earlier she escapes to her sickroom, Linda's eyes adjust to the non-human object world, a world in which her quilt's tassels are dancers and attendant priests, and in which medicine bottles are hatted men – in short, a world which makes visible the arbitrary cultural projections of gender. Having witnessed those gender operations at work in the cribbage game between Stanley and Beryl, she tries to communicate this insight to her mother via the metaphors and similes that are the code of dreams and stories.

Through such figuration the political dimensions of Linda's situation become apparent. Linda sees the dew-strewn grass lifting 'like a wave', the moonlit aloe 'rid[ing] upon it like a ship with the oars lifted'. This nautical image makes visible what has been implicit throughout the story: the domestic drama of the Burnells' house-move from Wellington to the hinterlands is a component scene in the narrative of global imperialism. With that visibility, accumulated details come into focus. Quarantine Island, whose lighthouse Kezia and Lottie spied from the storeman's cart, was still in operation when 'Prelude' was written and set, detaining ships arriving from the British Empire to protect New Zealand settlers from disease. The description of the sisters' coordinated attire at the start of the story becomes in retrospect more ominous than charming: 'Coats with brass anchor buttons and little round caps with battleship ribbons.'[31] Other parts of the pattern emerge: Pat's account of the ducks as the 'little Irish navy'; the Picton boat whose daily route sutures South Island to North; the racism directed towards Chinese immigrants.[32] Drawing the reader's attention to New Zealand's ubiquitous but unremarked colonial power structures, the emerging pattern invites us to recall when Kezia first saw the aloe's environs from the storeman's cart: '[T]hey were clanking through a drive that cut through the garden like a whiplash, looping suddenly an island of green.'[33] As extension of the road from Wellington to its agricultural exurbs, the drive is both the symbol and the vehicle of colonial expansion. Bisecting the garden, the 'whiplash' at once evokes the animal exploitation upon which the colonial settlement of New Zealand depends and the violence directed towards its indigenous peoples. It was the whipping of Te Ara, the son of a Māori chieftain, on the orders of a British ship captain that sparked the Boyd Incident in 1809; into the twentieth century, Māori children were whipped in government-run schools for speaking te reo. As metonymy for colonial violence, the whiplash stands in place of a history and culture otherwise absent from 'Prelude', as are the Māori themselves. By 'looping suddenly an island of green' – the banked grass mound on which the aloe rests – the whiplash drive suggests that the aloe's island is a miniature of New Zealand, implicating the Burnell's new homestead in the process of colonial violence, however occluded its power relations.

Linda's response to the aloe suggests that she recognizes the violence behind imperial power and sees the plant as a model for how that power might be repurposed. To Linda, the plant is a ship come to rescue her, as if British naval might were reassigned from protecting imperial economic interests to protecting Anglo-colonial women. Linda admires the menacing spines that adorn the aloe's leaves, reasoning that 'nobody would dare to come near the ship or to follow after'.[34] Little wonder that her heart should harden as she covets these evolutionary defences. For Linda, heteronormative sex is itself a form of violence. However kindly Stanley may treat her after intercourse, she finds him 'too strong for her' and 'frightening – really frightening'.[35] Linda hates 'things that rush at her', and Stanley, her too-loud, too-eager 'Newfoundland dog', is one such forceful presence.[36] Yet Linda's reaction to the power dynamics of gender remains internal. In response to Stanley's demands for attention, Linda longs to scream that he and the labour of obligatory childbearing are 'killing' her, but she says nothing. In the end, Linda submits to the demands of late Victorian colonial womanhood, confirming her mother's assessment that the aloe is going to bud, just as she herself will in a few months give birth.[37]

But even as she acquiesces, Linda conceives a trenchant analysis of her situation. 'I shall go on having children and Stanley will go on making money and the children and the gardens will grow bigger and bigger, with whole fleets of aloes in them for me to choose from', she thinks to herself.[38] Locating her position within colonialism's logic of constant increase, Linda proposes an ecofeminist insight: as a procreating colonial woman, however unwilling, she is the biological engine of empire. If the phrase 'fleets of aloes' reiterates the naval dimensions of Linda's fantasy of plant rescue only to accede to the procreative demands of patriarchy and empire, it does not foreclose the revolutionary potential her reverie awakens. Although the differences that emerge by reading the central plant of 'Prelude' as agave versus true aloe are significant, both readings converge in allowing Linda to envision new possibilities of female resistance. While Linda herself is unable to act upon these possibilities, the hope in 'Prelude' is that Kezia may someday do so.

To dismiss Kezia's behaviour as childlike is to ignore the radicality of her stance towards issues of gender and power. Kezia admires gentleness, not forcefulness, in men, as she recalls the storeman setting a bunch of grapes upon 'the leaves so tenderly that Kezia held her breath to watch'.[39] She is savvy enough to recognize the ruses of power, evading Isabel's designs that she be 'roped in under her government'.[40] Sharing her mother's aversions, Kezia 'hate[s] rushing animals like dogs and parrots' – both in actuality and in dreams when 'rushing, their heads swell e-enormous' – but unlike her mother, she speaks these truths aloud.[41] Kezia is attentive to the experience of non-human beings. Her part in the grotesque duck-slaughter scene is to voice a cry for justice, however impossible its realization: 'Put head back!'[42] This concern for non-human life is not restricted to the animal world. When making a matchbox surprise for her grandmother, Kezia provides the violet the company of a picotee on each side, taking pains 'not to cover their heads' with lavender.[43]

Kezia's care for non-human life suggests a capacity to envision the experience of other beings, but as one that she has yet to develop to the point of fully imagined becoming. To inhabit that capacity wholly was the joyful compulsion of Kezia's real-world creator, whose October 1917 letter to her friend Dorothy Brett is often taken for an aesthetic credo. It is easy to see why Mansfield's letter has informed so many animal studies: 'When I write about ducks I swear that I am a white duck with a round eye.'[44] Overlooked amid this recent interest is the fact that Mansfield's affirmation of becoming other begins not with fauna but with flora:

> What can one do, faced with this wonderful tumble of round bright fruits, but gather them and play with them – and become them, as it were. When I pass the apple stalls I cannot help stopping and staring until I feel that I, myself, am changing into an apple, too – and that at any moment I may produce an apple, miraculously, out of my own being like the conjurer produces the egg. When you paint apples do you feel that your breasts and your knees become apples, too?[45]

We see at once many of the elements of plant-based critique in 'Prelude': delight in the biologically evolved features of shape, texture and colour; the acknowledgement that these features are fundamentally sexual (knees being only slightly less eroticized than breasts in 1917); the recognition that these biological-sexual features have been captured within a market economy dependent upon their re-production. Mansfield's ambition is not simply to master artistic creation by 'produc[ing] an apple, miraculously, out of my own being'. Rather, its association with the marketplace suggests her desire that artistic production might upend the power relations inherent in commodity culture, upsetting the capitalist applecart.

Mansfield's paean to aesthetic creation is so compelling here that it nearly overshadows her account of where agency really lies: in the non-human natural being. Encountering the apples' vibrant presence, 'what can one do [...] but [...] become them?' The phrase 'I cannot help stopping and staring' initiates the metamorphosis whereby Mansfield becomes the non-human entity that she may replicate herself freely within art's limitless economy. Like Mansfield herself, Kezia is arrested by a non-human presence, albeit of a wilder kind than Mansfield's domesticated fruit and fowl. Referenced by the pronoun 'IT' – an analogue to 'THEY', the objects that conspire to haunt her mother – this spectral presence receives a single sentence in 'Prelude', when Kezia is alone in the family's abandoned house. The lengthier account of 'It' in 'The Aloe' hints at possibilities beyond the stereotypical childish fear of monsters:

> If [Kezia] began to call Lottie now and went on calling her loudly all the while she flew down the stairs and out of the house she might escape from *It* in time. It was round like the sun. It had a face. *It* smiled, but *It* had no eyes. *It* was yellow. When she was put to bed with two drops of aconite in a medicine glass *It* breathed very loudly and firmly and *It* had been known on certain particularly fearful occasions to turn round and round. *It* hung in the air. [...] *It* was at the top of the stairs; *It* was at the bottom of the stairs . . .[46]

While I do not wish to directly equate the *It* of 'The Aloe' with the aloe of 'Prelude', the correspondences are suggestive. *It* is eyeless; the aloe has a 'blind stem'.[47] *It* is 'round like the sun'; the aloe is lit by a dazzling full moon. *It* hangs 'in the air'; the aloe appears 'high above them, as though becalmed in the air'.[48] Though airborne, *It* simultaneously occupies the top and bottom of the stairs. Even while levitating, the aloe's roots cleave to the ground.

What I do claim is that the aloe of 'Prelude' constitutes an alien presence whose means of sensory input, lived experience and potential agency are so radically outside human comprehension as to provoke fear, much as 'It' frightens Kezia. The uncertainty driving Kezia's fear takes the form of questions that, with a shift in capitalization, could equally apply to aloe as to spectre: What does IT know, what does IT feel, what will IT do? Kezia's unspoken challenge is to learn to embrace and inhabit such radical alterity, to seek out the possibilities of untapped agency and unimagined alliances. If the dominant power structures relegate one to the status of object, what would it mean to envision solidarity among all beings so relegated, both human and non-human? What might be accomplished by an ecofeminism that is ecocentric, rather than anthropocentric?

Returning to the issue of species with which this chapter began, we must consider what impact the identity of the 'Prelude' aloe would have on the prospect of such a radical project of environmental justice. We have seen that when the botanical-cultural context is attended to, reading the plant as an agave highlights the threat of maternal mortality, while reading the plant as a true aloe emphasizes how traditional knowledge of medicinal plants enables female reproductive agency. Both plant interpretations illuminate how gender roles and colonial power structures intertwine, the agave by contrasting the reality of maternal mortality with the myth of the vanishing American, the true aloe by contrasting the military technology of barbed wire with centuries of plant knowledge accrued in colonial spaces that grant women reproductive agency. The two sets of readings are complementary, in that they engage a range of geographical settings, colonial experiences and women's histories. Were the species of plant in 'Prelude' fixed, the scope of the story's imaginative intervention in real-world concerns would be correspondingly limited. Fortunately, such fixity will never occur – not because the plant is an impossible hybrid or a 'symbolic monstrosity', but because the text is constructed as to be simultaneously agave and true aloe. This irreducible duality is what allows Mansfield's story to be botanically realist *and* formally modernist. In this way, 'Prelude' negotiates a course between what Lawrence Buell describes as the insistence of first-wave ecocriticism on ecological mimesis and second-wave ecocriticism's insistence that we can know the natural world only through our cultural representations of it.[49] This negotiation succeeds by virtue of the story's embodiment of the inherent virtuality of literary narrative, a virtuality Gilles Deleuze describes as 'Real without being actual, ideal without being abstract'.[50]

The species duality I am claiming at the heart of 'Prelude' is supported by a change Mansfield made as she revised 'The Aloe' into 'Prelude', as well as a plot development she considered but chose not to implement. The earlier story includes Kezia's observation that some of the plant's leaves 'looked as though they had been painted with broad bands of yellow'.[51] Mansfield removed this detail that would have weighted the scale towards the plant being an agave. She also chose not to pursue an idea in her working notes that had the Burnell family cutting down the burgeoning flower stalk in response to Linda's illness.[52] This action borrows a trope from newspaper anecdotes in which an invalid, upon learning that a century plant's blossoming heralds a death, conflates correlation with causality and cuts the flower-stalk to the ground.[53] While this textual trajectory supports the possibility that Mansfield wished to leave ambiguous the species of the central plant in 'Prelude', my argument does not rest on authorial intention nor on biographical circumstance. It would be as unshaken by, say, the publication of a letter in which Mansfield wrote that the aloe of 'Prelude' was a krantz aloe as it would by the discovery of an 1893 photo of Chesney Wold showing an agave's twenty-foot flower-spike. Rather, my argument relies on the fact that the meaning of any work of literature emerges contingently at the intersection of text, historical context and reader. It is through that contingent emergence that the literary text itself engages in its own process of becoming – of becoming world. To affirm this process is not to engage in utopian wishfulness, but to acknowledge the reciprocal relationship between thought and matter, seed and soil.

Notes

1 CW 2, p. 73.

2 Andrew Gurr, 'Katherine Mansfield: The Question of Perspectives in Commonwealth Literature', *Kunapipi*, 6, no. 2 (1984): 67–80.

3 Ibid., p. 74.

4 'aloe, n.' *OED*; Pedanius Dioscorides of Anazarbus, *De Materia Medica,* 3rd, rev edn, trans. and ed. Lily Y. Beck (Zurich: Georg Olms Verlag, 2017), pp. 186–7; Carol Linnaeus, *Species Plantarum*, vol. 1 (Stockholm: Laurentius Salvius, 1753), pp. 319–24.

5 Anne Pratt, *Flowers and their Associations* (London: Charles Knight and Co., 1840), pp. 284–5.

6 Ibid., pp. 285–6.

7 'Band to Greet a Flower', *Mataura Ensign*, 5 October 1912.

8 'A Century Plant', *Colonist*, 54: 13539, 5 October 1912.

9 Ibid.

10 'American Aloe', *Alexandra Herald and Central Otago Gazette*, 383, 10 September 1903.

11 Emmett Campbell Hall, 'The Sheriff of Aloe', *Star*, 7597, 6 January 1903.
12 'American Indian Magic', *Wanganui Chronicle*, 47: 12147, 20 February 1904.
13 Pratt, p. 284.
14 Thomas Campbell, *Gertrude of Wyoming; a Pennsylvanian Tale* (London: Longman, Hurst, Rees, and Orme, 1809), p. 33.
15 Jane Stafford and Mark Williams, *Maoriland: New Zealand Literature 1872–1914* (Wellington: Victoria University Press, 2006), pp. 142–70.
16 Walt Whitman, 'Pioneers! O Pioneers!' in *Leaves of Grass* (London: Putnam, 1897), pp. 183–6.
17 To be precise, the *Agave americana* reproduces sexually by flowering just once in its lifetime.
18 'A Century Plant.'
19 'Miscellaneous', *Timaru Herald*, 57: 6071, 3 October 1894.
20 CW2, p. 87.
21 See, for example, Fredric Jameson's account of how coincidence in modernist texts of the imperial centre differs from coincidence in colonial modernist texts; the former is an aesthetic compensation for the ungraspable totality of colonial subjects and spaces, whereas the latter is a plausible occurrence. Fredric Jameson, 'Modernism and Imperialism' in *Nationalism, Colonialism, and Literature*, intro. by Seamus Deane (Minneapolis: University of Minnesota Press, 1990), pp. 43–66. Given the importance of New Zealand agriculture to Britain's imperial economy, examining the coincidence of the *Agave americana* blooming in the settler colonial space of Mansfield's story would be a worthwhile undertaking for modernist studies and ecocriticism.
22 Paul Emms, 'Aloe marlothii', *PlantZAfrica*, South African National Biodiversity Institute, 2007, http://pza.sanbi.org/aloe-marlothii (accessed 3 March 2019); Alice Aubrey, 'Aloe ferox', *PlantZAfrica*, South African National Biodiversity Institute, 2001, http://pza.sanbi.org/aloe-ferox (accessed 3 March 2019); Andrew Hankey and Alice Notten, 'Aloe Arborescens', *PlantZAfrica*, South African National Biodiversity Institute, 2001, updated 2004, http://pza.sanbi.org/aloe-arborescens (accessed 3 March 2019). An aloe without a visible trunk is said to be *acaulescent*. Leonard E. Newton, 'Aloes in Habitat', in *Aloes: The Genus Aloe*, ed. Tom Reynolds (Boca Raton: CRC Press, 2004), pp. 3–14 (p. 4).
23 'South African War', *Hawke's Bay Herald*, 34: 11410, 16 December 1899; 'Untitled', *Lake County Press*, 1054, 5 March 1903.
24 'The Battlefields of Natal: The Views of a Lady Visitor', *Hawke's Bay Herald*, 35: 11666, 13 October 1900.
25 Aiden Forth, *Barbed-Wire Imperialism: Britain's Empire of Camps, 1876-1903* (Berkeley: University of California Press, 2017), pp. 138–41.

26 R. B. Bhat, 'Medicinal Plants and Traditional Practices of the Xhosa People in the Transkei Region of Eastern Cape, South Africa', *Indian Journal of Traditional Knowledge*, 13, no. 2 (2014): 292–8 (p. 294).
27 Sage-Femme Collective, *Natural Liberty: Rediscovering Self-induced Abortion Methods* (Las Vegas: Sage-Femme, 2008), p. 90.
28 In 'At the Bay' (1921), we will see the child to whom Linda gives birth, the infant boy whom she tells, 'I do not like babies' (CW2, p. 355).
29 CW2, pp. 86–7.
30 Cherry Hankin, *Katherine Mansfield and Her Confessional Stories* (London: Macmillan, 1983), p. 129.
31 CW2, p. 56.
32 CW2, p. 81.
33 CW2, p. 61.
34 CW2, p. 87.
35 Ibid.
36 Ibid.
37 Ibid.
38 CW2, p. 88.
39 CW2, p. 60.
40 CW2, p. 68.
41 CW2, p. 61.
42 CW2, p. 82.
43 CW2, p. 72.
44 *Letters* 1, p. 330.
45 Ibid.
46 CW1 p. 473.
47 CW2, p. 73.
48 Ibid.
49 Lawrence Buell, *The Future of Environmental Criticism: Environmental Crisis and Literary Imagination* (Oxford: Blackwell, 2005), pp. 17–36.
50 Deleuze's formulation repurposes Proust's description of memory. Gilles Deleuze, *Difference and Repetition*, trans. Paul Patton (New York: Columbia University Press, 1994), p. 208.
51 The yellow bands alone do not allow definitive identification, as there are striped aloes, including variegated forms of *Aloe arborescens*.
52 Katherine Mansfield, *The Aloe, with Prelude*, ed. Vincent O'Sullivan (Auckland: Port Nicholson Press, 1982), p. 163.
53 'Untitled', *Grey River Argus*, 17 April 1905.

6

Katherine Mansfield and American modernism

Chris Mourant

Katherine Mansfield, the New Zealand writer who spent her short adult life living and travelling in Britain and Europe, is rarely discussed in relation to American literature.[1] The recent volume of essays edited by Sarah Ailwood and Melinda Harvey, *Katherine Mansfield and Literary Influence* (2015), for instance, includes chapters examining Mansfield's debt to a range of writers, including Virginia Woolf, Elizabeth von Arnim, Colette, Chekhov, Dickens and Shakespeare, but none of them from the pantheon of American literature. Instead, we almost invariably position Mansfield in relation to British modernism and either English or European literary traditions, with Gerri Kimber and Janka Kascakova's volume *Katherine Mansfield and Continental Europe: Connections and Influences* (2015) being a good example of the latter trend. Mansfield's close but uneasy involvement in the networks of literary London, in particular, has determined how we have understood the development of her modernist writing style, with the trajectory of Woolf's career often serving as an indication of the path Mansfield's work might have taken had she lived beyond the age of thirty-four.

By resituating Mansfield to the Left Bank of Paris, however, it is possible to position her work within networks of influence centred on the 'lost generation' of expatriate American writers who dominated the Parisian literary scene in the early twentieth century. Mansfield's focused engagement with the work of these writers in the last months of her life not only suggests directions that her work might have taken had she lived longer but also reveals the literary influences that shaped her decision in the autumn of 1922 to enter George Ivanovich Gurdjieff's Institute for the Harmonious Development of Man.

Shakespeare and Company

Mansfield learnt of Gurdjieff's teachings and his plans to establish his Institute in Fontainebleau-Avon, a commune southeast of Paris, after attending a lecture in London in September 1922, given by the Russian mathematician and mystic P. D. Ouspensky. Battling worsening ill health, Mansfield was at this time desperate for not only a physical cure to her tuberculosis but also spiritual consolation, believing that if she could only find peace in her soul then her body might recover. Gurdjieff seemed to hold out the promise of this spiritual healing, and in the last months of her life Mansfield became convinced that he was 'the only man who understands there is no division between body and spirit'.[2] Gurdjieff taught his disciples that modern-day civilization had divided human nature, causing a disruption between the physical, emotional and intellectual 'centres' of the self; through a regime of conscious effort and voluntary suffering, he argued, the individual would be able to achieve the harmonious integration of those different 'centres' and thereby attain self-knowledge and a higher level of awareness.

In October 1922, en route to Fontainebleau, Mansfield spent several weeks in Paris, staying in the same place in which she had seen through the aerial bombardment of the city in 1918, the Select Hôtel on the Place de la Sorbonne. Mansfield offers the same account of the hotel across several letters to different correspondents, with some minor variations:

> I have a funny room on the 6th floor that looks over the roofs of the Sorbonne. Large grave gentlemen in marble bath gowns are dotted on the roof. Some hold up a finger; some are only wise. A coy rather silly looking eagle is just opposite perched on a plaque called Geologie. I like this view *fearfully*.[3]

October was a month of glorious weather in Paris. In her letters to her husband John Middleton Murry, Mansfield observes that 'there's just a light sailing breeze & the sun is really hot' and 'the sky is as blue as the sky can be'.[4] To S. S. Koteliansky, likewise, she writes that the weather 'is simply beautiful – clear, warm, still, so warm one can sit at the open window late at night, smoking a *good* cigarette. It is late summer, not autumn at all'.[5] In the first weeks of October 1922, at least, Mansfield was content, writing: 'I think for some reason Paris is nearer ones spiritual home than London. Why? But it feels nearer.'[6]

As well as leisurely smoking at the open window of her hotel room, Mansfield also reports in her letters that she spent these October days sitting in the sun in the Luxembourg Gardens, which were only a short walk away from the Place de la Sorbonne. Also within a ten-minute stroll was the famous bookshop

Shakespeare and Company, owned by Sylvia Beach and at that time located at 12 rue de l'Odéon. The bookshop had become famous throughout the literary world earlier in the year after publishing the first edition of Joyce's *Ulysses* in February. As well as a commercial enterprise, however, Shakespeare and Company also functioned as a lending library, servicing the many expatriate writers who gathered in Paris in the 1920s. Only ever in Paris for short spells of time, and often travelling through the city en route to elsewhere, Mansfield is rarely considered as a key figure in the avant-garde networks of the Left Bank; for instance, Shari Benstock's seminal study of these networks, *Women of the Left Bank: 1900–1940* (1986), which includes a chapter devoted to Beach and her bookshop, makes no reference to Mansfield, even as a writer on the margins or as someone passing through. However, the archival records for Shakespeare and Company show that Mansfield was involved briefly in these networks. The hundreds of readers' cards from the Shakespeare and Company lending library are now held at Princeton University. Among this archive collection is one reader's card in Mansfield's name which lists the books that were loaned out to her in October 1922 (Figure 1). The card misspells Mansfield's forename with a 'C', but we know this is indeed she as the address given is the Select Hôtel and the dates correlate with her time in Paris.

All the texts that Mansfield borrowed from Shakespeare and Company were by American authors. The three books borrowed on 6 October are all by Sherwood Anderson: the novels *Windy McPherson's Son* (1916) and *Poor White* (1920), and the short story cycle *Winesburg, Ohio* (1919); so too is the final text listed on the card, the short story collection *The Triumph of the Egg* (1921). Dorothy Canfield's *The Brimming Cup* was the bestselling novel of 1921 in America, and a huge commercial success. We know that Mansfield read this novel with enthusiasm as she writes to her father in November 1922 from Fontainebleau: 'I wonder if you happen to have come across a novel called "The Brimming Cup" by an American woman. The name of the writer is Dorothy Canfield. It seemed to me a most charming book and extremely clever.'[7] The novel *Peter Whiffle* (1922), by Carl Van Vechten, was an experimental work in which the author appears as a major character, and was almost certainly the earliest work of fiction to make a direct allusion to *Ulysses*. Van Vechten was a patron of the Harlem Renaissance and close friend of Gertrude Stein, whose book *Three Lives* (1909) Mansfield borrowed from Shakespeare and Company on the same day she was loaned *Peter Whiffle*. Anderson was also close to Stein at this time, after Sylvia Beach brokered an introduction in 1921 at Stein's infamous apartment on the rue de Fleurus. In her memoir, Beach recalls:

Sherwood told me that Gertrude Stein's writing had influenced him. He admired her immensely, and asked me if I would introduce him to her. [...] This meeting was something of an event. Sherwood's deference and the admiration he expressed for her writing pleased Gertrude immensely.[8]

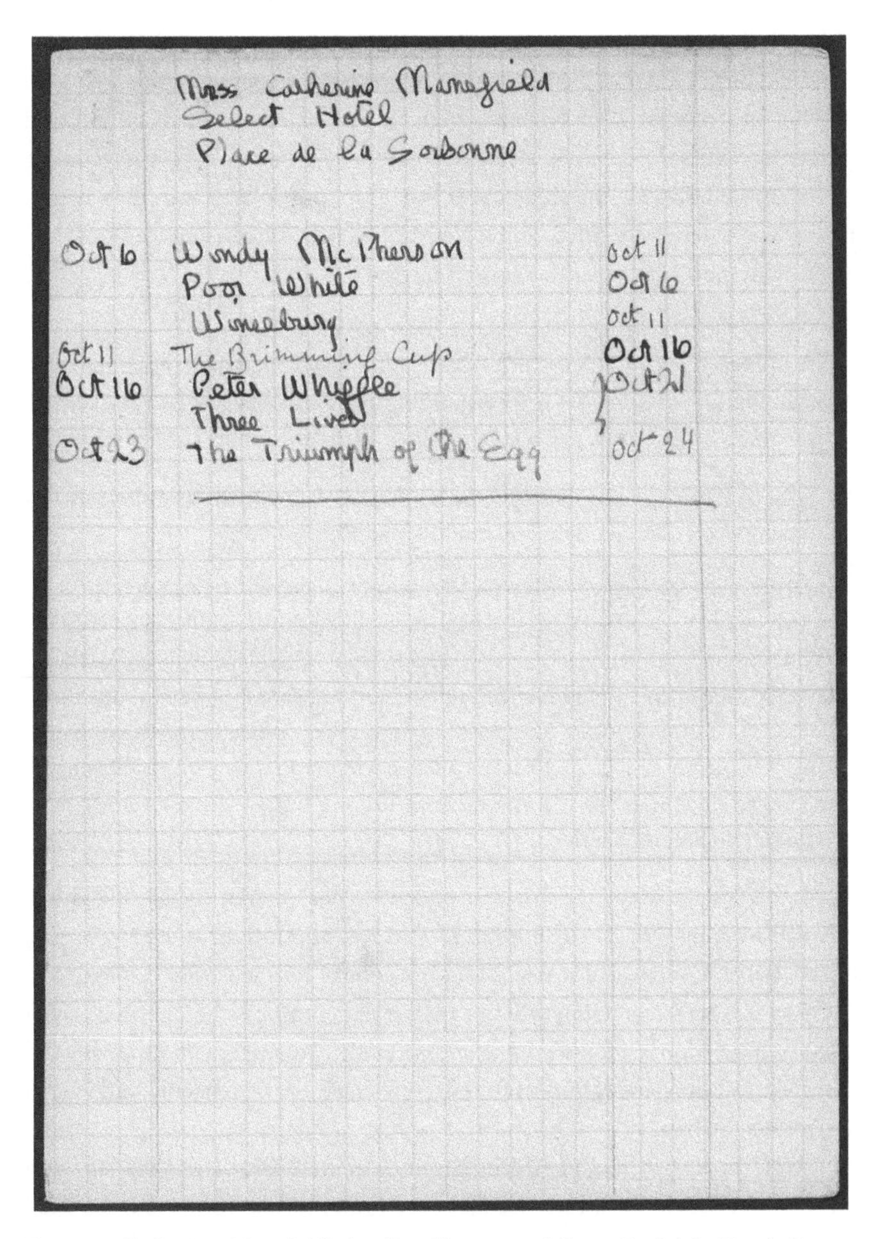

Miss Catherine Mansfield
Select Hotel
Place de la Sorbonne

Oct 6	Windy McPherson	oct 11
	Poor White	Oct 6
	Winesburg	oct 11
Oct 11	The Brimming Cup	Oct 16
Oct 16	Peter Whiffle	Oct 21
	Three Lives	
Oct 23	The Triumph of the Egg	oct 24

Figure 1 Katherine Mansfield's lending library card, box 43, Sylvia Beach Papers, Department of Rare Books and Special Collections, Princeton University Library.

Therefore, the Shakespeare and Company reader's card held in Mansfield's name reveals her intense interest in both popular and experimental American fiction at this time, in both the Dorothy Canfields of the day and also those writers, such as Carl Van Vechten and Sherwood Anderson, producing work from within the avant-garde networks of Sylvia Beach, Gertrude Stein and writers in their wider orbit of influence. This document indicates that, in the final months of her life, Mansfield began to focus her reading on modern American literature.

What is perhaps surprising, however, is the fact that Mansfield decided to borrow Stein's *Three Lives*, given that she had written a very unfavourable review of the book for the *Athenaeum* two years previously. Mansfield begins this review – derisively titled 'Some New Thing' – by dismissing Stein's formal experimentation with repetition, observing that

> Miss Gertrude Stein has discovered a new way of writing stories [which] is just to keep right on writing them. Don't mind how often you go back to the beginning, don't hesitate to say the same thing over and over again [...] just keep right on, and by the time you've done writing you'll have produced your effect.[9]

Focusing in particular on the second and longest of Stein's three stories, about the African-American woman Melanctha, Mansfield writes:

> [L]et the reader go warily, warily with Melanctha. We confess we read a good page or two before we realized what was happening. Then the dreadful fact dawned. We discovered ourselves reading *in syncopated time*. Gradually we heard in the distance, and then coming uncomfortably near, the sound of banjos, drums, bones, cymbals and voices. The page began to rock. To our horror we found ourselves silently singing [...] 'Melanctha' is negro music with all its maddening monotony done into prose; it is writing in real rag-time. Heaven forbid Miss Stein should become a fashion![10]

Deplorable in its overt racism, this review is also extremely short-sighted, rashly dismissing the 'syncopating time' that was about to grip the 1920s and, indeed, become very fashionable. Thinking about Mansfield's Shakespeare and Company reader's card alongside this review also prompts the question: given this strong aversion to Stein's work, expressed only two years previously, why did Mansfield feel the need to return to this book again? And, relatedly: did she, in fact, reread the book?

If we look at the dates at which these books were issued (on the left) and returned (on the right), we can see that *Poor White* was taken out and returned on the same day, 6 October. We might concede that Mansfield was a fast reader, but even for her this speedy turnaround seems far too quick to be feasible. And if we turn to Mansfield's letters from mid-October, we find ample evidence that – now very ill – she was not only struggling to write stories but also struggling to read. On 15 October, she writes to Dorothy Brett: 'I am sick all the time – and cold' and, as a result, 'work I can't at all for the present. Even reading is difficult.'[11] On the following day (the day she supposedly decided to take out *Peter Whiffle* and *Three Lives*), Mansfield writes to Murry: 'I don't want any more books at present of any kind. I am sick and tired of books and thats a dreadful fact.'[12] That morning, on 16 October, Mansfield left for Gurdjieff's Institute with her companion Ida Baker, who then returned to Paris to organize Mansfield's affairs from the Select Hôtel, forwarding on her letters, buying her warm clothes, and (we now know) borrowing and returning books on her behalf. On the day before her departure from Paris, Mansfield had written to Dorothy Brett: 'It's only while Ida is my legs that she is so present.'[13] As such, it seems highly likely that after Mansfield finished *The Brimming Cup* on 16 October she stopped choosing books from Shakespeare and Company, something that Ida took upon herself to do for Mansfield, perhaps making choices under the guidance of Sylvia Beach. Knowing that Mansfield had shown an intense interest in Anderson earlier in the month, Ida borrowed *The Triumph of the Egg* on 23 October, but received a letter from Mansfield the following day, commanding: 'Don't send the book. Why should you? I don't want any books at present' (at which point, as we can see from the reader's card, Ida swiftly returned it).[14] And a few days later, on 28 October, Mansfield abruptly ends another letter to Ida with this rebuke: 'I do not want to hear about Miss Beach.'[15] In the notes to Mansfield's *Collected Letters*, the editors Vincent O'Sullivan and Margaret Scott note that 'Ida was still at the Select Hotel in Paris' and suggest: 'Presumably she passed on some story relating to Sylvia Beach.'[16] We now know that there was no story, but that Mansfield simply did not want to hear about books that she was too ill or had no inclination to read.

While keeping these reservations in mind, however, we might surmise that Mansfield decided to return to Stein's work at this time as a result of her growing interest in Anderson. Stein's *Geography and Plays* had been published in the summer of 1922 with a preface written by Anderson, in which he praised her work unreservedly: he observed that 'the work of Gertrude Stein consists in a rebuilding, an entirely new recasting of life, in the city of words.'[17] And on 11 October 1922, the American periodical *The New Republic* published Anderson's 'Four American Impressions: Gertrude Stein, Paul Rosenfeld, Ring Lardner, Sinclair Lewis', in which he described Stein as 'a worker in words with the same loving touch in her strong fingers that was characteristic of the women of the kitchens of the brick houses in the town of my boyhood':

> She is making new, strange and to my ears sweet combinations of words. As an American writer I admire her because she, in her person, represents something sweet and healthy in our American life, and because I have a kind of undying faith that what she is up to in her word kitchen in Paris is of more importance to writers of English than the work of many of our more easily understood and more widely accepted word artists.[18]

This article was published on the very same day Mansfield returned three of Anderson's books to Shakespeare and Company, and it is entirely possible that Mansfield read the article before borrowing *Three Lives* five days later. This endorsement of Stein's experimental writing style may have confirmed Mansfield's suspicion, discernible behind the derision of her October 1920 review, that Stein had been successful in 'discover[ing] a new way of writing stories' and had thereby managed to produce an original 'effect'. By 'laying word against word, relating sound to sound, feeling for the taste, the smell, the rhythm of the individual word', as Anderson observes in his 'Impression' of Stein, she did 'something for the writers of our English speech that may be better understood after a time'.[19] For Anderson, Stein is 'the most important pioneer', ignoring the 'ridicule' and 'loud guffaws' of her day in order to produce something new and original.[20] Anderson argues that it is necessary therefore for 'writers, and particularly young writers, [to] come to understand a little of what she is trying to do'.[21] This may have convinced Mansfield to return to *Three Lives* again, and this renewed engagement with Stein's work may in turn indicate the direction that Mansfield's own writing might have taken had she lived beyond January 1923.

The Dial

Mansfield's interest in experimental American writers such as Stein, on the one hand, and popular, commercially successful authors like Canfield, on the other, reflects her negotiation of 'literary' and 'popular' marketplaces in the final phase of her career, as has been examined so astutely by Jenny McDonnell.[22] Mansfield had secured the literary agent J. B. Pinker in 1921 with the express purpose of trying to break into the American marketplace. On 16 August 1921 she had written to Pinker, stating: 'I am chiefly anxious to have serial publication arranged for my stories in America. I have not had any difficulty in disposing of the English rights, but America is so far an untouched market for my work.'[23] In particular, Mansfield was keen to secure publication of her stories in the American periodical *The Dial*, edited by Scofield Thayer from 1920 to 1925. Thayer was responsible for transforming *The Dial* from a liberal journal of opinion into one of the most important literary journals of the period. By 1922, the magazine's circulation had grown from 6,000 to 14,000, which extended the public profile and reach of modernism beyond the limited coteries of most 'little magazines' (by comparison, for example, the average circulation of *The Little Review* was approximately 1,500).[24] Even at the same time as an advert for the periodical published in 1924 informed prospective subscribers that *The Dial* 'will become a precious monument to the taste of the cultivated minority of the twenties', its circulation grew to just under 25,000.[25] If ever there was a publication that successfully managed to negotiate the mass market and the 'minority' tastes of modernism, therefore, *The Dial* was it: for any contributor, it was a magazine that promised both considerable cultural capital and dollars in the pocket. A typical issue of the magazine included letters from abroad (such as T. S. Eliot's from London, Ezra Pound's from Paris and Thomas Mann's from Germany), essays by the likes of George Santayana, book reviews by various hands (including Bertrand Russell, John Dos Passos, I. A. Richards and Conrad Aiken), artwork by Pablo Picasso and Wyndham Lewis, as well as poetry and short stories by the likes of Mina Loy, e. e. cummings, D. H. Lawrence and Virginia Woolf. In August 1921, the same month that Mansfield wrote to Pinker to ask him to become her agent, Murry had had a book review published in *The Dial*. And in the issue published the following month, in September 1921, the magazine printed a review by Malcolm Cowley of Mansfield's short story collection *Bliss and Other Stories*. Mansfield wrote to Pinker: 'Perhaps I may mention that The Dial gave me a long and pretty favourable review recently. I think they are *disposed* to take my stories.'[26] Alongside this review, the September 1921 issue of *The Dial* also contained the final instalment of Sherwood Anderson's long short story 'Out of Nowhere into Nothing', printed over twenty-one pages of the magazine issue and later included as the last story in *The Triumph of the Egg*. This would certainly have brought Anderson to Mansfield's attention.

Subsequently, Mansfield became an avid reader of *The Dial*, as evidenced in her letters. On 24 October 1921, for instance, she writes to Violet Schiff that the periodical 'is improved, I think' and 'there is always something in it', before commenting on work contributed to its pages by Lawrence and Eliot.[27] Later, referring to the November 1921 issue, Mansfield writes to Violet's husband Sydney Schiff: 'I do think The Dial is by far the most interesting magazine going today'.[28] This attentiveness to the contents of *The Dial* is also explained by the fact that Murry was finding regular publication in its pages: the October 1921 issue included his article 'The Commemoration of John Keats', and his 'Gustave

Flaubert' was the lead article in the December 1921 issue. Mansfield was keen to join Murry in the pages of the magazine, and in the last months of 1921 Pinker was working hard to secure publication of her story 'The Doll's House' in either *The Dial* or – failing that – a new little magazine published in Italy by American editors titled *Broom: An International Magazine of the Arts*.[29] This magazine, too, would have brought Anderson to Mansfield's attention. In an article published in the first issue, titled 'America Invades Europe', Anderson is cited as an example of a writer from whom 'the modern European world will get a better understanding of the new America's contact with herself, of her self analyses, self criticism, self transformation'; a writer who, 'without flashy brilliance, quietly touch[es] the bottom of things'.[30] This was followed with the publication of Anderson's story 'The Contract' in the second issue of *Broom*.

In January 1922, a notebook entry by Mansfield begins: 'Heard from Pinker the Dial has taken the Dolls House' and ends: 'Dreamed last night of a voyage to America'.[31] Mansfield had recorded a similar dream of a voyage to New Zealand from the previous night, and there is a striking, significant equivalence here between the two countries in her imagination: as countries that had both been colonized by Britain and in which the 'frontier' of vast open landscapes played such an important role in shaping human experience, New Zealand and America here occupy an analogous position in Mansfield's mind. This notebook entry is also important, though, because it highlights that, for Mansfield, possible publication in *The Dial* meant breaking new ground in the New World – it meant voyaging into the 'untouched market' of literary America. And this was a market dominated by Anderson. In December 1921, Anderson was announced as the winner of the first Dial Award. These prestigious awards were given annually until 1929: five went to poets (T. S. Eliot, Marianne Moore, e. e. cummings, William Carlos Williams and Ezra Pound), two to critics (Van Wyck Brooks and Kenneth Burke), and only one to a fiction writer (Anderson). Indeed, Anderson was the American fiction writer most closely associated with *The Dial* under Thayer's editorship, years that coincided with the critical acclaim that followed the publication of Anderson's best-known work, *Winesburg, Ohio* (1919). On its own, for instance, the January 1922 issue of *The Dial* included a thirteen-page article on Anderson by Paul Rosenfeld, a review of Anderson's *The Triumph of the Egg* by Robert Morss Lovett, and a 'Comment' piece about the first Dial Award. And we know that Mansfield read this issue of the periodical, because she writes to Koteliansky on 13 January 1922: 'What a supremely good piece of translation is this story by Bunin in The Dial', referring to the co-translation made by Koteliansky and Lawrence of Ivan Bunin's 'The Gentleman from

San Francisco', published in the January 1922 issue of the magazine (not the December 1921 issue, as claimed by the editors of Mansfield's *Collected Letters*).[32] The following issue of *The Dial*, moreover, opened with Anderson's 'I'm a Fool', a story that Mansfield almost certainly read after writing to Murry from Paris on 6 February 1922: 'Will you send me the Lit. Sup? And the Dial? Id be very glad of both.'[33] Having thought that 'The Doll's House' would be appearing in the periodical, Mansfield learnt in February 1922 that *The Dial* editors had withdrawn their offer of publication because the story had already appeared in the British periodical *The Nation and the Athenaeum*; the editors of *Broom* also decided not to publish the story. However, Mansfield continued to read *The Dial*. A letter written in May 1922 to Violet Schiff records a conversation about the April issue, and Mansfield was certain to see the (not particularly favourable) review of *The Garden Party and Other Stories* that appeared in the August issue of the magazine.[34]

Sherwood Anderson

The books that Mansfield borrowed from Shakespeare and Company in October 1922, combined with her sustained reading of *The Dial* over the previous year, indicates that she viewed Anderson as a potential influence in the future development of her own fiction. In particular, the publication of *Winesburg, Ohio* was a hugely significant moment in the history of the modern short story form, as Frank O'Connor argues in *The Lonely Voice*: 'It is from this remarkable little book that the modern American short story develops.'[35] As Anderson himself observed in his memoirs, 'in *Winesburg* [*sic*] I had made my own form. There were individual tales but all about lives in some way connected.'[36] By this method, Anderson looked to convey the 'feeling' that 'life is a loose flowing thing', because 'there are no plot stories in life'.[37] Mansfield had already begun to attempt something similar, publishing the interconnected stories 'Prelude' and 'At the Bay' across two short story collections, and following this with 'The Doll's House': all three stories were linked, depicting the same cast of characters. After J. B. Pinker's death in March 1922, his son Eric became Mansfield's agent and wrote to her suggesting that she consider writing a novel. Mansfield responded: 'I know myself well enough to assure you that the only safe moment for mentioning a novel by me is when you have the MS of it actually in your hands.'[38] Rather than aiming to write a novel, it seems far more likely that Mansfield looked to follow the example set by Anderson and publish a book of interconnected stories set in New Zealand. Moreover, Anderson's formal experimentation at the level of the sentence would have interested Mansfield. By composing his work through the 'unhurried repetition of words in slightly varied order', as Paul Rosenfeld notes in his article published in the January 1922 issue of *The Dial*, Anderson succeeded in creating 'a literature that approaches the condition of poetry, that is more and more a play of word-timbres, a design of overtones, of verbal shapes and colours, a sort of absolute prose'.[39] This resonates with Mansfield's own aim, stated in 1916, to write 'a kind of special prose [...] trembling on the brink of poetry'.[40] Indeed, we can see a similar experiment with repetition in Mansfield's 'The Doll's House' when the narrator tells us of the freshly painted doll's house: 'But perfect, perfect little house! Who could possibly mind the smell? It was part of the joy, part of the newness.'[41]

In addition to its formal inventiveness, Anderson's work would have interested Mansfield due to its depiction of modernity in America, a country gripped by the individualism and industrialism of capitalism. As Anderson himself observed, *Windy McPherson's Son* is 'the story of a young boy who became a sort of minor captain of industry and sickened of it. More or less it was my own story':

> Working in factories I had seen and felt there a curious diminution in men, the result of this separateness, this isolation, this 'individualism' – seen and felt it in the men as they came to the factories in the morning and left them for their homes at night. There was a certain power in us that could not get itself expressed.[42]

Anderson liked to repeat the same tale of his 'own story': one day, he simply got up and left his factory job and, in a daze, wandered out of town along the railroad before coming to the decision that he would become a writer. In this self-mythology, Anderson sets himself against the alienation of capitalist America. As Rosenfeld observes, Anderson's fiction responds to the 'sickness of soul' in contemporary America:

> Everything in raw America stimulated ugly ambitiousness, exploitations of human beings and of the soil. [...] The census reports proclaimed tens upon tens of millions of inhabitants. But there were no living human lives. There were automatons gyrating about, repeating sentences written by unconsciously lying reporters in the newspapers. No one knew the truth. No one knew what he felt, what the man reading the newspaper next to him felt. No one felt, at all.[43]

In Anderson's fiction, Rosenfeld continues, 'loneliness, that he thought a desolation all his own, is sensed in a million tight, apart bodies.'[44] As Frank

O'Connor also observes, the 'two terrible words, "alone" and "lonely", ring out in almost every story in *Winesburg, Ohio*, and with them the word "hands" – hands reaching out for a human contact that is not there.'[45] At the close of the story 'Adventure', for instance, Alice Hindman turns her face to the wall and tries 'to force herself to face bravely the fact that many people must live and die alone'.[46] And in the opening story to the collection, titled 'Hands', a man's touching of others is viewed with suspicion, so that his hands become symbolic only of his loneliness and isolation from his fellow man. As Rosenfeld notes, Anderson 'knows that when in writing he searches for touch with his fellows, he feels his way blindly in the dark'.[47] Throughout Anderson's fiction, individuals are disconnected from one another and lost in a modern world unmoored by increasing industrialization and mechanization. This disconnection leads to 'misunderstanding', a key word throughout Anderson's oeuvre. The story 'Surrender' in *Winesburg, Ohio*, for example, begins: 'The story of Louise Bentley [...] is a story of misunderstanding'.[48]

We can see these ideas at play in Anderson's 'Out of Nowhere into Nothing', first published in *The Dial* across three instalments in July–September 1921, the final instalment appearing alongside Cowley's review of Mansfield's *Bliss*. The main character of this story, Rosalind Wescott, is cut off from all those around her and yearns for something more vital and beautiful than the life she is living. This desire is symbolized by the gulls that Rosalind watches circling over the Chicago River, 'graceful, living, free things. They were triumphant.'[49] Through free indirect discourse, Anderson tells us: 'She was weary. [...] Where was the wonder of life? It was not within herself, not in the ground. It must be in the sky overhead.'[50] In both the country and city, Rosalind has been surrounded by people 'who lived physically but who in spirit were dead': 'A sea of faces floated up to her. They were the faces of dead people. [...] They too could not break through the walls of themselves to the white wonder of life.'[51] This resonates with a passage from Anderson's novel *Poor White*, in which he reiterates the idea of 'misunderstanding':

> All men lead their lives behind a wall of misunderstanding they have themselves built, and most men die in silence and unnoticed behind the walls. Now and then a man, cut off from his fellows by the peculiarities of his nature, becomes absorbed in doing something that is personal, useful and beautiful. Word of his activities is carried over the walls.[52]

Rosalind becomes aware of such men who, despite the alienating effects of modernity, 'had kept some precious thing alive in themselves', and she tries to reach out to them: 'Rosalind had an almost irresistible desire to put out her hand and touch his hand. She wanted to shout, crying – "I am here. I am not dead. I am alive." Instead she stood in silence, staring at him.'[53]

Behind her own wall of separation, therefore, Rosalind reverts to silence, but she is 'hungry, hungry, always hungry – for companionship'.[54] Rosalind is 'very lonely' but acutely aware of 'the thing beyond words, beyond passion – the fellowship in living, the fellowship in life'.[55] However, Rosalind is unable to connect with others, and while her vital inner life burns unnoticed, the monotony of her outer life is deadening. She fears that death might 'overtake her and live within her while her body is still alive', reflecting: 'She was so much alive and yet not alive.'[56] Likewise, Rosalind's lover, Walter Sayers, 'lived and did not live'.[57] Attempting to overcome this stultifying life that is 'not alive', Rosalind's story ends with her expressing the wish to be 'naked, new born'.[58]

The idea of self-division, of being 'alive and yet not alive', would have resonated with Mansfield, who wrote to Koteliansky on 19 October 1922, 'I am a divided being': 'I am always conscious of this secret disruption in me [...]. What is important is to try & learn to live – really live, and in relation to everything – not isolated (this isolation is death to me).'[59] One week after returning two of Anderson's books to Shakespeare and Company, therefore, Mansfield echoes his emphasis on the 'secret' life lived behind walls of isolation. On the day she returned these books, Mansfield also wrote a letter to Murry, in which she observed:

> I feel the only thing to do is to get the dying over – to court it, almost (Fearfully hard, that) and then all hands to the business of being reborn again. What do I mean exactly? Let me give you an instance. Looking back, my boat is almost swamped sometimes by seas of sentiment. 'Ah what I have missed. How sweet it was, how dear how warm, how simple, how precious.' And I think of the garden at the Isola Bella and the furry bees and the house wall so warm. But then I remember what we really felt there. The blanks, the silences, the anguish of continual misunderstanding. Were we positive, eager, real – alive? No, we were not. We were a nothingness shot with gleams of what might be. But no more. Well, I have to face everything as far as I can & see where I stand – what *remains*.
>
> For with all my soul I do long for a real life, for truth, and for real strength.[60]

Like Rosalind, Mansfield here expresses a desire to be 'reborn', to overcome the 'blanks, the silences', the 'nothingness' and 'anguish of continual misunderstanding': only then might one be 'positive, eager, real – alive'. This letter clearly echoes the language of Anderson's fiction, recalling the 'silences' in his many stories set at night, the 'misunderstanding' between individuals disconnected from one another, and the desire felt by characters such as Rosalind to transcend the walls of modern-day isolation in order to feel more 'alive'.

Dorothy Canfield

On the day she penned the letter quoted above, Mansfield borrowed Dorothy Canfield's novel *The Brimming Cup*. This novel is striking for the parallels we find in it with Mansfield's own work. At a significant point in the novel, for instance, the characters gather to watch the 'night-blooming cereus in its one hour of glory': 'Once a year, just once, it puts forth a wonderful exotic flower of extreme beauty.'[61] This recalls the aloe in Mansfield's 'Prelude' that flowers once every one hundred years. Canfield's novel also includes a 'delightful and enchanting' doll's house that becomes the focus for the protagonist's memories of her childhood.[62] These parallels suggest to me that Canfield was directly influenced by Mansfield's work, and it is no wonder that Mansfield found the novel 'a most charming book and extremely clever'.[63] The title and central image of *The Brimming Cup*, for instance, echoes Mansfield's 'Bliss' (1918), in which Bertha reflects: 'Oh, why did she feel so tender towards the whole world tonight? Everything was good – was right. All that happened seemed to fill again her brimming cup of bliss.'[64] The protagonist of Canfield's novel, Marise Crittenden, likewise desires 'to be so filled with some emotion, something great and fine, that I would be an urn too full, gushing up in a great flooding rush'.[65]

Water imagery is central to the novel. Throughout her life, Marise has experienced the same recurring dream, in which she is 'the current' of a river, 'the wind, not the bird blown by it; the wave itself'.[66] This dream of 'freedom and power and momentum' seems impossibly out of reach when Marise becomes a wife and mother, that is, until the arrival in her small town of Vincent Marsh, a wealthy young man who encourages Marise to pursue her desires without regard for anyone else. Vincent represents the materialism and aggressive individualism of modern-day America.[67] In deciding between Vincent and her husband Neale, Marise must make a choice between 'selfish, possessive, never-satisfied' and passionate desire and selfless, giving love.[68] In the course of making this decision, she asks: 'Was there any deep spiritual reality which counted at all, which one human being could give to another? Did we really live on desert islands, cut off so wholly from each other by the unplumbed, salt, estranging sea?'[69] Marise does not choose the superficial life that Vincent embodies, but instead comes to see herself 'before the vastness of the whole, of which she and her children were only a part'.[70] At the end of the novel, standing out in the open at night with her family around her, 'their faces and hearts upraised silently to receive the immensity above and about them', Marise becomes aware of 'feeling herself one with the great current, advancing with an irresistible might, majesty and power, in which she shared, to which she gave her part'.[71] It is not passionate, possessive love that helps Marise to realize her dream, as she had once thought, but the love that she gives selflessly to others. By turning against modern-day materialism and individualism, therefore, Marise is able to connect with the world around her and feel part of its 'vastness'.

Two days before Mansfield returned Canfield's novel, she wrote a notebook entry reflecting on the illness that was destroying her, in which she observed:

> By health I mean the power to live a full, adult, living, breathing life in close contact [with] what I love – the earth and the wonders thereof, the sea, the sun. All that we mean when we speak of the external world. I want to enter into it, to be part of it, to live in it, to learn from it, to lose all that is superficial and acquired in me and to become a conscious, direct human being. I want, by understanding myself, to understand others. [...] To be rooted in life – to learn, to desire to know, to feel, to think, to act. That is what I want. And nothing less. That is what I must try for.[72]

This was composed on Mansfield's thirty-fourth birthday. In this passage, Mansfield expresses the same desire as Canfield's protagonist to 'enter into' the natural world, 'to be part of' the universal vastness, to connect with others and 'lose all that is superficial'. Two days later, she wrote to Murry telling him that she would be going to Fontainebleau. The way in which Mansfield arrived at and articulated this decision, I want to suggest, cannot be disentangled from her reading at this time. In her letters and notebook entries, we can register the influence of Anderson and Canfield in the language Mansfield uses to express her sense of what it means to be truly 'alive': by living 'in relation to everything', Mansfield hoped to break through the walls of modern-day 'isolation' and overcome 'the anguish of continual misunderstanding'. Undoubtedly, Mansfield was predisposed to the kind of vague mysticism preached by Gurdjieff. However, uncovering her reader's card from Shakespeare and Company and her interest in *The Dial* over the preceding year reveals the particular literary influences that helped determine Mansfield's decision to enter Gurdjieff's Institute. This changes how we understand Mansfield's final months. Rather than being beholden solely to Gurdjieff's vague esoteric doctrine, Mansfield's motivations for travelling to Fontainebleau can be traced to her sustained and focused reading of modern American fiction.

Notes

1 I would like to thank Andrew Thacker, for making me aware of the Shakespeare and Company reader's card held in Katherine Mansfield's name, and Joshua Kotin from The Shakespeare and Company Project at Princeton University, for so patiently and helpfully answering my questions and for providing permission to reproduce the image of Mansfield's reader's card included in this chapter.

2 *Letters* 5, p. 296.

3 *Letters* 5, p. 283.

4 *Letters* 5, pp. 288, 295.

5 *Letters* 5, p. 286.

6 *Letters* 5, p. 284.

7 *Letters* 5, p. 317.

8 Sylvia Beach, *Shakespeare and Company* (London: Faber and Faber, 1956), pp. 42–3.

9 CW3, p. 675.

10 CW3, pp. 675–6.

11 *Letters* 5, p. 300.

12 *Letters* 5, p. 302.

13 *Letters* 5, p. 301.

14 *Letters* 5, p. 308.

15 *Letters* 5, p. 312.

16 Ibid.

17 Sherwood Anderson, 'The Work of Gertrude Stein,' in Gertrude Stein, *Geography and Plays* (Boston: The Four Seas Company, 1922), p. 8.

18 Sherwood Anderson, 'Four American Impressions: Gertrude Stein, Paul Rosenfeld, Ring Lardner, Sinclair Lewis,' in *Sherwood Anderson/Gertrude Stein: Correspondence and Personal Essays*, ed. Ray Lewis White (Chapel Hill: The University of North Carolina Press, 1972), pp. 24–5.

19 Ibid.

20 Anderson, 'The Work of Gertrude Stein,' pp. 6, 8.

21 Ibid., p. 6.

22 Jenny McDonnell, *Katherine Mansfield and the Modernist Marketplace: At the Mercy of the Public* (Basingstoke: Palgrave Macmillan, 2010).

23 *Letters* 4, p. 263.
24 Christina Britzolakis, 'Making Modernism Safe for Democracy: *The Dial* (1920–9)', in *The Oxford Critical and Cultural History of Modernist Magazines, Volume II: North America 1894–1960*, eds Peter Brooker and Andrew Thacker (Oxford: Oxford University Press, 2012), p. 86.
25 Ibid., p. 92.
26 *Letters* 4, p. 298.
27 *Letters* 4, p. 303.
28 *Letters* 4, p. 330.
29 James B. Pinker Papers, Northwestern University, letter from Carl Brandt to J. B. Pinker (25 November 1921).
30 Emmy Veronica Sanders, 'America Invades Europe', *Broom: An International Magazine of the Arts*, 1, no. 1 (November 1921): 92.
31 *Notebooks* 2, pp. 315–16.
32 *Letters* 5, pp. 13–14.
33 *Letters* 5, p. 48.
34 *Letters* 5, p. 175.
35 Frank O'Connor, *The Lonely Voice: A Study of the Short Story* (London: Macmillan, 1963), p. 41.
36 Sherwood Anderson, *Sherwood Anderson's Memoirs* (New York: Harcourt, Brace and Company, 1942), p. 289.
37 Ibid.
38 *Letters* 5, p. 135.
39 Paul Rosenfeld, 'Sherwood Anderson', *The Dial*, 72, no. 1 (January 1922): 30, 37.
40 *Notebooks* 2, pp. 32–3.
41 CW2, p. 415.
42 Anderson, *Memoirs*, pp. 283–4.
43 Rosenfeld, pp. 39–40.
44 Ibid., p. 34.
45 O'Connor, p. 40.
46 Sherwood Anderson, *Winesburg, Ohio: A Group of Tales of Ohio Small-Town Life* (New York: The Modern Library, 1947), p. 134.
47 Rosenfeld, p. 36.
48 Anderson, *Winesburg, Ohio*, p. 88.
49 Sherwood Anderson, *The Triumph of the Egg: A Book of Impressions from American Life in Tales and Poems* (New York: B. W. Huebsch, 1921), p. 217.
50 Ibid., p. 237.
51 Ibid., pp. 266, 238.
52 Sherwood Anderson, *Poor White* (New York: B. W. Huebsch, 1920), p. 227.
53 Anderson, *The Triumph of the Egg*, pp. 183, 193–4.

54 Ibid., p. 202.
55 Ibid., pp. 188, 265.
56 Ibid., pp. 185, 204.
57 Ibid., p. 220.
58 Ibid., p. 266.
59 *Letters* 5, p. 304.
60 *Letters* 5, p. 294.
61 Dorothy Canfield, *The Brimming Cup* ([1919] London: Virago, 1987), pp. 77, 80.
62 Ibid., p. 271.
63 *Letters* 5, p. 317.
64 CW2, p. 148.
65 Canfield, p. 13.
66 Ibid., p. 166.
67 Ibid., p. 167.
68 Ibid., p. 269.
69 Ibid., p. 268.
70 Ibid., pp. 268–9.
71 Ibid., p. 313.
72 *Notebooks* 2, p. 287.

7

'A god instead of a mortal'

Katherine Mansfield and the Orphic mysteries

Erika Baldt

'The moderns had never written anything one wanted to read about death': so Virginia Woolf wrote in 'Mrs. Dalloway in Bond Street' in 1922.[1] Though neither readers nor the character herself would consider Clarissa Dalloway an authority on such matters, her opinion certainly rings true when we consider how many modernists turned to classical antecedents as a way to process and express the death and destruction of the early twentieth century. Woolf later wrote in 'On Not Knowing Greek' that 'when thus stirred by death, by betrayal, by some other primitive calamity, Antigone and Ajax and Electra behave in the way in which we should behave thus struck down; the way in which everybody has always behaved',[2] and her contemporaries like H. D., T. S. Eliot and James Joyce seemed to feel the same way.[3] But what of Katherine Mansfield, who claimed to have 'no patience' for what she saw as a self-conscious obsession with death in the work of Eliot and his ilk?[4] I will argue that not only did Mansfield have a similar preoccupation with ancient beliefs about the afterlife but that she also seemed to reference specific Greek texts even before some of her colleagues did. Though there is no evidence that she shared Woolf's 'wish to know Greek',[5] I will show that it is not only possible but also probable that Mansfield encountered what were known as the Orphic mysteries through her associates and that stories such as 'An Indiscreet Journey'[6] and 'Bliss'[7] bear striking resemblance to artefacts associated with the mysteries: the gold tablets of the archaic period.

The gold tablets and modern times

Ancient Greeks believed that after death and a proper burial, souls retired to the Underworld, ruled by Hades and his queen Persephone. In some accounts they were transported across the river Styx by Charon the ferryman.[8] In others they simply arrived, and, 'as soon as the soul [...] left the light of the sun',[9] it was faced with a choice of which direction to take – right or left – and from which spring to drink – the waters of memory or the waters of forgetfulness. Bad souls went to the left and faced either immediate punishment or hundreds of years of repentance until they earned another chance. Good souls went to the right towards relaxation and eventually reincarnation. Even the good souls, though, could undo all of their goodness if they drank from the wrong spring – forgetfulness instead of memory – and forgot all of the positive lessons they had learnt in life.[10] Those initiated into the Orphic mysteries, however, received secret instructions that would allow them to make the correct choice of path and spring and therefore avoid any waiting or even reincarnation. If the soul of the initiate followed directions, it would 'become a god instead of a mortal'.[11] To help them remember these instructions, initiates purchased and were buried with what are now known as the gold leaves or tablets: short texts printed on very thin sheets of gold that acted as mnemonic devices, or, as Sarah Iles Johnston, translator of the tablets, puts it, 'crib-sheet[s] for the soul's most final of exams'.[12] Though the tablets are dated to around the fourth century BCE, they were not excavated from graves in Greece and Southern Italy until the early nineteenth century, and even when the first one was discovered, it was not understood. It eventually made its way to the British Museum in the late nineteenth century, and by that time, more gold leaves had been found, transcribed and connected to 'Orphic and Bacchic' mystery cults,[13] Orpheus being 'nearly always the oldest of the Greeks, and [...] the main source of religious truth for Pythagoras, Plato, etc'.[14]

Yet this information is both specific and esoteric. How would Mansfield have come by it? I believe there are three possibilities. The first, as the previous references to her work would suggest, is through Virginia Woolf. Jane Ellen Harrison included an appendix on the tablets in her *Prolegomena to the Study of Greek Religion*, first published in 1903,[15] and she was well-known to Woolf.[16] Woolf and Mansfield did not meet, however, until 1916, after 'An Indiscreet Journey' had already been written.[17] The second, increasingly likely, source is D. H. Lawrence, with whom Mansfield and Murry experienced an intense relationship after meeting him in 1913.[18] Even though Lawrence's *Etruscan Places* was not published until after both of their deaths, it is possible that he may have shared with Mansfield some early interest in the subject. Lawrence, for example, writes of figures in Etruscan tomb paintings 'saluting the mysterious egg'[19] and according to Harrison, 'We may say with certainty that the cosmic egg was Orphic' and was offered to the dead.[20] Mansfield's story 'Feuille d'Album' of 1917 ends with the protagonist holding out an egg to the woman he has been pursuing,[21] which may be a coincidence, but there are other indications that Lawrence's interests may have been Orphic in nature and shared with Mansfield. For example, Fritz Graf notes that 'the actual worship of the phallus' became 'the center of the mysteries that the Greeks took over from the Egyptian cult of Osiris',[22] and in 1916 Mansfield suggested that Lawrence 'should call his cottage The Phallus' due to his preoccupation with the subject.[23]

However, it is the third possibility that is the most compelling. A. R. Orage, as Gerri Kimber notes, 'had been a theosophist for many years, with interests also in mystical literature', and according to Kimber, 'from her first meeting with Orage in February 1910 through to the end of 1911, Mansfield now became part of the close-knit theosophical community surrounding Orage and [Beatrice] Hastings'.[24] Theosophy, which garnered some popularity on both sides of the Atlantic at the turn of the twentieth century, combined the study of the spiritual beliefs of various cultures with an interrogation of unexplained natural phenomena.[25] Orage was a prominent member of the British Theosophical Society for several years, contributing a number of articles to *The Theosophical Review*, one of the society's many publications, before taking up his best-known post as editor of *The New Age*. While at times critical of them, he was nonetheless well-versed in theosophy's foundational texts, stating in 'What is Man?' in 1906, for example, that

> I for one will never demand that the amazing and inspiring world of the *Secret Doctrine* shall be cribbed within the narrow cell of my formal mind. On the other hand, I will not pretend that my formal mind holds the *Secret Doctrine* as fact. It refuses to do so, and therefore I honour and despise it.[26]

The Secret Doctrine is H. P. Blavatsky's two-volume, over 1000-page treatise on theosophy in which she describes the 'inventors of letters; none of them dies but still lives, and they are the first Initiators into, and Founders of the Mysteries',[27] including Orpheus, 'the possessor of the *phorminx*, the 7-stringed lyre, which is the seven-fold mystery of initiation'.[28] Of all Mansfield's associates, it was Orage who would have been most familiar with, at the very least, the culture that produced the gold tablets, and I believe that it is Orage who most likely introduced Mansfield to the mysteries, especially considering that his spiritual interests seem to have been inseparable from his public persona. The artist Jacob Epstein declared that Orage 'went about like a Greek philosopher or rhetor, with a following of disciples',[29] and Paul Selver insisted in his 'reminiscences' on his time at *The New Age* that 'the Orage magic was no mere legend'.[30] Even Beatrice

Hastings, who bitterly claimed that 'Orage [knew] neither Greek nor Latin', described the milieu in which Orage moved as '"Initiate" circles',[31] suggesting that the man himself developed his own mystery cult of which Mansfield was, for a short time, at least, a member.

Although there is no evidence in her letters or notebooks that she received any kind of education from him in theosophy or the ancient mysteries, from 1911 Mansfield's published work does show what I would argue is Orage's influence on that score. According to Antony Alpers, 'Someone on the *New Age*, probably Orage, must have handed her a volume of Theocritus and suggested that she might make an amusing pastiche of the XVth Idyll'.[32] That 'amusing pastiche' was Mansfield's 'The Festival of the Coronation (With apologies to Theocritus)' of 1911,[33] and she revisited ancient Greece for inspiration when she returned to the magazine in 1917. Plato was a favourite of Orage,[34] which may explain why, after several years of hard feelings against him,[35] Mansfield included a 'fragment' called 'Cephalus', a dozen lines about the character from Plato's *Republic*, in the 'Pastiche' she contributed to *The New Age* in April of that year.[36] Cephalus, as Alan Bloom explains, is an old man who, now that he is coming closer to death, begins to fear what comes next:

> The tales told by the poets about punishments in another world for injustices committed in this one concerned Cephalus little when he was younger. He was inclined to laugh them off; accordingly, he worried little about injustices he might be committing. Only as death and death's perspective approaches does fear cause him to become concerned about his duties to men and gods.[37]

This description could just as easily apply to Mansfield herself, for while her interpretation of the character in the fragment is tongue-in-cheek, focusing as it does on his 'admirable exit'[38] from the conversation with Socrates, she herself was preoccupied even before 1917 with the same questions about death and the afterlife as Cephalus.

It is here that we come closer to bridging the gap between how Mansfield would have come to know about the gold tablets and why they would have resonated with her. Fritz Graf notes that in *The Republic* Plato describes mysteries and rites performed by followers of Orpheus for those like Cephalus 'who were still alive but who might fear that the old stories about punishment after death were true after all'.[39] The idea that there might be an initiation that could result in 'calming the fears [individuals] felt regarding the world of the dead'[40] would undoubtedly have been attractive to Mansfield during this period in her life. She witnessed the devastating effects of the Great War in February of 1915 when she visited the French front,[41] and the experience was followed by the death of her brother later in that year.[42] However, her own personal fascination with death seems to have begun even before that, as she wrote on 2 January 1915 that 'I don't feel like a girl any more, or even like a young woman. I feel really quite past my prime. At times the fear of death is dreadful',[43] and it continued for years. In 1917 she was thinking about Cephalus[44] and writing 'Feuille d'Album', and in February 1918, less than ten days before she finished 'Bliss' and sent it to Murry, Mansfield acknowledged in a notebook that she might have 'real consumption' that could kill her.[45] Her drawing on the mysteries, I would suggest, is her way of trying, like Cephalus, to calm her own fears about 'the world of the dead'.

1915: 'An Indiscreet Journey' through the Underworld

In her essay '"By what name are we to call death?": The Case of "An Indiscreet Journey"', Josiane Paccaud-Huguet likens the story to a mystery play, a 'secular version' of 'a timeless narrative, often of religious inspiration, concerning, for example, the joy of the Nativity or the passion of Christ' that 'will celebrate both joy and a "cry against corruption"'.[46] I would suggest that Mansfield *was* reworking a mystery, but that of the ancient Greeks. The story bears uncanny similarities to the text of several of the gold tablets, grouped together by scholars as geographic for their description of the landmarks of the Underworld and the route the initiate should take through a series of obstacles or challenges.[47] For example, the text of the second tablet states:

> You will find to the left of the house of Hades a spring
> and standing by it is a white cypress.
> Do not even approach this spring!
> You will find another, from the Lake of Memory,
> cold water pouring forth; there are guards before it.
> Say, 'I am a child of Earth and starry Sky.
> but my race is heavenly. You yourselves know this.
> I am parched with thirst and am dying; but quickly grant me
> cold water flowing from the Lake of Memory.'
> And they themselves will grant you to drink from the sacred spring.
> And thereafter you will rule among the other heroes.
> This is the work of Memory. When you are about to die
> To die write this
> enwrapped...darkness[48]

Similar instructions appear on several tablets, but the basic landmarks remain consistent, and, I would argue, also appear in 'An Indiscreet Journey' as well.[49] As Paccaud-Huguet puts it, the narrator of that story undergoes a 'descent into hell' as she travels from Paris to the front to meet her lover,[50] and her journey follows these directions set out in the tablet for initiates navigating the underworld.

The first parallel is the change in the trees. In Paris, the trees are dark: 'A little steamer hooted on the river; a cart with two horses at a gallop flung past. The rapid swirling water; the tall black trees on the far side.'[51] As she journeys on, however, the landscape changes, and she remarks on 'these dark woods lighted so mysteriously by the white stems of the birch and the ash.'[52] Here, the description of the trees echoes the 'white cypress' of the tablets, of which, scholars have suggested, either 'the tree's whiteness [signals] the inverted nature of the Underworld' or 'the tree's color [...] makes it stand out better in the gloom of the Underworld.'[53] In both cases, the eerie illumination of the trees is the first indication that the individual has entered a new and different world.

The next step for the initiate is to address the guards at the Lake of Memory, something Mansfield's narrator does as well. She must pass two, as she calls them, 'gods', relying on her passport and a [fabricated] letter from her 'Aunt Julie' to gain her passage to the Front. As Johnston notes, 'The one who desires access often has to prove that he is from a special family or group',[54] which Mansfield's narrator does: 'God II. held up a finger to me, and I produced Aunt Julie's letter and her card. But he did not seem to feel the slightest interest in her. He stamped my passport idly, scribbled a word on my ticket, and I was on the platform again.'[55]

Finally, there is the question of what to drink and where. Johnston argues that 'the idea of the dead being thirsty is nearly universal';[56] however, the tablets suggest that there are two choices of spring, the first of which must be avoided. Mansfield's narrator faces a similar dilemma in the cafe where she meets her lover and his friends, although the first opportunity to drink is less of a choice, as the waiter knocks over a bottle in a scene that certainly seems otherworldly: 'An amazed silence. Through it the drip-drip of the wine from the table on to the floor. It looked very strange dropping so slowly, as though the table were crying.'[57] This small moment can be read as a reference to the mythological Cocytus, one of the five rivers of and first access point to the Underworld, which was believed to have been formed by the tears of the wicked.[58] As per the tablet, the narrator and her companions thus do not drink this first offering but travel to another café in search of Mirabelle, which, after much ado, they are finally able to obtain: '"Ah, at last!" The blue-eyed soldier's happy voice trickled through the dark. "What do you think? Isn't it just as I said? Hasn't it got a taste of excellent – *ex-cellent* whiskey?'"[59] Mirabelle, an eau-de-vie,[60] is the ideal choice to usher in the narrator's new [after]life.

According to the tablets, the initiate who successfully negotiates all of these obstacles 'will rule among the other heroes'.[61] Mansfield's narrator passes all the tests, but the 'heroes' with whom she has surrounded herself are either the walking wounded or law breakers,[62] and the story ends before any such reward is obtained. However, as Johnston argues, 'The Gold Tablets don't say much about what ultimately awaits the initiate; as mnemonic devices they focus on the task that needs to be done rather than its reward.'[63] Perhaps working through the journey was, in itself, enough for Mansfield, the story becoming her response to a 'world going nowhere, a war nobody wanted, and a pervasive disempowerment of individuals' which had 'increased markedly the plausibility of the claims of life beyond death, and for the need for a "New Age" of creative thinking and feeling, compassion, health, wholeness, and humanity'.[64] However, Mansfield's personal need for 'health' and 'wholeness' did not cease with the completion of 'An Indiscreet Journey'. As I suggested earlier, her awareness of her own mortality only grew more intense as time passed, possibly leading her to revisit the tablets for the creation of 'Bliss' as a way to once more interrogate 'the claims of life beyond death'.

1918: 'Bliss', a Makarismos

There are several references to death and rebirth in Mansfield's 1918 story 'Bliss': the fire, like a 'nest of baby phoenixes', Bertha's feeling that she 'was taking leave of [her friends] for ever', and Eddie Warren's fear that he was '*driving* through Eternity in a *timeless* taxi'.[65] Yet, like 'An Indiscreet Journey', the story itself seems to feature specific elements of the *lamellae aureae*, Bertha's journey following the form of what scholars refer to as the 'purity' tablets in which 'the soul will speak to the Queen of the Underworld herself, rather than her guards'.[66] See tablet five, for example:

> I come pure from the pure, Queen of the Chthonian Ones,
> Eucles, Euboleus and the other immortal gods.
> For I also claim to be of your happy race.
> But Moira overcame me and the other immortal gods
> And the star-flinger with lightning.
> I have flown out of the heavy, difficult circle,
> I have approached the longed-for crown with swift feet,

> I have sunk beneath the breast of the Lady, the Chthonian Queen,
> I have approached the longed-for crown with swift feet.
> 'Happy and blessed, you will be a god instead of a mortal.'
> A kid I fell into milk.[67]

The text of the tablet represents the soul of the departed describing to Persephone, 'the Chthonian Queen', the events leading up to her arrival in the Underworld in an attempt to establish a connection and receive her blessing, and several of the images within this particular tablet appear at the beginning of Mansfield's story. Bertha's desire to 'bowl a hoop'[68] in the opening paragraph connects to the initiate's emergence from the 'heavy, difficult circle', while her centrepiece of a blue dish 'with a strange sheen on it as though it had been dipped in milk'[69] echoes the last line of the tablet. Indeed, the description of Bertha's walk home parallels the initiate's explanation of her own death:

> What can you do if you are thirty and, turning the corner of your own street, you are overcome, suddenly, by a feeling of bliss – absolute bliss! – as though you'd suddenly swallowed a bright piece of that late afternoon sun and it burned in your bosom, sending out a little shower of sparks into every particle, into every finger and toe? . . .[70]

A sudden change in the individual's state is common to both texts, and the 'little shower of sparks' Bertha imagines corresponds to the 'star-flung'[71] lightning bolt with which the initiate had been 'overcome'. Bertha herself is dressed in white[72] as initiates were always depicted,[73] and her question 'Why be given a body if you have to keep it shut up in a case like a rare, rare fiddle?'[74] can be interpreted as a reference to the Orphic understanding of body and soul. According to Plato's *Cratylus*: 'The Orphic poets [...] were under the impression that the soul is suffering the punishment of sin, and that the body is an enclosure or prison in which the soul is incarcerated, kept safe [...] until the penalty is paid.'[75] Like the Orphics, Bertha sees herself as existing within 'an enclosure or prison' from which, she hopes, she will be freed at her party if she can impress the guest of honour, Pearl Fulton, or, for our purposes, Persephone.

If, as Daniel A. Weiss suggests, Laura of 'The Garden Party' is the innocent Persephone encountering death for the first time,[76] Pearl Fulton, I would argue, is the more mature Persephone who has become the queen of the underworld. Although throughout the story she is associated with the moon, which would suggest the goddess Artemis,[77] the connection is actually Orphic. According to Robert Graves, the moon is central to Orphic creation myths in which the goddess Night lays an egg from which the world begins: 'Night's silver egg means the moon, silver being the lunar metal.'[78] The silver fillet she wears in her hair[79] further reinforces the connection and is similar to those worn by the gods in ancient texts,[80] while the description of her as one who 'lived by listening rather than seeing'[81] would fit an existence in the gloom of the underworld. Then, of course, there is her encounter with Harry, which is marked by violence:

> She saw . . . Harry with Miss Fulton's coat in his arms and Miss Fulton with her back turned to him and her head bent. He tossed the coat away, put his hands on her shoulders and turned her violently to him. His lips said: 'I adore you,' and Miss Fulton laid her moonbeam fingers on his cheeks and smiled her sleepy smile. Harry's nostrils quivered; his lips curled back in a hideous grin while he whispered: 'To-morrow,' and with her eyelids Miss Fulton said: 'Yes.'[82]

Harry's seizing of Pearl without her vocalized consent (only her eyelids say 'yes') is reminiscent of Hades' abduction of Persephone, and even the couple's names seem to echo those of their Greek counterparts.

Harry himself shares the characteristics of being 'fierce and jealous of his rights' which the ancient Greeks also attributed to Hades,[83] and his relationship with Bertha, too, is marked by what she perceives as a sort of gratuitous violence. In conversation 'He made a point of catching Bertha's heels',[84] and in interactions with others he has what Bertha identifies as a 'passion for fighting'.[85] It would not be outside the realm of possibility, then, to consider both Pearl and Bertha as conquests of Harry/Hades, especially since, according to Züntz, some traditions hold that Persephone was only one of many maidens forcefully abducted by the god.[86]

While Bertha is unaware for most of the story of the relationship between her husband and Pearl Fulton, she spends much of her time attempting to forge a deeper connection with the other woman. Much like an initiate, with whom Persephone was believed to share a relationship 'of an intimacy virtually unparalleled',[87] Bertha believes that she and Pearl Fulton are communicating on another level: 'What she simply couldn't make out – what was miraculous – was how she should have guessed Miss Fulton's mood so exactly and so instantly. For she never doubted for a moment that she was right, and yet what had she to go on? Less than nothing.'[88] Indeed, when Pearl does give the 'sign' that Bertha has been waiting for, 'all Bertha could do was to obey'.[89] Furthermore, her repetition of the image of 'bliss' burning in her bosom could refer to 'hav[ing] sunk beneath the breast of the Lady, the Chthonian Queen', or to the last enigmatic line of the tablet, 'a kid I fell into milk'. According to Johnston, to 'fall into milk' or 'leap into milk' means to be 'in the midst of abundance, or to make a new beginning. [...] Particularly in the context of the preceding lines on tablet no. 5 [...] the line makes general sense as part of a makarismos – a statement of the initiate's bliss.'[90] Both tablet and story, then, represent the individual's performance of 'bliss'.

We know, however, that the story does not conclude with Bertha feeling 'happy and blessed', but rather confused and dismayed as she wonders 'what is going to happen now?'[91] As is the case with 'An Indiscreet Journey', the text is silent about the future for the protagonist. Mansfield's own future was uncertain as well, as her health began to deteriorate even more quickly, and, as for her characters, it seems unlikely that the gold tablets ultimately provided Mansfield with the answers she craved, focusing as they did on how to die, rather than how to live. As her own death came closer and closer, Mansfield's attitude towards mortality, and to the beliefs surrounding it, changed drastically:

> Perhaps to people who are not ill all this is nonsense. They have never travelled this road. How can they see where I am? All the more reason to go boldly forward alone. Life is not simple. In spite of all we say about the mystery of Life when we get down to it we want to treat it as though it were a child's tale.[92]

The concern was no longer for the mysteries of death but the 'mystery of Life', and perhaps Mansfield came to the realization that there was no text that could help her navigate her path through it.

And yet, according to Orage at least, the vocabulary of the tablets was still with her at the end. During her final days at Fontainebleau she described for him a story, the theme of which was a common one of a husband and wife negotiating their current relationship with past experiences, but the treatment was Orphic: 'Think of how they would try to lay the ghosts in each other and in themselves. Suppose them to be jointly competing for the divine laurel and living and loving as an art.'[93] In this new story the 'ghosts' would be mere memories instead of constant companions. The 'longed-for crown' of the tablets would become the poet's laurel wreath, sacred to Apollo, god of the sun,[94] rather than Persephone, 'the Chthonian Queen'. Finally, the only initiation required would be 'an initiation into truth'.[95] Orage's response, 'Where is the writer with the keys of initiation upon him?',[96] suggests that he could no longer be her guide, and though Mansfield may not have found what she needed in him or in the tablets, she was perhaps ready at last to 'go boldly forward alone'.

Notes

1 Virginia Woolf, 'Mrs. Dalloway in Bond Street', in *The Complete Shorter Fiction of Virginia Woolf*, ed. Susan Dick, 2nd edn (Orlando: Harcourt, 1989), pp. 152–9 (p. 155).

2 Virginia Woolf, 'On Not Knowing Greek', in *The Common Reader* (New York: Harcourt, Brace and Company, 1925), pp. 39–59 (p. 44).
3 See, for example, H. D., *Asphodel*, ed. Robert Spoo (Durham: Duke University Press, 1992); T. S. Eliot, 'The Waste Land', in *Collected Poems, 1909–1962* (London: Faber and Faber, 1963), pp. 61–86; James Joyce, *Ulysses*, ed. Hans Walter Gabler with Wolfhard Steppe and Claus Melchior (New York: Vintage, 1986).
4 *Letters* 2, p. 318. In the same letter to Woolf dated 12 May 1919, Mansfield wrote of Eliot: 'These dark young men – so proud of their plumes and their black and silver cloaks and ever so expensive pompes funebres – Ive no patience'.
5 Woolf, 'On Not Knowing Greek', p. 39.
6 CW1, pp. 439–51.
7 CW2, pp. 141–53.
8 Robert Graves, *The Greek Myths: Complete and Unabridged Edition in One Volume* (Mt. Kisco: Moyer Bell Limited, 1960), pp. 120–3.
9 Fritz Graf and Sarah Iles Johnston, 'The Tablets: An Edition and Translation', in *Ritual Texts for the Afterlife: Orpheus and the Bacchic Gold Tablets*, 2nd edn (New York: Routledge, 2013), pp. 1–49 (p. 9).
10 Sarah Iles Johnston, 'The Eschatology behind the Tablets', in *Ritual Texts for the Afterlife*, pp. 94–136 (p. 102).
11 Graf and Johnston, p. 9.
12 Johnston, p. 94.
13 Fritz Graf, 'A History of Scholarship on the Tablets', in *Ritual Texts for the Afterlife*, pp. 50–65 (pp. 52–4).
14 D. P. Walker, 'Orpheus the Theologian and Renaissance Platonists', *Journal of the Warburg and Courtauld Institutes*, 16, no. 1–2 (1953): 100–20 (p. 105), http://www.jstor.org/stable/750229 (accessed 9 May 2018).
15 Jane Ellen Harrison, *Prolegomena to the Study of Greek Religion*, 2nd edn (Cambridge: Cambridge University Press, 1908).
16 See, for example, Virginia Woolf, *The Diary of Virginia Woolf, Volume One: 1915–1919*, ed. Anne Olivier Bell (San Diego: Harcourt Brace & Company, 1977), p. 188, and Virginia Woolf, *A Room of One's Own* (London: Hogarth Press, 1928).
17 *Letters* 1, p. 324, n. 1.
18 *Letters* 1, p. 131.
19 D. H. Lawrence, 'Etruscan Places', in *D. H. Lawrence and Italy: Sketches from Etruscan Places, Sea and Sardinia, Twilight in Italy*, eds Michael Squires et al. (New York: Viking Press, 1972), p. 40.
20 Harrison, p. 629.
21 'Blushing more crimson than ever, but looking at her severely he said, almost angrily: "Excuse me, Mademoiselle, you dropped this." And he handed her an egg'. CW2, p. 97.

22 Fritz Graf, 'Dionysiac Mystery Cults and the Gold Tablets', in *Ritual Texts for the Afterlife*, pp. 137–66 (p. 148).
23 *Letters* 1, p. 262.
24 Gerri Kimber, '"A child of the sun:" Katherine Mansfield, Orientalism and Gurdjieff', in *Katherine Mansfield and Russia*, eds Galya Diment, Gerri Kimber and Todd Martin (Edinburgh: Edinburgh University Press, 2017), pp. 41–65 (pp. 49–50).
25 See, for example, the main 'objects' of the Theosophical Society in Anon., *The Theosophical Movement 1875–1925: A History and a Survey* (New York: E. P. Dutton & Company, 1925), p. 20.
26 A. R. Orage, 'What Is Man?', *The Theosophical Review*, 39, no. 231 (November 1906): 237–42 (p. 240).
27 H. P. Blavatsky, *The Secret Doctrine, Vol. Two: Anthropogenesis* (London: The Theosophical Publishing Company, 1888), p. 267.
28 Ibid., p. 529.
29 Paul Beekman Taylor, *Gurdjieff and Orage: Brothers in Elysium* (York Beach: Weiser Books, 2001), p. 15.
30 Paul Selver, *Orage and the New Age Circle: Reminiscences and Reflections* (London: George Allen & Unwin, 1959), p. 15.
31 Beatrice Hastings, *The Old New Age: Orage and Others* (London: Blue Moon Press, 1936), pp. 18–19.
32 Antony Alpers, *The Life of Katherine Mansfield* (1980; repr., Oxford: Oxford University Press, 1982), p. 125.
33 Katherine Mansfield, 'The Festival of the Coronation (With apologies to Theocritus)', *The New Age*, 9, no. 9 (29 June 1911): 196.
34 Taylor, p. 61.
35 See, for example, *Letters* 1, p. 172: 'No, you won't find anything of mine in the New Age because I won't send them a line. I think Orage is too ugly'.
36 Katherine Mansfield, 'Pastiche. Fragments', *New Age*, 20, no. 25 (19 April 1917): 595.
37 Alan Bloom, 'Interpretive Essay', in *The Republic of Plato*, 2nd edn (New York: Basic Books, 1968), p. 314.
38 Mansfield, 'Pastiche. Fragments', p. 595.
39 Graf, 'Dionysiac Mystery Cults', p. 145.
40 Ibid., p. 144.
41 CW4, p. 159: 'The French soldiers are "pour rire". Even when they are wounded they seem to lean out of their sheds and wave their bandages at the train. But I saw some prisoners today – not at all funny'.
42 See CW4, p. 169, n. 4. Leslie Beauchamp died on 6 October 1915.
43 CW4, pp. 147–8.
44 CW4, p. 223. The name Cephalus appears with 'New Age 19.4.17' in Mansfield's 1917 notebook among some of the other sketches that make up 'Pastiche. Fragments'.

45 CW4, p. 241.

46 Josiane Paccaud-Huguet, '"By what name are we to call death?": The Case of "An Indiscreet Journey"', in *Katherine Mansfield and World War I*, eds Gerri Kimber et al. (Edinburgh: Edinburgh University Press, 2014), pp. 13–25 (p. 19).

47 Johnston, p. 131.

48 Graf and Johnston, p. 7.

49 The first reference to the tablet in Mansfield's work may be in her poem 'The Earth-Child in the Grass', published in 1912, in which the grass says to the speaker:

> Foolish little earth-child!
> It is not yet time.
> One day I shall open my bosom
> And you shall slip in – but not weeping.

Both the name 'earth-child' and the image of slipping into or below the earth resonate with the initiate's journey to the underworld. See CW3, p. 80.

50 Paccaud-Huguet, p. 14.

51 CW1, p. 439.

52 CW1, p. 440.

53 Johnston, p. 109.

54 Ibid., p. 113.

55 CW1, p. 444.

56 Johnston, p. 117.

57 CW1, p. 447.

58 Anon., *A Commentary, Mythological, Historical, and Geographical, on Pope's Homer and Dryden's Aeneid of Virgil: with a Copious Index* (London: John Murray, 1829), p. 317, books.google.com (accessed 13 October 2018).

59 CW1, p. 451.

60 In French, 'eau-de-vie' literally means 'water of life'. It is a type of clear alcohol that was originally created as a cure for cholera. R. W. Apple, Jr., 'Eau de Vie: Fruit's Essence Captured in a Bottle', *The New York Times*, 1 April 1998, https://www.nytimes.com/1998/04/01/dining/eau-de-vie-fruit-s-essence-captured-in-a-bottle.html (accessed 23 April 2019).

61 Graf and Johnston, p. 7.

62 One of the soldiers in the cafe has just 'got the bandage off' his eyes, while the narrator and her friends are breaking the rules by even being out at night: 'The clock on the wall struck half-past eight; and no soldier is allowed in a cafe after eight o'clock at night.' See CW1, pp. 447, 449.

63 Johnston, p. 116.

64 Paul Morris, 'Mansfield and Her Magician', in *Katherine Mansfield's Men*, eds Charles Ferrall and Jane Stafford (Wellington: Katherine Mansfield Birthplace Society, 2004), pp. 75–95 (p. 77).

65 Mansfield, 'Bliss', in CW2, pp. 149, 151, 146.

66 Johnston, p. 121.

67 Graf and Johnston, p. 13.

68 CW2, p. 141.

69 CW2, p. 142.

70 Ibid.

71 Harrison, p. 669. Where Graf and Johnston translate the line as 'star-flinger with lightning', Harrison uses 'star-flung thunderbolt'. Both suggest the 'shower of sparks' found in the text.

72 CW2, p. 145.

73 Jan N. Bremmer, 'Divinities in the Orphic Gold Leaves: Euklês, Eubouleus, Brimo, Kybele, Kore and Persephone', *Zeitschrift für Papyrologie und Epigraphik*, 187 (2013): 35–48 (p. 43).

74 CW2, p. 142.

75 Plato, *Cratylus*, trans. by Benjamin Jowett, http://classics.mit.edu/Plato/cratylus.html (accessed 25 October 2018).

76 Daniel A. Weiss, 'The Garden Party of Proserpina', *Modern Fiction Studies*, 4, no. 4 (Winter 1958–9): 363–4.

77 Graves, p. 82.

78 Ibid., pp. 30–1.

79 CW2, p. 147: 'And then Miss Fulton, all in silver, with a silver fillet binding her pale blonde hair, came in smiling, her head a little on one side'.

80 Urania Molyviati-Toptsis, 'Vergil's Elysium and the Orphic-Pythagorean Ideas of After-Life', *Mnemosyne*, 47 (February 1994): 33–46. See n. 23, p. 41: 'J. Conington-H. Nettleship in the commentary on the *Aeneid* 6.665 (1963) observe that the white fillets are a mark of consecration, being worn by the gods and by persons and things dedicated to them'.

81 CW2, p. 148.

82 CW2, p. 151.

83 Graves, p. 121.

84 CW2, p. 145.

85 CW2, p. 147.

86 Günther Zuntz, *Persephone: Three Essays on Religion and Thought in Magna Graecia* (Oxford: Clarendon Press, 1971), pp. 401–2: 'Popular imagination appears to have conceived of young maidens as a favorite prey of [Hades]; thus the lord of the Netherworld won his queen.'

87 Bremmer, p. 48.

88 CW2, pp. 148–9.

89 CW2, p. 149.

90 Johnston, p. 129.

91 CW2, p. 152.

92 CW4, p. 434.

93 A. R. Orage, 'Talks with Katherine Mansfield at Fontainebleau', *Century Magazine* (November 1924): 6.

94 Graves, pp. 78, 82. Mansfield also expressed a wish to be 'a child of the sun' during the same period Orage describes here. See CW4, p. 434 and Kimber, p. 41.

95 Orage, 'Talks with Katherine Mansfield at Fontainebleau', p. 2.

96 Ibid.

8

'But the smile undid them'

Bergsonian perceptions of impermissible comedy in Katherine Mansfield's 'Psychology'

Nick Hocking

Building on the illuminating comparative readings of 'Katherine Mansfield's fiction' and the philosophy of Henri Bergson advanced to date,[1] in this chapter I suggest that the resonances between them extend to their complex treatment of comedy, and an enduring marginalization by critics of this dimension of their work. I shall work backwards from the notion of a late modernist aesthetic of 'mirthless' and 'self-reflexive laughter',[2] in order to examine Bergson's *Laughter* alongside Mansfield's short story 'Psychology', suggesting that, taken together, they represent a distinctive precursor to mid-twentieth-century iterations of tragicomedy, and do so insofar as they share a recognition of comedy's dangerous potential to nullify as well as innervate their texts. The comic modulations of 'Psychology' work as polyvalent disruptions of Mansfield's undoubtable commitment to a Bergsonian aesthetic of richly drawn, individuated and fluid experience – disruptions which impel more vexed, more surprising, more affectively pliant and, in all senses, more *moving* interplays between the vital and the mechanical than are to be found in configurations of the tragicomic genre in which those two elements resolve into a relatively stable compound.

Despite the pervasive and widely established impact of Bergsonian ideas on the writers, publications, institutions and social networks around which the British modernist aesthetic took shape, and despite Bergson's book-length study of the subject, *Laughter*, culminating in 'his only systematic treatment of aesthetics, primarily drawing upon dramatic forms',[3] his theory of comedy was not widely embraced. Mary Ann Gillies's seminal study of Bergson's reception among British modernists concludes that 'it does not appear to have had much impact on the writers generally recognised as having an affinity to Bergson'.[4]

While she excludes Mansfield from her survey of British modernism, it is perhaps significant that Joseph Conrad – the one writer in whose texts she does find evidence of a theoretical interest in *Laughter* and an appreciable debt to it in his use of humour – was, like Mansfield, an immigrant, whose cultivation of naturalized English literary codes was thus the more self-consciously artful and whose sensitivity to its racial and colonial contexts was sharper; why this should matter will, I hope, become clear as my argument advances. Similarly, if, as Gerri Kimber suggests, the quintessential constituents of Mansfield's style are her 'use of symbolism, literary impressionism and humour',[5] then it can be said that comedy is *the* element regularly occluded when considering the literary significance of her work, for, although 'humour is frequently present in Mansfield's short stories [...] this is one aspect of her writing continually glossed over by many of her critics'.[6]

Indeed, in her inaugural reading of the Bergsonian dimensions of Mansfield's works, Angela Smith noted that a limitation of her approach was that Mansfield's 'pervasive sense of humour may be obscured, though this is never the case in any of her writing',[7] and, accordingly, her otherwise acutely sensitive applications of Bergson's ideas overlook his concepts of comedy, laughter and humour. Notwithstanding this acknowledged blind spot, Smith's reading of 'Psychology' shapes my own, below, in most essential respects, and can be said to anticipate several of the departures I shall make from it.

First, I agree with Smith's judgement that the most salient elements of 'Psychology' are its sharp 'Fauvist juxtapositions'[8] – of theme, 'the social against what is unspoken', and of method, richly associative symbolism against sharp satirical caricature of 'the code[s] of practice' of 'class and gende[r]'.[9] The point of departure for my own interpretation will be the nature of the story's 'ironic reversal[s]' ('things not the people go to bed, and overtly sexual imagery is reserved for the two friends' mental imagery').[10] The pervasiveness of doubling, inversion and dramatic irony derives from the fact that the male and the female protagonist embark upon a debate about the relationship between psychopathology and literature in order to cover over the extrusion of their own suppressed feelings (for each other) upon their 'business-like public sel[ves]'.[11] But whereas Smith applies a Freudian framework to the comedy, arguing that its ironic evocation of the couple's true motivations are conveyed by 'parapraxis, dreams, body language, repetition and indirection',[12] and thus brings out the meaning of the comedy in terms of the repressed content it brings to light, I believe that a sharper sense of the tensions and ambiguities present in the story is imparted by reading the glitches in the couple's interactions through Bergson's definition of the comic – 'something mechanical encrusted upon the living'.[13] I do so in order to explore the savage effects of Mansfield's 'fauvist juxtapositions' as a primarily formal transgression – an attempt to hold together the two fundamental modalities of art that Bergson insisted were radically incompatible.

'Life', comedy and art

If, as is well known, 'Bergson aims, throughout his career, to *contest* the mechanical, habitual and automatic that threaten to encrust themselves upon the living',[14] his concept of comedy is only conducive to this project insofar as it remains a limit case among the arts, its exteriority to the 'genuine art forms'[15] marking a conceptual and pragmatic threshold.

Laughter culminates in an extended treatise on aesthetics where Bergson attempts to bound the corrosive effects of comedy by defining it as the constitutive outside of the artistic realm per se. Bergson argues here that comedy is concerned above all with 'the surface of the social body', the 'group' being its subject but also its audience and its beneficiary ('unconsciously [...] it pursues a utilitarian aim of general improvement'),[16] and thus it plays upon and corrects whatever in human life is common, generic and stereotypical; ergo, comedy cannot truly belong to the category of art, whose guiding aims are the highest degree of formal perfection and the deepest intuition of vital existence. Nevertheless, because the phenomenon of laughter arises from a society's desire to produce a higher degree of flexibility, vitality and aesthetic responsiveness among its members than is strictly necessary (to fulfil their productive functions), the comic spirit can be said to 'com[e] into being just when society and the individual, freed from the worry of self-preservation, begin to regard themselves as works of art'.[17] In this sense, comedy 'is situated on the border-line between art and life'.[18] But Bergson's border is a conceptual barbed wire fence. He does not suggest that any mediation between art and life occurs at this limit; no third term is produced, no conceptual interdependence is illuminated.

Ultimately, then, if *Laughter* adumbrates an aesthetic theory which is unusual in taking comedy as its point of departure, it does so in order to re-establish, at the level of genre, a fundamental, ahistorical and non-reversible distinction between the mechanical and the vital. And Bergson's contribution to the history of aesthetics is to demonstrate that a generic division between comedy and genuine art is both necessary in theory and inevitable in practice. Having no use for the rich particularity of phenomena – worse, having a tendency to (de)compose the unique and particular into freshly moulded stereotypes for its own purposes – comedy is wholly inimical to the intuitive sympathy and sharpened sensory attunement necessary to create or respond to works of poetic genius: '[Comedy] is the ONLY one of all the arts that aims at the general; so that once this objective has been attributed to it, we have said all that it is and all that the rest cannot be.'[19] Implicit in Bergson's somewhat neoclassical classification of comedy, therefore, is a strong case for the impracticability of tragicomedy.

As I shall argue later, Bergson's ideas on comedy had their most direct and tangible influence on writers of late modernist tragicomedy, who productively transgressed his division between comedy and 'the rest', and (not unrelatedly) either scorned or were indifferent to his vitalist philosophy. The contrariety of Mansfield's fiction, and 'Psychology' in particular, derives partly from the fact that *Laughter* is permitted to erupt while a Bergsonian 'affirm[ation of] the transformative energies diffused in living beings'[20] remains in flow.

The historic catastrophe of tragicomedy

Boucher has argued that 'tragicomedy emerges in distinctively modern moments of deep socio-cultural crisis, where the post-traditional disintegration of the metaphysical foundations of cultural formations is particularly evident',[21] and claims that the two historical moments in which the genre has risen to salience, 'the short period from the 1580s to the beginning of the English Civil War' and 'the mid-point of the terrible twentieth century' are marked by a combination of traumatic social conflict and the fracturing of underlying metaphysical certainties.[22] His dating of the second wave of tragicomic forms from the mid-twentieth century tallies broadly with Tyrus Miller's claim that from the late 1920s a distinctive 'tragicomic vision' emerged through 'reflection upon a peculiar type of laughter as the zero degree of subjectivity – a condition shared by the artist, his [*sic*] characters, and his reader/spectators', a historically distinct mode that he dubs 'late modernism'.[23] Foster, however, dates the tragicomedy revival earlier, citing the example of Ibsen's *The Wild Duck* (1884), and she emphasizes the historical usurpation of aristocratic hegemony by the bourgeoisie as the determinate factor in its rebirth:

> In the modern age it is almost impossible to write tragedy, especially within the realistic convention, which emphasizes ordinary human beings from the middle

> or lower classes speaking unexalted language and possessing failings that often seem more embarrassing than lethal. Any attempt to write tragedy today is likely to produce melodrama instead. But though the dramatic form *tragedy* no longer exists, what is *tragic* in human experience has found its aesthetic home in tragicomedy, where it is simultaneously subverted, protected, and rendered more painful by its peculiar relation with the comic. Ibsen seems to have realized this paradox in writing *The Wild Duck*.[24]

Whether Bergson is best understood as a prophet of doom or an early opponent of tragicomedy's ominous reappearance, I read *Laughter* as a severe but implicit opponent of the emerging modalities of modern(ist) tragicomedy. Moreover, his antipathy is both more thoroughgoing and more intellectually productive than that of his historical forebears. Sir Philip Sidney may stand as a representative example of the latter, having complained that such 'mongrel' forms failed *both* as tragedy and as comedy: 'Neither right Tragedies, nor right Comedies [...] neither the admiration and commiseration, nor the right sportfulness, is by their mungrell Tragy-comedie obtained'.[25]

For Bergson, tragic drama and its contemporary tributaries 'plumb the depths' of the poet's 'inner nature' in order to cultivate 'a fuller view of reality'[26] replete with 'profound [but] dimly apprehended truth[s]'.[27] By contrast, because, in his eyes, comedy derives from the uncanny resemblance of a living being to a mere automaton, it remains necessarily at the level of surface and generality – the only vista from which Bergson believes a person, in all their complexity and uniqueness, can come to resemble 'a regular talking-machine'.[28] He is clear that shifts – though *not* amalgamations – between comic and tragic effects are possible; but the danger lies in the asymmetry of the processes involved, for although a comic writer will 'endanger and in the end [...] sacrifice all that was laughable' if they suggest a connection between comic speech, action or logic and causes which lie 'deep-seated' in a living soul,[29] ultimately there is no element of the human personality which (once subjected to repetition, caricature, incongruous transposition, etc.) cannot be stripped of its depth and its vitality, and thus made all the more profoundly laughable:

> The feelings we have matured, the passions we have brooded over, the actions we have weighed, decided upon, and carried through, in short, all that comes from us and is our very own, these are the things that give life its ofttimes dramatic and generally grave aspect. What, then, is requisite to transform all this into a comedy? Merely to fancy that our seeming freedom conceals the strings of a dancing-Jack.[30]

The neglect of *Laughter* among Bergson's modernist proponents is rather less surprising, then, in light of the book's far-reaching insight that what went under its definition of comedy had to be bracketed off, not only conceptually but also in practice, in order to preserve the aesthetic forms (impressionism, symbolism, and their high modernist reformulations) which provided refuge from the bourgeois rationalization of social relations.

The birth of late modernism: Bergson contra Bergson

The foregoing point also accounts for an inverse phenomenon: the book's influence upon writing which in other respects stands in opposition to Bergsonism. Most famously, Wyndham Lewis, pre-eminently hostile to the central tenets of Bergson's philosophy ('this psychological time, or duration, this mood that is as fixed as the matter covering it, is as romantic and picturesque as it is "local colour" and usually as shallow a thing as that'),[31] recognized that the reversibility of Bergson's terms was *the* essential discovery of *Laughter*: 'from [the comic] point of view all men are necessarily comic: for they are all *things*, or physical bodies behaving as *persons*'.[32] Rearticulated in this form, Bergson's theory of comedy provided a foundation for artistic and polemical response to modernism: a 'curious mélange of mimicry and violent rejection',[33] which, according to Tyrus Miller, inaugurates the late modernist *dépaysement* in which 'modernism's unique authorial voice endures, but degraded to the tinny broadcasts of a stereotyped discourse'.[34] Stereotyping, by means of habitual repetition, is one of the most fundamental comic processes in Bergson's account and, as such, foreign to all genuine art: 'The hero of a tragedy represents an individuality unique of its kind. It may be possible to imitate him, but then we shall be passing, whether consciously or not, from the tragic to the comic'.[35] Prompted by Bergson's prohibition, then, Lewis reconnects modernist literary form and Bergsonian comic techniques to their common conditions of possibility:

> Loosen[ing] the modernist dominance of form and allow[ing] a more fluid, dialogic relation with the immediate historical context [...] at the cost of abandoning the modernist gold standard: form as the universal currency in which aesthetic value could be measured and circulated.[36]

Similarly, in the work of Samuel Beckett, 'the habitual and the automatic become progressively more central' both thematically and formally.[37] The eponymous hero of *Murphy*, for example, 'in keeping with Henri Bergson's definition of the comic, exhibits a mechanical inelasticity, an inability to adjust to the modern bureaucratic, commercial London that lies outside his mind [...] [and] that maladjustment is equally a feature of Beckett's composition'.[38] And, in his foreword to Djuna Barnes' *Nightwood*, perhaps fearful that the work sits uneasily with the 'rhythmic unity, [...] writerly value, [...] moral cohesion [and] disinterested awareness' of high modernism, T. S. Eliot is at pains to inoculate its readers against 'the impression of automatism' and allay any 'suspicion' of the 'mechanistic qualities' of its characters:[39] 'Sometimes in a phrase the characters spring to life so suddenly that one is taken aback, as if one had touched a wax-work figure and discovered that it was a live policeman.'[40] For all of these writers, then, *Laughter* provided the conceptual ballast with which to sail free of the artistic values which had predominated since on or around December 1910, when British Bergsonism was at its zenith.

'Here the poetry has escaped': Lewis and Mansfield versus Aiken and Mansfield

In what follows, I do not claim an exact homology between Mansfield's fiction and the 'mirthless laughter' of the abovementioned late modernists. Nonetheless, it is suggestive, and a little surprising, that Mansfield herself expressed a considerable fascination with Wyndham Lewis and his work, writing to Anne Drey in 1921, 'I regret not knowing him. He's one of the few people Id very much like to have had for a friend.'[41] Indicative as this may be of certain subcutaneous resonances between their works, the obvious difference is that Mansfield, as Kimber rightly notes,[42] also consistently displays an ardent commitment to the post-1910 aesthetic dispensation, in particular (post)impressionism and symbolism. As she wrote to Dorothy Brett, 'its queer I feel that as an artist in spite of his passions and his views and all that he lacks a real *centre*.'[43] Ultimately, her interest in Lewis is tempered (in both senses) by the pseudo-eschatological 'aim' of realizing her particular inner vision through ongoing creative refinement of her life and work:

> What I *aim* at is that state of mind when I feel my soul and my mind are one. Its awfully terribly difficult to get at. Only solitude will do it for me – But I feel Wyndham Lewis would be inclined to call the soul tiddley ompom. It's a mystery, anyway. One aims at perfection – knows one will never achieve it and goes on aiming as though one knew the exact contrary.[44]

The crux of her attitude to Lewis is that, even as she asserts her concern about a deficiency at the heart of Lewis's work, she enfolds her own commitment to the 'soul' of art within his comedy of human machines behaving, absentmindedly, as if they were persons. In other words, she exposes her deeply felt sense of repeatedly failing to live up to her own (and her era's) literary standards to the 'dancing Jack' effect – sketching The Artist as a character who 'goes on' with their work 'as though [(s)he] knew the exact contrary', pulled along on the strings of his/her professional jargon.

My contention, then, is that Mansfield's stories enact a war between two incompatible aesthetic approaches, which might retrospectively be termed 'high modernist' and 'late modernist', but which were prefigured in Bergson's rigid distinction between comic invention and genuine art. Arguably, among her contemporaries, the critic who was most attuned to this conflict was the poet, critic and short story writer Conrad Aiken.[45] In a 1921 review of *Bliss and Other Stories* he praised in the highest terms the 'genius' of her prose style, which he termed 'narrative lyric' owing to its 'chromatic vividness' of language and form, and (echoing Bergson's notion of the artist as adept in the rich inner harmonies of the sensible universe) attributed this quality to her possessing a 'sensibility intense to the point of febrility, ecstatically aware of texture and hue, magnificently responsive, most of all to the sound of life'.[46] Having testified to Mansfield's remarkable gifts, he then adds a sharp qualification to his judgement of her actual achievements in the short story form. Where her style fails to 'respond' to her theme, and here he cites the 'comparative triviality' of 'Psychology' as an example, 'Miss Mansfield resorts to cleverness, *esurient humor*, or even, as in the termination of "Bliss," to the trickery of disguise [...] here, we feel, *the poetry has escaped*' (my italics).[47] As with his endorsement, his reservations too mirror Bergson's distinction between the genius of the artist and the more superficial ingenuity of the comedian:

> Any poet may reveal himself as a wit when he pleases. To do this there will be no need for him to acquire anything; [...] it seems rather as though he would have to give up something [...] by simply resolving to be no longer a poet in feeling, but only in intelligence.[48]

Mansfield responded sympathetically to Aiken's distinction between the stories in *Bliss* that glisten with poetic brilliance and those, such as 'Psychology', which 'resort' to wit, comic misrecognitions and (unrestrained) humour, writing 'to thank [him] *particularly* for pointing out so justly where I have failed', before exclaiming: 'Queer – isn't it – how helpful it is to know that someone else sees what is wrong in one's work.'[49] The implication is surely that Aiken has been among the few, perhaps the first, to identify a defect of which the suffering author has long been aware.

'How sure are you that psychology *qua* psychology has got anything to do with literature at all?': Funny impressions, self-reflexivity and inner itching

We need not accept Aiken's judgement that in stories such as 'Psychology' Mansfield's comic modulations drive her lyricism, and thus her genius, off the page. But I would maintain that behind all the 'fauvist juxtapositions' that Smith highlights in the story, the crucial one (that cuts across the theme, tone and structure of the piece) is the shocking contact between her lyrically wrought, free indirect discourse and touches of comedy which do indeed threaten to reduce the hard-won freedom of the narrative voice to the status of a 'talking-machine'.

Smith describes 'Psychology' as a 'self-reflexive story',[50] one that offers neither the illusory objectivity of 'realism' nor 'the authenticity of an authorial personality'.[51] I think this is broadly right, but leaves open the question of where the self that reflects is to be located. Surely not coincidental, in this regard, is the fact that the primary focalizer is a female writer whose claim to literary significance rests, she thinks, on her 'exquisite sense of real English comedy'.[52] Like the 'self-reflexive laughter' of late modernist form that implicates writer, character and reader, my sense is that the story's self-reflexivity resides in the fact that the authenticity of the authorial personality is not abandoned but brought within the (comic) narrative frame where it nonetheless continues to function as the witness to its own comedic voidance.

On the proximity between Freud's concept of the uncanny and Bergson's of comedy, Alenka Zupancic has proposed that the difference is simply a matter of the framing: the uncanny effect emerges from 'a collapse of reality (as fundamentally the reality of desire)'.[53] This means that uncanny texts stage the unravelling of their symbolic coordinates as a drama and focalize this sense of collapse through the sufferings of a rounded (desiring) protagonist. With the comic mode, as described by Bergson, such an unravelling of meaningful symbolic reality does not produce the sense of collapse because, although the text no longer derives its coherence and legibility from the verisimilitude of complex, rounded characters or the authority of a narratorial voice, those functions are nonetheless fulfilled by radically impersonal mechanisms, comic processes which give the impression of running like clockwork. For Zupancic, indeed, comedy is best defined as a joyous ascension to 'the structure of the drive'.[54] And on this point her Hegelian-Lacanian reading is extremely close to Bergson, for whom the world of comedy is animated by a single character trait, an 'inner itching',[55] which is not treated as an integral part of the central character's personality but rather exists with the character as a 'parasitic organism [...] endowed with an independent existence'.[56] It is the 'itching' itself that takes on the function of

> the central character, present though invisible, to which the characters in flesh and blood on the stage are attached. At times it delights in dragging them down with its own weight and making them share in its tumbles. More frequently, however, it plays on them as on an instrument or pulls the strings as though they were puppets.[57]

The scenario in 'Psychology' concerns an ambitious young male writer, thirty-one, paying the latest of an increasingly habitual series of visits to the townhouse of a similarly driven woman of thirty. The ostensible purpose of their meetings is to lay open their thoughts, feelings and impressions regarding the future course of English letters. Yet above and beneath the voices of the two writers, with their asseverations of aesthetic refinement and intellectual disinterestedness, it is arguably the inner itch that provides the story's true agency, not least because of the text's mimetic conceit, whereby the pair's 'secret selves' call out to each other through erotically charged direct speech that contrasts sharply with the stilted dialogue and solemn free indirect discourse in which the characters go about the business of, in Lewis' words, 'physical bodies behaving as persons':

> Just for a moment both of them stood silent in that leaping light. Still, as it were, they tasted on their smiling lips the sweet shock of their greeting. Their secret selves whispered:
>
> 'Why should we speak? Isn't this enough?'
>
> 'More than enough. I never realized until this moment . . .'
>
> 'How good it is just to be with you. . . .'
>
> 'Like this. . . .'
>
> 'It's more than enough.'
>
> But suddenly he turned and looked at her and she moved quickly away.[58]

These sharp, quick exchanges between personified drives have a force and a frankness which accentuates the absence of these qualities from the voices of the characters themselves. For example, ellipses in the man's speech indicate the presence of an inner itch that intrudes when the entanglement of stereotypically 'high' and 'low' forms of consumption (such as reading and feeding) are brought to light: '"Always reading while I feed . . . my habit of looking upon food as just food . . . something that's there, at certain times . . . to be devoured . . . to be . . . not there." He laughed'.[59] These breaks in the flow of the sentence do not produce anacoluthon though: the syntactical coherence of his speech remains intact; only there is a sense that it is the product of halting, laboured expression rather than of spontaneous thoughts flowing from live interactions between neurons, breath and lips. That is to say, the fluid motion of their dialogue is being sacrificed for the sake of semantic and syntactic coherence. The life generated by their encounter is contained, but only just, by a rudimentary switch mechanism, its presence replaced by absence before it can disrupt the habitual sequence of the meeting. The comedy generated by these characters, insofar as their words and actions suggest rigidity, mechanization and absentmindedness, derives from the simple irony that their theorization of literature and their self-regardingly solemn experiment in authentic, vivid communication is all too obviously used as a means of holding themselves aloof from the erotic impulses which they experience in relation to each other.

This brings us to one of the central images in 'Psychology', one that crystallizes the moment at which the debate over the place of 'psychology *qua* psychology' in modern fiction is undercut by the two characters' own sudden, savage awareness of dramatic irony:

> On the talk went. And now it seemed they really had succeeded. She turned in her chair to look at him while she answered. Her smile said: 'We have won.' And he smiled back, confident: 'Absolutely.'
>
> But the smile undid them. It lasted too long; it became a grin. They saw themselves as two little grinning puppets jigging away in nothingness.[60]

Of this passage, Aimee Gasston notes that 'the object world robustly endures while the couple in the story flounder', and argues that this is an instance of Mansfield 'introducing the uncanny (and its accompanying state of attunement, angst) to habitual perception so that it is disrupted, so that things can be seen anew'.[61] I suggest that the accompanying sense of attunement might better be described as Bergsonian laughter than Heideggerian angst, because with the latter a dawning sense of unreality and inauthenticity bears within it the promise of still more authentic and individualized being-in-the-world, whereas in the former case the very notions of authenticity and individuality are subjected to laughter. But Mansfield gives neither of us firm grounds for our own diagnosis.

Certainly, the image of the two 'eager, serious'[62] protagonists reduced via a fixed smile to the aspect of 'grinning puppets' is almost explicitly Bergsonian in its illustration of the way an 'exquisite sense' of comedy exposes, amplifies and builds upon the first signs that human intercourse (the confident, reciprocal smile of self-mastery) contains a trace of artificiality. Yet the paradox of the text's self-reflexivity is that it is hard to differentiate, intellectually or intuitively, the inhuman pleasures of the comic tableau from the rendering in free indirect discourse of the living, breathing existential angst of the comedian.

Conclusion – talent borrows, genius often forgets a citation

I will end by pushing that indeterminacy a little further, without resolving it, by invoking Jacqueline Jones's term, 'citational character'.[63] She coins it to label an aspect of Mansfield's writing practice which the author herself highlighted in a letter to Murry dated 14 March 1918. Describing the protagonist of 'Bliss' – another story which Conrad Aiken singled out as an excessively clever failure – she confides to her husband that she has created a voice for her central character which she feared was not quite 'permissible' to her (modernist) readership:

> Bertha, not being an artist, was yet artist manqué enough to realise that those words and expressions were not & couldn't be hers – They were, as it were *quoted* by her, borrowed [...] . . . Yet she'd none of her own . . . But this I agree is not permissible – I cant grant all that in my dear reader.[64]

This technique, impermissible as it is, localizes the ironic distance within the character's own sense of *failure* at a deeper level of consciousness that exists only as the self-reflexivity that occurs at the place of a 'lack' (*manqué*) beneath their stereotyped identity. Jones, however, offers a spiritualization of Mansfield's own reading, sublimating the comedic *prima materia* of lack, imitation and depersonalization into a form of ironic epiphany:

> It could be argued that Bertha is possessed by Katherine Mansfield's own creative spirit in an almost occult way.
>
> While Mansfield makes her supra-narrator withdraw from view, s/he becomes 'ghostly' and, as I have noted, at times covertly operates in the text by providing the reader with information ahead of Bertha. [...] If in 'Bliss' Bertha is never given full access to memory and consciousness her limited (or false) consciousness is, ironically, *revealed* via epiphany.[65]

The seeming difference between the two readings is only that Jones reintroduces 'that portion [of human personality] which interests our sensibility [and] appeals to our feeling', the portion which according to Bergson is not 'capable of becoming comic',[66] and does so by invocation of an implied authorial voice. The notion of an authorial voice is used very exactly here as an animating force, a 'spirit attendant on a person' (an etymologically sound definition of '*genius*'), that emerges autochthonously within the text as a guarantor of meaning, at the moment the character becomes a comic object for itself.

Jones's reading tentatively touches on a point which Aiken was not willing to concede: the moments when 'esurient humour' ruptures the vibrant lines of her 'narrative poetry' are the moments where Mansfield guiltily draws her poor 'dear reader' to the edge of the abyss between living meanings and machinic iterations. They bring us to the crux of Bergson's distinction between the two types of art, as well as between individuated personality and stereotypical 'character'. But we arrive there and are brought to a halt, without the authority to confirm the presence, absence or even the possibility of an authentically comedic 'genius'.

Notes

1 Angela Smith, *Katherine Mansfield: A Literary Life* (Basingstoke: Palgrave, 1991); Eiko Nakano, 'One or Many: Bergsonian Readings of Katherine Mansfield's Modernism' (unpublished doctoral thesis, University of Stirling, 2005); Louise Edensor, 'Creative Evolution: Symbolist Representations of Bergson's Duration in the Works of Katherine Mansfield' (unpublished MA dissertation, The Open University, 2010); Jacqueline C. E. Jones, 'Katherine Mansfield and Memory: Bergsonian Readings' (unpublished doctoral thesis, University of Edinburgh, 2016); Clare Hanson, 'Katherine Mansfield and Vitalist Psychology', in *Katherine Mansfield and Psychology*, eds Clare Hanson, Gerri Kimber and Todd Martin (Edinburgh: Edinburgh University Press, 2016), pp. 23–37.

2 Tyrus Miller, *Late Modernism: Politics, Fiction, and the Arts between the World Wars* (Berkeley: University of California Press, 1999), p. 64.

3 Simon Yuill, 'Bend Sinister: Monstrosity and Normative Effect in Computation Practice', in *Fun and Software: Exploring Pleasure, Paradox and Pain in Computing*, ed. Olga Goriunova (New York: Bloomsbury, 2014), p. 49.

4 Mary Ann Gillies, *Henri Bergson and British Modernism* (Montreal: McGill-Queen's University Press, 1996), p. 169.

5 Gerri Kimber, *Katherine Mansfield and the Art of the Short Story* (Basingstoke: Palgrave Macmillan, 2015), p. 2.

6 Ibid, p. 63.
7 Smith, p. 163.
8 Ibid., p. 121.
9 Ibid., p. 120.
10 Ibid., p. 117.
11 Ibid., p. 119.
12 Ibid., p. 117.
13 Henri Bergson, *Laughter: An Essay on the Meaning of the Comic*, trans. Cloudesley Brereton and Fred Rothwell (London: Temple of Earth Publishing, 2008), p. 14a.
14 Ulrika Maude, 'Chronic Conditions: Beckett, Bergson and Samuel Johnson', *Journal of Medical Humanities*, 37, no. 2 (2016): 193–204 (p. 193).
15 Bergson, p. 52b.
16 Ibid., p. 9a.
17 Ibid.
18 Ibid., p. 46b.
19 Ibid.
20 Hanson, p. 36.
21 Geoff Boucher, '*Measure for Measure* after Zizek's Lacanian Dialectics', in *Lacan, Psychoanalysis and Comedy*, eds Patricia Gherovici and Manya Steinkoler (Cambridge: Cambridge University Press, 2016), pp. 156–83 (p. 156).
22 Ibid., p. 158.
23 Miller, p. 58.
24 Verna A. Foster, 'Ibsen's Tragicomedy: *The Wild Duck*', *Modern Drama*, 38, no. 3 (1995): 287–97 (p. 287).
25 Sir Philip Sidney, *An Apologie for Poetrie* (London: Alex Murray and Son, 1868), p. 65.
26 Bergson, p. 51b.
27 Ibid., p. 50a.
28 Ibid., p. 23b.
29 Ibid., p. 52a.
30 Ibid., p. 26a.
31 Wyndham Lewis, *Time and Western Man*, quoted in Gillies, p. 133.
32 Wyndham Lewis, 'The Meaning of the Wild Body', in *The Wild Body: A Soldier of Humour and Other Stories* (London: Penguin Classics, 2004), p. 158.
33 Miller, p. 76.
34 Ibid., p. 120.
35 Bergson, p. 50b.
36 Miller, p. 31.
37 Maude, p. 193.
38 Miller, p. 180.

39 Ibid., pp. 123–4.
40 Elliot, quoted in Miller, p. 123.
41 *Letters* 4, pp. 231–32.
42 See n. 5, above.
43 *Letters* 5, p. 142.
44 Ibid.
45 On the relationship between Aiken and Mansfield, see Sydney Janet Kaplan, 'Seated Between "Geniuses": Conrad Aiken's Imaginative and Critical Responses to Katherine Mansfield and Virginia Woolf', in *Katherine Mansfield and Virginia Woolf*, eds Christine Froula, Gerri Kimber and Todd Martin (Edinburgh: Edinburgh University Press, 2018), pp. 42–54.
46 Conrad Aiken, *Bliss and Other Stories*, in *A Reviewer's ABC: Collected Criticism of Conrad Aiken* (London: W. H. Allen, 1961), p. 292.
47 Ibid., p. 292.
48 Bergson, p. 34a.
49 *Letters* 4, p. 304.
50 Smith, p. 117.
51 Ibid., p. 121.
52 CW2, p. 194.
53 Alenka Zupancic, *Why Psychoanalysis?: Three Interventions* (Uppsala: Nordic Summer University Press, 2008), p. 54.
54 Ibid., p. 55.
55 Bergson, p. 44b.
56 Ibid., pp. 43b-44a.
57 Ibid., p. 7b.
58 CW2, p. 193.
59 CW2, pp. 194–5.
60 CW2, p. 196 (both quotes).
61 Aimee Gasston, 'Phenomenology Begins at Home: The Presence of Things in the Short Fiction of Katherine Mansfield and Virginia Woolf', *Katherine Mansfield: Masked and Unmasked*, special issue of *Journal of New Zealand Literature*, 32, no. 2 (2014): 31–51 (pp. 43–4).
62 CW2, p. 194.
63 Jones, p. 209.
64 *Letters* 2, p. 121.
65 Jones, p. 209.
66 Bergson, p. 46a.

Literary influence and life writing

9

'Something sensational and new'

Katherine Mansfield's engagement with the literary marketplace in London, 1908–9

Katie L. Jones

Studies of Katherine Mansfield's literary and professional development typically identify her 1910–11 association with the socialist periodical *The New Age* as the beginning of her life as a professional author.[1] By focusing so heavily on Mansfield's contributions to *The New Age*, critics such as Jenny McDonnell and Patrick D. Morrow have largely overlooked the impact of her earliest work (including her 1907 publications in the Australian periodical *The Native Companion*).[2] They have also attributed much of her early success to the influence of specific mentors (including *The New Age*'s principal editor, A. R. Orage and its unofficial co-editor, Beatrice Hastings). The dominant narrative has taken a rather restricted view of Mansfield's professional development, suggesting that her 1910–11 involvement with *The New Age* acted as an 'apprenticeship', and that the relationship between the writer and Orage was a 'master/student binary'.[3]

Emphasizing the influence of Orage and his role in shaping the young writer's literary style risks understating Mansfield's active engagement with the literary field as an aspiring professional author, and her efforts to ensure the marketability of her work. This chapter seeks to revise the view that Mansfield was moulded into a professional writer by Orage (and others at *The New Age*); it will instead demonstrate that her literary development was already well underway by the time she became an official contributor to *The New Age*. In order to do this, I will focus on Mansfield's first tumultuous year as an adult in London in 1908–9, taking account of how the writer looked to engage with trends in the literary and musical scenes as she struggled to discover a writing style that would appeal to audiences and readers.

London, 1908–9: Adapting to new surroundings

In August 1908, having spent an unsettled eighteen months in Wellington, Mansfield arrived back in London where she was welcomed by her close friend, Ida Baker. Mansfield stayed at Beauchamp Lodge, Paddington – a hostel that accommodated unmarried female music students. Despite her longstanding urge to return to the city that had first inspired her connection with the works of Oscar Wilde, Walter Pater and Arthur Symons, the development of her own writing soon became hindered by the distractions of London life. According to Baker, Mansfield's 'many acquaintances' in Beauchamp Lodge were 'too constant' and 'their attentions suffocat[ed] her and prevent[ed] her from working'.[4] Having spent the whole of 1907 and the first half of 1908 yearning to return to London, her involvement with a widening social circle, coupled with the financial constraints of independent living, resulted in a period of personal and literary instability for Mansfield in the months following her arrival.[5]

For Mansfield, London represented an uninhibited space in which she could explore her conflicted identity and cultivate her developing aesthetic vision. Shortly after her arrival, she embarked on an intense (but ill-fated) three-month romance with the violinist Garnet Trowell, which resulted in her work, letters and diary entries taking on an almost overwhelmingly sentimental tone. Throughout the brief relationship with Trowell (which, according to Vincent O'Sullivan and Margaret Scott, 'dominated her life' at that time),[6] Mansfield wrote a series of love letters which she embellished with romantic poetry. One such letter, sent to Trowell on 29 October 1908, reveals her infatuation with the young musician:

> My most Beloved One – […] My soul is full of love for you. Your letter this morning did so satisfy me – that – oh, I had strength to conquer the world – and I wrote four poems which I send you tonight. They are to be set to music […]. I wrote them for you – truly […]. Beloved – I must copy out those poems – & then start work. […] I am forever your devoted wife.[7]

Though it is difficult to reconcile this mawkish style of writing with the sharp, satirical tone that would characterize her 1910–11 Bavarian sketches in *The New Age*, there is yet a discernible mindfulness in these apparently artless, effusive letters to Trowell. Mansfield's creative output was naturally informed by her working knowledge of the literary field, and her personal writings too reveal her alertness to the elements that make up a love letter. In his analysis of Mansfield's post-1911 letters to the man who became her second husband, John Middleton Murry, C. K. Stead comments on the self-consciousness of Mansfield's most intimate writings:

> She is trying always from a distance to manage Murry's emotions – to keep her hold on him. She's very demanding. She needs constant responses, and gets them. [...] His letters to her [...] often look like sad imitations of hers, or attempts to give her what she wants. [...] But she keeps him acting up to the fiction that they are an Eloise and Abelard, perfect lovers kept apart by unavoidable circumstances, exchanging letters that may one day be published.[8]

The same can be said of Mansfield's love letters to Trowell. Many of Mansfield's diary entries from this period have direct addressees and appear to be draft versions of letters that she intended to send; this may help to explain the excessively 'rehearsed' quality of her romantic correspondence with Trowell.[9]

In the letter to Trowell quoted above, Mansfield explains that the words of one of the enclosed poems, 'By the Sea Shore', should be set to 'strange MacDowell, Debussy chords'.[10] Mansfield is perhaps alluding here to the tendency for these composers to produce compositions invoking the free-flowing rhythm of poetry; she conceives of the opening verse of 'In the Church' as a 'strange organ-like passage' which is 'almost recitative at the beginning'.[11] According to O'Sullivan and Scott, Mansfield's desire to set her poetry to the chords of American composer Edward Alexander MacDowell was motivated by popular trends in music towards the end of the nineteenth century: they state that 'the "poetical" compositions of [...] Edward MacDowell [...] were in vogue at this time, particularly in Germany'.[12] It seems fitting that Mansfield should have chosen the compositions of MacDowell to accompany her early romantic poetry because, according to E. Douglas Bomberger's biography of the composer, by the late nineteenth century MacDowell's emotionally intense melodies were perceived as over-sentimental.[13] Claude Debussy also appears to have been an obvious choice for Mansfield, as his compositions were renowned for their 'literary allusions and parodistic references to poetry that he set to music'.[14]

Another of Mansfield's enclosed poems, 'The Lilac Tree', was clearly written in the style of a romantic nocturne – a brief and highly expressive composition, structured according to rhythm and melody:

> The branches of the lilac tree
> Are bent with blossom – in the air
> They sway and languish dreamily,
> And we, pressed close, are kissing, there
> The blossoms falling on her hair –
> Oh, lilac tree, Oh lilac tree
> Shelter us, cover us, secretly.[15]

Despite the fact that it arguably lacks the depth of some of her later poetry, this poem's vivid emotional style evokes the musicality of Debussy, since the rhapsodic content of the verse is accompanied by a simple, musical-style beat.[16] In her letter, Mansfield describes the poem as being 'full [of] a rhythmic grace', adding that it would 'suit Tom's composition'.[17] Garnet's twin brother Tom (Arnold) Trowell – a gifted cellist and composer – had a growing reputation in London at this time, and his compositions were attracting favourable reviews from local publications such as the classical music magazine, *The Strad*: 'Mr Arnold Trowell has written a considerable number of short pieces for the violoncello, and his contributions are [...] always melodious, and [...] will appeal to lovers of sentiment.'[18] The poems that Mansfield sent to Garnet are intimate pieces that complement a romantic letter, but they also reveal Mansfield's desire to extend the distribution of her work towards a different (and wider) public audience.

At this point in her life, Mansfield was looking to integrate her musical interests and her literary career and, according to Ida Baker, she would often put on small public performances to supplement her annual allowance:

> Katherine was able to use her great gift for recitation, mimicry and music, as in those days hostesses often provided entertainment for their guests. When Katherine's gift was discovered through the friends she had made at the lodge, she was soon offered professional invitations, at a guinea an evening.[19]

As Baker suggests, the financial incentive for staging these public recitals would certainly have motivated the struggling Mansfield, but it is clear from her letters of this time that the idea of reciting (or 'performing') her poetry also appealed because it presented an ideal opportunity to promote her own work to a wider audience. The poems that Mansfield sent to Trowell in her letters reveal her intention to create expressive pieces for public performance rather than literary texts to be printed in the pages of a magazine or newspaper. They are, for this reason, more than simply overwrought juvenilia: as Gerri Kimber and Angela Smith note, these poems are 'stepping stones' in her early career'.[20] In another letter to Trowell, she describes her desire to combine her talent for writing with the art of public recitation:

> I have a strange ambition – I've had it for years – and now, suddenly here it is revived [...] It is to write – and recite what I write – in a very fine way [...]. Revolutionise and revive the art of elocution [...]. I could then write just what I feel would suit me – and could popularise my work – and also I feel there's a big opening for something sensational and new in this direction.[21]

Mark S. Morrisson describes how the oral performance of poetry in 1908–9 reflected a pre-modernist concern with authorial presence, which was to be 'mediated by the reciter'.[22] By identifying performative verse recital as the most suitable medium for delivering her material in the public sphere, the twenty-year-old Mansfield was demonstrating an astute awareness of the emerging verse-recitation scene within the London literary marketplace and, even at this early stage of her career, she was actively looking to negotiate her position within it.

W. B. Yeats and the vogue for verse recitation

London's evolving culture of recitation owed much to the influence of W. B. Yeats, whose verse dramas had played a key role in ensuring that his poetry reached wider audiences during the 1890s.[23] As Morrisson notes, Yeats's distinctive reading style, coupled with his desire to express the rhythm of poetry above all else during his recitals, helped to position oral performance as 'a component of literary appreciation'.[24] Yeats lectured extensively on the musical qualities of poetry to audiences in London between 1901 and 1904, often staging public recitals of his own material (alongside the West End actress Florence Farr) to accompany his speeches.

Together with the dramatists Isabella Augusta ('Lady') Gregory and Edward Martyn, Yeats published the 'Manifesto for Irish Literary Theatre' in 1897, in which he set out his proposal to establish a national theatre for Ireland. Building on their manifesto, the three figures co-founded the Irish Literary Theatre in 1899, staging a performance of Yeats's verse drama *The Countess Cathleen* (1892) on 8 May to mark the theatre's opening.[25] Joseph Holloway – an Irish theatre critic who kept meticulous records of every performance that he attended – commented on Yeats's ability to convey the rhythmic quality of his material to the audience during this first showing of *The Countess Cathleen*: 'It was not acting in the ordinary sense, but a laudable attempt "to lend to the beauty of the poet's rhyme the music of the voice" in half chant-like tones.'[26]

According to Yeats, the practice of 'chant-verse' allowed reciters to explore 'an endless variety of expression' during their performances.[27] Often accompanied by music played on a psaltery – a stringed, harp-like instrument designed to resemble the range of the speaking voice – Farr would intone Yeats's verses in a style that sought to emphasize the unique rhythm of his poetry.

On 8 December 1900, at the Irish Literary Society in London, Farr and Yeats staged a public rendition of his poem 'The Lake Isle of Innisfree' (1890) and a section from *The Countess Cathleen*. During the event, Farr and Yeats emphasized the musical quality of language by chanting each verse – an approach that drew mixed responses from audiences at the time including, most notably, George Moore: 'The theories of the author regarding the speaking of verse I hold to be mistaken [...]. Many times I prayed during the last act that the curtain might come down at once.'[28] Despite the fact that public renditions of his verse dramas were not always received favourably by audiences, Yeats participated in the advancement of the verse-recitation scene through his enterprising poetry recitals, his lectures on oral performance and his verse plays – all of which brought poetry readings to the attention of new audiences.

Ronald Schuchard recognizes Yeats as the principal driving force behind the 'educating [of...] London audience[s] in the "lost" arts of musical speech, symbolic scenery, and rhythmical acting' during the pre-war era.[29] The impact of Yeats and his verse dramas contributed to a surge in the popularity of public readings in London at the turn of the century, facilitated by the opening of fourteen new theatres in the West End between 1880 and 1900.[30] Inspired by the success of Yeats, the Poetry Recital Society (later renamed the Poetry Society) was founded by Galloway Kyle in February 1909 with the aim of introducing ideals of elocution to verse recitation. Lady Margaret Sackville was appointed president of the Society, and on 24 February 1909 she delivered a lecture entitled 'The Art of Speaking Verse' at the group's inaugural meeting (which was later published in the May 1909 issue of *The Poetical Gazette*). In her speech, Sackville commended the efforts of Yeats and the Irish National Theatre Society to find new ways of expressing the rhythm of poetry in their recitals; as Schuchard notes, Sackville had been a strong 'advocate of chanted verse since she first attended one of Yeats's Monday evenings in 1902'.[31] Described by Morrisson as 'an institution of the verse-recitation movement', the Poetry Society was an important platform for the period's aspiring poets to deliver readings and performances of their work to audiences they would otherwise have struggled to attract.[32]

By the time of Mansfield's arrival in 1908, London's theatre and musical performance scenes were thriving and she soon found herself immersed in the culture of the metropolis, attending numerous concerts, plays and silent film screenings. Mansfield's letters around this time are filled with references to the musical and dance recitals that she attended. In October 1908, she recalls feeling 'staggered' by the tone and intensity of a performance by Venezuelan pianist Teresa Carreño at the Bechstein Hall (after which Mansfield was invited backstage to meet the musician).[33] She attended concerts of nineteenth-century music at the Queen's Hall, Greek classical dances at the Palace Music Hall, as well as staging her own informal evenings of 'recitation, mimicry and music'.[34] Two years before his death in 1939, Yeats wrote that 'I have spent my life in clearing out of poetry every phrase written for the eye, and bringing all back to syntax that is for ear alone'.[35] As the following section will demonstrate, Mansfield shared a similar aspiration throughout 1908–9 as she looked to fashion an identity for herself through the oral performance of her work.

Mansfield: A shrewd negotiator

Despite the fact that she was often distracted by her new bohemian London lifestyle, Mansfield remained creatively productive and alert to literary trends and professional opportunities during this time.[36] The poems that Mansfield enclosed in her letters to Trowell were deeply personal, and most were intended as lyrical accompaniments to his brother's musical pieces, but they give the impression that she viewed him as both a lover and an 'ideal reader'; she was certainly aware that Trowell's position with a touring orchestra company and his growing musical reputation could facilitate the delivery of her written 'performance pieces' to large audiences across Europe.[37] Claire Davison suggests that the pieces Mansfield enclosed in her letters to Trowell foreshadow her future role as a contributor to avant-garde magazines:

> 'Brief forms' [like…] the prelude, nocturne or rhapsody […] were often a direct off-shoot of industrialisation: the rise of 'little magazines' [brought] essays, prose poems and sketches to new enthusiastic readers, where the focus was more often on self-contained pieces rather than on publication in serial version.[38]

Behind her romantic hyperbole one can discern a shrewd young writer looking to cultivate a favourable position for herself in the popular literary marketplace and to advance her career by making the most of her connections.

In his discussion of Mansfield's literary output during this 1908–9 period, Antony Alpers speculates that she was suffering from a lack of direction in her writing:

> What did she *do* with all these pieces? [… Her friend] Margaret Wishart [...] recalled no rejections in London. […] She was a girl in a hostel writing things, struggling quite alone to discover a form, with no idea where to turn for the critical guidance that every young writer needs.[39]

There are certainly signs that Mansfield was in an experimental phase of writing during this time and that she may have had difficulty in adapting her material to appeal to a market outside her own inner circle. However, her early creative efforts were not altogether unsuccessful. For example, the poem 'October' (later renamed 'November') became Mansfield's first published work in England, appearing in the 'Table Talk' column of the *Daily News* on 3 November 1909.[40] 'October', which was dedicated to Mansfield's sister Vera Beauchamp (and sent to her as a birthday gift), was written on the date of Vera's birthday, 22 October 1908 – more than a year prior to its publication. Mansfield does not appear to have written it with the primary intention of submitting it to journals or newspapers. Yet the poem hardly seems suitable as a birthday gift, primarily due to its sombre, impersonal tone and its negative portrayal of London:

> The dead leaves fall, a silent, shivering cloud.
> Through the grey haze the carts loom heavy, gigantic
> Down the dull street … Children play in the gutter,
> Quarrel and cry; their voices are flat and toneless.[41]

Mansfield's relative inactivity in sending her work out to prospective publishers throughout 1908–9 does not necessarily support Alpers's description of her as a writer struggling to discover a sense of direction. Wishart insists that Mansfield wrote 'masses of short stories' while living at Beauchamp Lodge, none of which were submitted for publication.[42] However, this does not mean that she was a naïve and directionless aspiring author in need of a guiding light in the form of A. R. Orage, as Mansfield's focus was firmly fixed on the development of her musical 'performance pieces' rather than on short fiction or fictional sketches of the sort that would eventually launch her *New Age* career. In suggesting that Mansfield was a young woman plagued by feelings of uncertainty about the form that her work should take during this time, Alpers focuses exclusively on the short stories, ignoring Mansfield's enterprising engagement with the contemporary musical literary scene, to which she wished to contribute something 'sensational and new'.[43]

George Bowden: A teacher of singing and elocution

The final months of 1908 were turbulent, necessitating a period of transition for the young writer. Mansfield's relationship with Trowell came to an end in December, after which she discovered that she was pregnant with his child.

On 2 March 1909, Mansfield impulsively married music teacher George Bowden, only to leave him on the night of their wedding. She promptly returned to Trowell, who rejected her upon hearing of her recent marriage. Mansfield's relationship with Trowell had satisfied her both personally and professionally; it seems likely that her initial attraction to Bowden was driven by a similar interest in his position as a singing and elocution teacher, though her decision to marry him barely a month after their first meeting was, according to Kimber, 'solely to seek legitimacy for her unborn child'.[44] Finding herself pregnant and alone, Mansfield turned to the reputable music teacher in an attempt to restore some sense of social respectability to her situation. The turning point in Mansfield's life would come in May 1909 when Annie Beauchamp, concerned about her daughter's recent marriage and erratic sexual behaviour, sent Mansfield off to the spa town of Bad Wörishofen in Bavaria, where she later suffered a miscarriage. Her experiences as an enforced 'cure guest' at the Pension Müller between mid-June and the end of July 1909 provided the inspiration for the Bavarian sketches that would appear in *The New Age* the following year.

In December 1909, having spent the last six months in Germany, Mansfield returned to London and moved in with her 'husband of convenience', George Bowden.[45] Though their relationship at this stage was not a romantic one, the arrangement was favourable for Mansfield; Bowden provided a sense of stability that had been absent throughout the turbulent 1908–9 period of Mansfield's life, and his encouragement of her work would eventually lead to the writer's first association with an avant-garde periodical. The relationship also presented Mansfield with a platform to perform her own material in front of an audience. In his roles as vocal coach and elocution teacher, Bowden conducted musical concerts and delivered lectures to classes of men – many of whom were training to become church ministers – instructing them on how to strengthen their speaking voices. In his 'Biographical Note on Katherine Mansfield' (1947), Bowden makes several references to Mansfield's participation at these events:

> She [...] collaborated with me in a concert at one of the institutions at which I held a lectureship, delighting a large audience of college men and relatives and friends by her recital of some of her sketches.[46]
>
> Both in the little work she did with me and in the public recital of some of her own sketches given at one or two of my concerts, the use of her voice was quite unselfconscious.[47]
>
> K. M. talked freely of her writing and would show me what she was doing at the time. I did not, I think, see any of her earlier work of which, judging by her resources in the way of sketches for recital there must have been a good deal.[48]

The details of these events are scarce; Bowden's biographical piece offers no specific information on the number of recitals performed by Mansfield, nor does it provide the dates of these events. We do not know which of her sketches Mansfield selected for the performances. Nevertheless, Bowden's record offers an intriguing insight into Mansfield's short-lived, but fruitful, engagement with oral literary performance at this early stage of her career. Bowden's suggestion that she had a considerable number of sketches in reserve for these public recitals also reinforces Margaret Wishart's claim that Mansfield had been writing productively for a number of years, despite the relative absence of publications between 1908 and 1909.

Conclusion: The lasting impact of verse recitation on Mansfield

Less than a year before her death, Mansfield wrote a letter to Ida Baker expressing her desire to perform her work to large audiences: 'I intend, next Spring, to go to London, take the Bechstein Hall and give readings of my stories. I've always wanted to do this, and of course it would be a great advertisement.'[49] Her ambition to perform endured throughout her career, but it was during her first year as a twenty-year-old in London that she discovered a market for her performance pieces. From her turbulent relationship with Garnet Trowell to her misguided marriage to George Bowden, Mansfield surrounded herself with individuals who could facilitate her introduction into London's musical and literary performance spheres. Mansfield's participation in the emerging verse-recitation scene within London's literary marketplace shaped her literary output during this period; rather than producing works designed for publication in a journal or magazine, her late-1908 creative pieces were imitative of the wider culture with which she was engaging. The poems that Mansfield sent to Trowell in October and November 1908 ('In the Church', 'On the Sea Shore', 'The Lilac Tree', 'A Sad Truth', 'A Song of Summer' and 'The Winter Fire') were all conceived as performance pieces. As this chapter has shown, early biographers of Mansfield (such as Alpers) have often overlooked the seminal influence of verse recitation on her storytelling. Along with recent revisionist accounts by Kimber (2016) and Mourant (2019), this chapter stresses the importance and influence of Mansfield's early years as a writer, and argues that her engagements with London's artistic and cultural scenes between August 1908 and May 1909 – a period characterized by burgeoning live performance movements – certainly left their mark on her subsequent creative output.

Notes

1 The four-volume Edinburgh University Press edition of Mansfield's writings (which includes a complete collection of her fiction, from the first story written in 1898 to the final piece created in 1922), along with Gerri Kimber's *Early Years* biography, challenges this approach by emphasizing the significance of her pre-1910 work to her development as a writer. Chris Mourant's recent study of Mansfield's position within periodical culture also highlights the importance of her formative experiences with *Queen's College Magazine* (1904–5) and *The Native Companion* (1907) before going on to explore her engagements with *The New Age* in 1910–11.

2 In her introduction to *Katherine Mansfield and the Modernist Marketplace: At the Mercy of the Public* (Basingstoke: Palgrave Macmillan, 2010), Jenny McDonnell briefly mentions Mansfield's pre-1910 publications before going on to make *The New Age* the focus of her opening chapter. Similarly, Patrick D. Morrow opens *Katherine Mansfield's Fiction* (1993) with a selection of stories from *In a German Pension* (1911), with subsequent chapters following a chronological order. Selections of Mansfield's stories typically omit any work written or published before 1910 (beyond an occasional footnote reference).

3 McDonnell, pp. 34, 37.

4 Ida Baker, cited in Antony Alpers, *The Life of Katherine Mansfield* (New York: The Viking Press, 1980), p. 72.

5 Mansfield received a weekly allowance of forty shillings from her father which, according to Baker, was insufficient as it left her with only ten shillings each week after the rent had been paid. Mansfield was eventually forced to sell her cello for the small sum of £3 to support her income, of which Baker remarks in her book of memoirs: 'Her need must have been serious indeed for her to let this happen.' Interestingly, Mansfield denied the claim that financial pressures had forced her to sell the instrument, instead declaring to Baker that she had 'finally decided to be a writer instead of a musician' (Baker, p. 41). Describing the impact of Mansfield's hectic social life on her writing at this time, Baker states: 'She was constantly overwhelmed by the students, who would sit for hours on end in her room with or without invitation. She met undesirable men, and was unable to refuse invitations. [...] It was becoming increasingly impossible to get on with her task of writing.' In Ida Baker, *Katherine Mansfield: The Memories of LM* (London: Michael Joseph, 1971), p. 41.

6 *Letters* 1, p. 57.

7 *Letters* 1, pp. 80–1. To Garnet Trowell, 29 October 1908. The four poems that Mansfield attached to this letter were 'In the Church', 'On the Sea Shore', 'The Lilac Tree' and 'A Sad Truth'; all four were posthumously published in Miron Grindea, ed., *Adam International Review*, nos. 370–375 (1972–73).

8 C. K. Stead, *Answering to the Language: Essays on Modern Writers* (Auckland: University of Auckland Press, 1989), p. 170.

9 In a diary entry dated 21 October 1908, Mansfield wrote a detailed account of her short trip to Paris for a friend's wedding. This entry appears to have been written as a draft letter for Trowell, as she addresses the recipient: 'Observe me then dearest on the Newhaven platform' (CW4, pp. 94–7).
10 *Letters* 1, p. 80.
11 Ibid.
12 *Letters* 1, p. 83.
13 E. Douglas Bomberger, *MacDowell* (Oxford: Oxford University Press, 2013), p. 166. MacDowell was also an early student of the Venezuelan pianist Teresa Carreño, whom Mansfield greatly admired.
14 Arthur Wenk, *Claude Debussy and the Poets* (Berkeley: University of California Press, 1976), p. 5.
15 Katherine Mansfield, 'The Lilac Tree', in *Letters* 1, p. 82.
16 Debussy produced an orchestral composition entitled *Nocturnes* (or *Trois Nocturnes*) in 1899, having borrowed the term from the American artist James McNeill Whistler. Mansfield may have taken inspiration from Debussy's use of an artistic expression to describe his music, as she was also looking to combine elements of different artistic fields in her performance pieces.
17 *Letters* 1, p. 80.
18 Anon. 'Editor's Table', *The Strad*, 20, no. 237 (1 January 1910): 335.
19 Baker, p. 39. It is unclear whether Mansfield recited any of her own work during these early performances.
20 CW3, p. 3.
21 *Letters* 1, p. 84. To Garnet Trowell, 2 November 1908.
22 Mark S. Morrisson, *The Public Face of Modernism: Little Magazines, Audiences and Reception, 1905–1920* (Wisconsin: University of Wisconsin Press, 2001), pp. 64–5.
23 Ibid., p. 73.
24 Ibid., p. 64.
25 The Irish Literary Theatre closed in October 1901, staging seven productions in total: *The Countess Cathleen* (Yeats), *The Heather Field* (Edward Martyn), *The Bending of the Bough* (George Moore), *Maeve* (Martyn), *The Last Feast of the Fianna* (Alice Milligan), *Diarmuid and Grania* (Yeats and Moore) and *Casadh an t-Sugáin* (Douglas Hyde). The closure eventually led to the formation of the Abbey Theatre (the National Theatre of Ireland), which opened on 27 December 1904 with productions of *On Baile's Strand* and *Cathleen Ní Houlihan* by Yeats and *Spreading the News* by Lady Gregory.
26 Robert Hogan and Michael J. O'Neill, eds, *Joseph Holloway's Abbey Theatre: A Selection from his Unpublished Journal, 'Impressions of a Dublin Playgoer'* (Carbondale and Edwardsville: Southern Illinois University Press, 1967), p. 7. Irish architect Joseph Holloway (1861–1944) was responsible for designing the Abbey

Theatre prior to its 1904 opening and he would become one of its most faithful visitors, regularly attending plays and rehearsals over a fifty-year period. His critical comments and reviews of each performance are recorded in 221 volumes of his journals.

27 W. B. Yeats, 'Speaking to the Psaltery', in *Essays and Introductions* (London: Macmillan, 1961), pp. 13–27 (p. 18).

28 George Moore, 'The Irish Literary Theatre', in *Samhain*, ed. W. B. Yeats (Dublin: Sealy Bryers and Walker, 1901). Cited in Ronald Schuchard, *The Last Minstrels: Yeats and the Revival of the Bardic Arts* (Oxford: Oxford University Press, 2008), p. 38.

29 Ronald Schuchard, 'W. B. Yeats and the London Theatre Societies, 1901–1904', *The Review of English Studies*, 29, no. 116 (November 1978): 415–46 (p. 416).

30 Rebecca D'Monte, *British Theatre and Performance: 1900–1950* (London: Bloomsbury, 2015), p. 15.

31 Schuchard, *The Last Minstrels*, p. 257.

32 Morrisson, p. 56. By 1912, the Poetry Society had gained a reputation as an elitist group that offered favourable reviews to those who agreed to purchase advertising space in their associated newsletter, *The Poetical Gazette*. Morrisson's study offers a detailed analysis of the Society's exclusionary approach to poetry, and the complex ways in which aspiring experimental writers engaged with the group in order to expand their own readership. He identifies the popular poetry recitals of the founder of the Futurist movement, F. T. Marinetti, as an example of how the 'bourgeois principles [of the Poetry Society] could accommodate avant-garde poetic practices as well' (Morrisson, p. 71).

33 *Letters* 1, p. 64.

34 Baker, p. 39. It is also significant to note that Ezra Pound, who would become one of the principal figures of the early modernist movement, arrived in London in August 1908 – the same month as Mansfield. A close friend and outspoken admirer of Yeats, Pound provided regular contributions to *The New Age* between 1911 and 1922 (though he never appeared in the same issue as Mansfield). His ideas on the role of rhythm in poetry were central to the 1912 formation of the poetic movement Imagism, with one of its key principles being 'to compose in the sequence of the musical phrase, not in sequence of a metronome'. In F. S. Flint, 'Imagisme', *Poetry*, 1, no. 6 (March 1913), 198–200 (p. 199).

35 W. B. Yeats, 'An Introduction for my Plays', in *Essays and Introductions* (London: Macmillan, 1961), pp. 527–30 (p. 529).

36 Poems composed in the months following Mansfield's arrival in London include 'October' (September 1908), 'You ask me for a picture of my room', 'In the Church', 'On the Sea Shore', 'The Lilac Tree', 'A Sad Truth' (October 1908), 'The Winter Fire' (November 1908), 'Revelation' and 'The Trio' (December 1908). With the exception of 'October', all of these poems were unpublished at the time of her death.

37 Mansfield's letters to Trowell are sometimes reminiscent of her earlier correspondence with the editor of *The Native Companion*, E. J. Brady. On 17 September 1908, she told her lover: 'I shall send you what work I have; it's very little just now' (*Letters* 1, p. 61). A year before she sent this letter to Trowell, Mansfield wrote to Brady, 'I send you some more work – practically there is nothing local' (*Letters* 1, p. 26).

38 Claire Davison, 'Foreword', in Gerri Kimber, *Katherine Mansfield and the Art of the Short Story* (Basingstoke: Palgrave Macmillan, 2015), p. 2.

39 Alpers, p. 80.

40 Mansfield wrote this poem while living at Beauchamp Lodge but by the time of its publication she had been staying at the Pension Müller in Bavaria for six months.

41 Katherine Mansfield, 'October (To V.M.B)' in CW3, pp. 61–2.

42 Margaret Wishart, cited in Alpers, p. 77. It is impossible to determine the accuracy of Wishart's statement as she claims that Mansfield went on to destroy the majority of these short stories.

43 *Letters* 1, p. 84.

44 Gerri Kimber, '"That Pole outside our door": Floryan Sobieniowski and Katherine Mansfield', in *Katherine Mansfield and Continental Europe: Connections and Influences*, eds Janka Kascakova and Gerri Kimber (Basingstoke: Palgrave Macmillan, 2015), pp. 59–83 (p. 60).

45 CW1, p. 544.

46 George Bowden, 'A Biographical Note on Katherine Mansfield'. Alexander Turnbull Library, Wellington, New Zealand. qMS-0262, p. 14.

47 Bowden, p. 10.

48 Ibid., p. 12.

49 *Letters* 5, p. 160. To Ida Baker, 30 April 1922.

10

'From my life I write to you in your life'

Katherine Mansfield, Philip Larkin and Yiyun Li

Kathleen Jones

In the letters of Philip Larkin, Katherine Mansfield's name is one of those authors mentioned most frequently. His correspondent, friend and lover, Monica Jones, was amused to find how often 'a little of KM shakes a letter out of you to me'.[1] It was not so much the stories that fascinated Larkin, but Mansfield's life as recorded in her notebooks and letters. The legacy of a writer's autobiographical work – notebooks, journals and letters – is usually considered to be less important than their creative work as an influence on the literary output of other authors. Larkin's engagement with Mansfield's autobiographical writing has not been part of the critical discourse around his poetry or his fiction. Fascinated by Mansfield's life and her relationship with John Middleton Murry – a man he despised, in spite of his self-confessed identification with him – Larkin saw parallels with his own relationships and the way they were recorded. 'I shld like', he wrote, 'to look into this conversion of life-into-art-business, & also the Journal v. Stories business.'[2] Larkin kept a journal all his life, but we will never know how he approached the transformation from autobiography to poetry (what Anne Sexton called turning 'rats' into 'star'[3]), because most of his own journals were destroyed after his death. The letters are virtually all that we have.

A connection between a misanthropic English poet who died in 1985 and a contemporary Chinese novelist in the United States might seem unlikely, but the Chinese author Yiyun Li shared Larkin's obsession with Mansfield's life, first reading Mansfield's fiction as a student in Beijing. When she later emigrated to the West she found the Margaret Scott edition of Mansfield's notebooks in a second-hand bookshop in London. She herself had kept a journal from a very young age and in it she began to enter into a dialogue with Mansfield and to ask questions about the nature of autobiography, identity and belonging.

Shortly afterwards, quite by chance, Li also bought a copy of Larkin's *Letters to Monica* and was astonished to find frequent references to Mansfield. The duologue became a three-way conversation. Like Larkin, Li's own work has been influenced by Mansfield's letters and notebooks, and Li's autobiography *Dear Friend, from My Life I Write to You in Your Life*, published in 2017, draws heavily on the writing of both authors.

Mansfield's letters and notebooks have been influencing writers ever since Murry first published extracts from them shortly after her death in 1923. Murry was acting on an instinct that her life and how she lived it would be just as influential as her work. He was right. Mansfield herself was well aware of the intimate quality of diaries and letters, observing that, 'they breathe, they speak, they bring the person before you'.[4] They contained the 'nearness' that she was trying to achieve in her stories. Keeping a journal is part of almost every writer's daily routine – it is part of the 'life into art' transformation process. The writer is shaping their life onto the page as well as collecting impressions and emotions to hoard for later use, letting off steam and arguing things out with themselves. It was something that Mansfield was supremely good at. 'Nothing', she recorded, 'affords me the same relief'.[5]

Li writes,

> There are telling details from her journals, passing thoughts, gnawing pains, brilliant sentences that would later find places in her stories. My favourites are the expense lists: mostly entries for daily food, but unfailingly there are envelopes, letter paper, stamps, and sometimes telegrams, altogether more costly than food. Other small expenses I like to read about too – curtains, boot polish, hair pins, 'bill with sewing woman', 'safety pin for Jack', and 'laundry(!)'.[6]

She notes that it is this accumulation of everyday detail, what Mansfield called 'the life *in* the life of it',[7] that creates reality for the reader. It's a technique Li tries to replicate in her own stories, where her narrative structure closely follows Mansfield's.

Larkin's reaction to the notebooks was just the same. He was exposed to Mansfield's fiction while he was still at school. His father loved the stories and her work was on his parents' bookshelves alongside D. H. Lawrence and Aldous Huxley. The young Larkin also read Mansfield's letters in the highly edited Murry edition. At first he wasn't complimentary about her – 'Katherine Mansfield is a cunt', he wrote to his friend Jim Sutton, in his characteristically abrasive and profane style. He observed that she 'luxuriated in emotion far too much', adding: 'She's a woman & I'm a tied-up bugger, but anyone who can spew out their dearest and closest thoughts, hopes and loves to JM Murry must be a bit of an anus.'[8] Murry, a leading 'man of letters' during the 1930s, had, by the 1940s, become one of the most despised literary figures of the time, good for a bit of undergraduate ridicule. Larkin wrote an early bit of unflattering doggerel which begins:

> We're Middleton Murry & Somerset Maugham
> Vive la compagnie!
> We both try to write in a 'spiritual form',
> Vive la compagnie![9]

During his time at Oxford Larkin read the Ruth Mantz biography, published in 1933, although he was not to know how heavily this had been influenced by Murry. This censored and sentimentalized narrative of Mansfield's early life 'endeared' her to Larkin, 'being in a similar condition of mental struggles myself'. He admits that he would like to read her letters again, and more significantly that he 'share[s] a hell of a lot of common characteristics with her'.[10] This is quite an admission. But the Mansfield that Larkin liked was the one who was sharp, capable of saying sarcastic things at parties, the girl who didn't give a damn – except in private – the Mansfield who, in 1916, snatched Lawrence's work from the hands of his critics and marched out of the Café Royal triumphant. Since Larkin refers to them, it also seems that he read Mansfield's notebooks, in the early Murry edition, though there's no indication of the date, and that he also read Murry's autobiography, *Between Two Worlds,* which had been published in 1936.

Experiments in fiction

In the beginning, Larkin stated that his ambition was to write fiction. 'The writing of novels has always been my ultimate ambition',[11] he told his first publisher, admitting that he wanted to be a novelist, 'in a way I never wanted to be a poet'.[12] He began at Oxford when he was only nineteen and his first novel *Jill* was written while he was still an undergraduate and published in 1946.

The protagonist of *Jill* is a young man called John, a working-class boy, out of his social depth at Oxford, whose story bears a strong resemblance to Murry's account of his undergraduate experience in *Between Two Worlds*. John is clumsy and inept in his relationships with women, and is writing a novel which involves the invention of a fifteen-year-old sister called Jill, who is at boarding school, and the construction of her fictional journal and letters as well as the inclusion of a complete short story. The hero then, by a tremendous coincidence, meets a fifteen-year-old girl called Jill in real life, but she turns out not to be the same person as his fantasy after all. You can't help being reminded of Murry's 're-invention' of Mansfield after her death – something Larkin had strong opinions about.

Larkin's second published novel *A Girl in Winter* made its appearance in 1947 and features a girl called Katherine, who has come to England to live, though we learn very little about her origins, though her grandfather, like Katherine Mansfield's ancestor, was a silversmith. The novel was, by Larkin's own admission, an exploration of loneliness and social isolation. Katherine has a relationship with a young man that has been constructed mainly by the exchange of letters. The name and the broad circumstances can't be a total coincidence.

How do we quantify the influence of one writer on another? A few echoes, a sense of engagement, a series of intertextual links, a self-confessed involvement? Since Larkin was reading so much of Mansfield at the time it's impossible not to make connections. Larkin admitted that in his novels he was trying to write 'poetic prose' in the style of Mansfield, with the same depth of observation. He wrote to his friend Jim Sutton that he wanted to write with that 'double-distilled purity of essence-of-Mansfield'.[13]

James Booth, Larkin's colleague at Hull for seventeen years, and literary adviser to the Philip Larkin Society, talks about this in his biography of Larkin quoting a section from Larkin's second novel as an example of this kind of writing:

> From the stone facades pigeons fluttered down on to the pavements and waddled uneasily about, casting a wary eye at him, but he paid no attention to them. The wind blew and a whole wall of ivy danced in the sun, the leaves blowing back to show their white undersides. So in him a thousand restlessnesses yearned and shook.[14]

To emphasize the point, Larkin quotes Mansfield's notebooks, in one of his letters, as an example of what he is trying to achieve: 'On the wall of the kitchen there was a shadow, shaped like a little mask with two gold slits for eyes. It danced up and down'. That sentence, 'or pair of sentences', he writes, 'about the shadow on the wall seems to me to contain such a lot; the suggestion of a gaiety, sinister because heartless, at the very centre of life – yet only a mask! What looks through it is still a mystery'.[15]

Larkin began to change his mind about Mansfield's fiction writing when he reread her letters and diaries in new editions and discussed them, and the stories, in detail with his friend and lover Monica Jones. Mansfield, as a writer, is now in Larkin's opinion better than Virginia Woolf who is 'wooden and dead' by comparison. But although he has come to admire her fiction, Larkin declares that he would still rather 'read her journals etc than many of the stories'.[16] 'Her effect on me', he writes, 'was visionary [...] the world glowed with imparted radiance'.[17] He also admires her 'vivid exultance'.[18]

Interrogating the self

With a personal journal, there is always the issue of truth. It can be argued that a journal is written as a dialogue with the writer's own self and so can be relied on to be more truthful, but Woolf famously said that no one writes a journal without being aware of the 'supposed reader' looking over their shoulder.[19] Journal keepers lie, dissemble and disguise. Larkin was prepared to believe that Mansfield was writing truth when she recorded her thoughts and feelings. His friend Monica Jones had a different opinion. 'I know too much about that kind of writing-in-a-diary. [...] I know when she's writing the truth & when she's making it up, I've done it all myself.'[20]

Needing certainty, Li also feels an obligation to look for truth. Although she acknowledges that 'all people lie, in their writing as much as in their lives', she holds on to what she knows is 'an unrealistic belief: there is some irrefutable truth in each mind, and the truth is told without concealment or distortion in a letter or in a journal entry'.[21] Li finds Mansfield's truth in shopping lists and small domestic details, also discussing the self-reflective aspects of reading autobiographical texts. 'Our admiration and scrutiny of another person reflect what we love and hate to see in ourselves.'[22] When Li read in Mansfield's notebooks that 'she loved Chekhov so much she wanted to adopt a Russian baby and name him Anton, her emotional transparency embarrassed me. I felt the urge to laugh because I was terrified to recognise even a residue of myself in her.'[23]

Li, reading Larkin's letters alongside Mansfield's journals and letters, noticed that Larkin had also begun to interrogate his own life through Mansfield's.[24] In a letter to Monica Jones he admits:

> KM's Journal can hardly help arousing questions within oneself of a disagreeable nature.
>
> Q. What is your aim in life?
>
> A. Oo- ah–
>
> Q. Ten years ago you were determined 'to write', weren't you?

A. Yes.
Q. What's happened to that determination?

Larkin can only provide evasive answers to the questions he imagines Mansfield asking, ending 'Oh go and boil yr head'.[25]

Some of the questions that Mansfield's notebooks posed, for Larkin, were about his relationships with women. A lot of Mansfield's problems, Larkin commented, were brought about by 'loving [. . .] a slippery emotional character like Murry, who played up to all her all-for-love-two-children-holding-hands line of talk but was quite content to live apart from her and indeed found actual cohabitation with her a bit of a strain'.[26] He admits in letters to friends that some of the things he hated in Murry were characteristics that Larkin shared with him, particularly the inability to cohabit with someone. 'To read KM's dreams of a shared life with Murry – this perturbs me greatly [...]. To live quietly and complementarily with another would be extraordinary – almost impossible.'[27]

Reading Mansfield's journals not only made Larkin re-examine his life and question his own creativity but they also inspired him:

> She is one of the few people [. . .] who set things moving, swinging, quietly, harmoniously, inside one, as if some thaw was taking place. And again it makes you dreadfully miserable, since you apprehend life more keenly and since you know (or I know) that she's so far ahead in unselfish observation and transcription.[28]

Mansfield's notebooks unsettled Larkin and left him with conflicting emotions, perhaps because he was confronted, not only by her skill at translating everyday events into art but also by her dedication to self-improvement. He measured himself against that dedication and found himself wanting.[29]

Transforming life into art

In 1954, reading Murry's new 'Definitive' edition of Mansfield's *Journal* Larkin is struck, like Li, by her perceptions of the world around her and by the fact that Mansfield felt 'not only an artistic obligation to record them, but a moral obligation to "live up to" them'. He was referring back to Mansfield's statement: 'To me life and work are two things indivisible. It's only by being true to life that I can be true to art.'[30] Monica Jones argued that this was Mansfield self-dramatizing, but Larkin thought differently. 'It reads to me more like the ordinary reaction of any person who sees anything beautiful [...] to struggle towards a state of mind in which such perceptions would be more common, and in which they would be of some practical use.' He adds that 'I am quite sure nobody has ever written to touch her, not even Lawrence'. And that, coming from Larkin was quite an accolade. Larkin went further. 'I shd like to look into this conversion of life-into-art business & also the Journal v Stories business.'[31] For him these are the important issues about Mansfield. The stories, he argues, are less successful than her autobiographical writing, though it has to be noted that he was not a fan of the short story form in general. 'I think a short story should be either a poem or a novel. Unless it's just an anecdote.'[32]

Larkin, in thinking about this 'life into art' business, put his finger on exactly why Mansfield is such a great writer:

> She was enormously aware of things unquestionably more pure, more significant, more beautiful than she was herself & of the problem of translating them by means of art, by catching hold of their tiny significant manifestations. [...] This seems to me to depend enormously on the fact that she did not distinguish between life and art. [...] You have to think like that to be a writer, just as you have to believe your soap is the best in the world if you're a soap-seller. [...] If you don't believe that good art is better than bad life, then bugger off.[33]

Larkin may even have been thinking about Mansfield when he wrote the last lines of his poem *An Arundel Tomb:* 'Time has transfigured them into/Untruth. [...] The stone fidelity/They hardly meant/' has come to prove 'our almost instinct almost true:/ that what remains of us, is love'.[34] It is difficult to read that without thinking of Mansfield's words in that final letter to Murry: 'No other lovers have walked the earth together more joyfully, in spite of all.'[35] Larkin was struck by that letter when he first read it, and it remained in his memory. He quoted it in one of his own and commented that it was written on the day before he was born.[36] Larkin's lines in *An Arundel Tomb* read like a cynical response to the public illusion of perfect relationship that death seems to create. He was scathing about love – this is from one of his unpublished poems: 'In our family/Love was disgusting as lavatory./And not as necessary.'[37] Larkin was continually irritated by the portrayal of Mansfield and Murry's relationship as pure and true. 'There is something suspect about it', he observed, 'it's perfect, & therefore untrue.'[38]

Larkin eventually gave up writing fiction for publication towards the end of 1949. 'Novels', he wrote, 'are about other people, and poems are about yourself. I didn't know enough about other people, I didn't like them enough.'[39] We will never know how he approached the 'life into art business' because all except one of his adult journals were destroyed after he died by friends who wanted to protect his reputation. Apart from a juvenile diary, the only one that survives concerns his holidays with Monica Jones, begun in 1967 and running to three hundred pages. It is in the form of a conversation, with entries by Jones and responses by Larkin sometimes being written on facing pages. This is ironic, since Larkin became 'increasingly impatient' of holidays, as he grew older, writing that 'they seem a wholly feminine conception, based on an impotent dislike of everyday life and a romantic notion that it will all be better at Frinton or Venice'.[40] It seems fitting that the only journal of his to survive describes his holidays with the woman he spent his life with, but could never quite decide to marry.

Place and identity

Larkin died when Li was thirteen years old and still at school in Beijing. She studied sciences at Peking University and in 1996 – ten years after Larkin's death – she came to the United States as an immunologist. It wasn't until 2003 that her first short story was published in the *New Yorker* and she began to study for an MFA degree in Creative Non-Fiction and Fiction. Her first collection of short stories, *A Thousand Years of Good Prayers*, was published in 2005, to great acclaim, and she was compared by reviewers to Chekhov and Alice Munro. Li went on to become professor of Creative Writing at Princeton University. In 2012, after a breakdown, she decided to spend a year reading memoirs, journals and biographies because she found them comforting.

In her hotel room, Li read Mansfield's notebooks over and over again. She was riveted by them and, like Larkin, regarded Mansfield's writings on creativity and the process of writing as some of her most important work. As Li read the notebooks, she began to see a parallel between herself and that other girl who came to the West from a foreign country desperate to write, both of them exiles, journal keepers, letter writers, authors of short stories. The identification was so strong that she underlined passages in the notebooks and afterwards wondered, 'Are they her thoughts or mine?'[41] She noted the difference between Mansfield's 'cool, at times cruel, command in her short stories', and the 'unrestrained wildness' in her letters and notebooks.[42] Li found that the latter presented her with a dilemma.

> I would prefer to distrust her. But it would be dishonest not to acknowledge the solace of reading them. Not having the exact language for the bleakness I felt, I devoured her words like thirst quenching poison. Is it possible that one can be held hostage by someone else's words?[43]

Her memoir *Dear Friend, from My Life I Write to You in Your Life* came out of this experience, written after a period of suicidal despair and hospitalization. She describes it as a period of self-interrogation, and the memoir is not so much a straightforward autobiographical text, as an exploration of her own creativity through the medium of other writers' lives, including Mansfield and Larkin. The title is a line from one of Mansfield's early attempts at the novel, the story of Rewa, in Notebook 1 of the Margaret Scott edition, and continues, 'and yet it seems that we never meet on any definite ground, that I found you in the borders of Noman's Land, that our hands met and knew each other there',[44] which seems to encapsulate what every creative writer does – they send out a letter from their own lives to those of their readers, a connecting thread they hope will be grasped in friendship.

The first part of the memoir consists of fragments from Li's journal, which she has kept since she was at school. For Li, 'the Journal was – and remains – a long argument with myself: a lucid voice questioning judiciously, and a more forceful voice speaking defiantly, sometimes in reply, other times in digression'.[45] There are brutal, fundamental questions. Why write? Why live? As the narrative develops into longer passages of reflection, she explores her relationships with her homeland, her family, with literature and the process of integration into American society. The structure she adopts echoes the fragmented, collage-like texture of Mansfield's notebooks.

Like Mansfield, Li has a problem with belonging. She had abandoned her own culture for a European life, eventually settling in the United States. For Li it has to be an absolute abandonment, 'done with such determination it is a kind of suicide'. She refuses attachment. 'To own – a house, a life on a quiet street, a language, a dream – is to allow oneself to be owned too.'[46] She feels that she no longer belongs anywhere and quotes another favourite author, the Irish John McGahern, with envy: 'The people and the language and landscape where I had grown up were like my breathing.' She longs to feel that, but, '[the] paths I walked by myself in Beijing are gone. Even if the city had remained unchanged, I have turned away from the people and the language and the landscape.'[47] But, like Mansfield's renunciation of New Zealand, Li remains haunted by her homeland, though she considers the word 'claustrophobic and insincere'. She points out the etymology of the word 'haunt', with its origins in the word 'home'. 'When we feel haunted, it is the pull of our old home we're experiencing', and she acknowledges the possibility that 'the past has become homeless, and we are offering it a place to inhabit in the present'.[48]

Also like Mansfield, Li has a problem with identity. She is Chinese, American, a writer, a scientist, a daughter, a sister, a mother, a wife, a friend, an exile, a depressive, a survivor, charting a passage through her life dragging them all in her wake. Mansfield was aware of her own 'difference' throughout her life in Europe. She was the 'little colonial' who could never quite belong, the 'hotel proprietor' with a hundred and one identities. Both Mansfield and Li had been desperate to leave the countries of their birth, but both suffered feelings of fragmentation and alienation in their adopted habitations. Li abandoned her language and her culture, writing only in English, leaving her journals and letters behind in Beijing. Mansfield, on the other hand, felt compelled to revisit New Zealand in prose, re-creating her homeland in fiction. Exile, with its distance and unique perspective, has played a big part in both their works, both fictional and autobiographical.

Another New Zealand writer, Janet Frame, pointed out that all writers are exiles, wherever they may live, and spend their whole lives on a long journey, writing themselves back to an unnamed 'lost land'.[49] Perhaps this is because creative writers have to stand outside their own experience and look at it objectively in order to write about it. They are always trying to get back to the 'lost land', those moments experienced and gone, at the core of their imaginative lives. Edward Said went further, in his memoir *Out of Place*, claiming that every author is involved in making 'a home of words' to dwell in.[50] Journal or notebook-keeping is part of this process of building not only a space to inhabit creatively but also an identity, snatching meaning from fleeting moments, giving permanence to thoughts and feelings by putting them down on paper, forming a mirror image of the person wielding the pen. It is a kind of literary 'selfie' – a form of photography that Larkin was addicted to.

Larkin was also given to disowning the place of his birth and upbringing. In 1954 he wrote a poem called 'I Remember, I Remember', which describes the poet and a friend on a train that stops unexpectedly in Coventry station. The friend observes '"You look as if you wished the place in Hell"', and Larkin responds: '"I suppose it's not the place's fault," I said./"Nothing, like something, happens anywhere"'.[51] Larkin also wrote an essay, 'Not the Place's Fault', which is a companion piece to the poem, although not so satirical in tone.[52] He describes his childhood in Coventry, his family, early reading and friendships, the lack of girls and the beginning of his life as a writer. It is a fascinating reflection that suggests he could have been 'a candidly emotional and autobiographical writer', rather than one who disguised any self-reference and jeered at his own pretensions. Larkin later refused to have this essay reprinted, telling Faber editor

Charles Monteith that 'in some curious way that [essay] exposes more of me than I want exposed, although heaven knows there is nothing scandalous in it'.[53] He also refused to let Blake Morrison include it in *Required Writing: Miscellaneous pieces 1955–1982*, telling him that 'I think I said just a little more about myself than I really want known'.[54] Larkin later left ambiguous instructions in his will that allowed his former secretary and lover, Betty Mackereth, to feed his diaries and journals (more than thirty of them) into a paper shredder as instructed by Monica Jones. Only one early notebook has been preserved, from his early years in Coventry as well as the travel diary shared with Jones, post-1967, as already noted.

Conversations with the 'other'

For Li, brought up and educated in China, journal writing had an unusual difficulty – the problem of the 'I' word. She admits that she hates it. 'The moment that "I" enters my narrative my confidence crumbles.' In the Chinese language, the 'I' word is not often used and under the Maoist regime such individualism was not encouraged. It was usual to use the impersonal pronoun, or to use 'we'. In China, Li observes, 'Living is not an original business.'[55]

Li explores the reasons why we're so fascinated by writers' lives. In letters and journals, she explains, we enter into a conversation with this 'other' who then becomes, Li warns, falsely familiar. When we read Mansfield's private words, she writes: 'When we experience her most vulnerable moments with her, and when her words speak more eloquently of our feelings than we are able to', she speaks to us as a friend.[56] But such familiarity is deceptive; we can never really 'know' this 'other' through their writing. According to Li, the reading of autobiography, like the writing of it, is self-reflective: 'Our admiration and scrutiny of another person reflects what we love and hate to see in ourselves.'[57] There's an identification, a transference. She observes that Larkin, '[in] analysing Mansfield's life and love affairs' was 'talking about himself'.[58] But so is Li.

She finds herself arguing with both of them, defending Mansfield against Larkin's accusations, sometimes disagreeing with Larkin's defence of Mansfield against other critics:

> I was aware that my obsession with them reflected what I resent in myself: seclusion, self-deception, and above all the need – the neediness – to find shelter from one's uncertain self in other lives. For Mansfield, it was Chekhov; for Larkin, it was Mansfield and Hardy.[59]

Finding Mansfield's notebooks was a life-changing moment for Li. She was staying in a hotel in London, depressed and unsure where her life was going and she gave herself up to reading, hardly leaving her room:

> For a while I read them to distract myself. 'Dear friend, from my life I write to you in your life', [...]. I cried when I read the line [...] It reminds me why I do not want to stop writing. The books one writes – past and present and future – are they not trying to say the same thing?

'What a long way it is from one life to another', she observes, 'yet why write if not for that distance'?[60] It's a long way from Beijing to the United States, from a life in China to a life in America. It's impossible not to suspect that the 'Dear Friend' Li writes to is her other self, an attempt to bridge that distance with words, just as Mansfield tried to draw New Zealand to her with her pen, a country which was at times 11,500 miles too far away.

Li destroyed most of her own journals and letters before she left China. Others she put in sealed boxes and has never opened them. 'One crosses the border', she says, 'to become a new person.'[61] That person speaks a new language that takes on new meanings, which gives her work a unique voice. But in renouncing the mother-tongue, a great deal gets erased from memory. This loss, she admits, 'is my sorrow and my selfishness'.[62] Mansfield recognized, late in her brief career, how essential such connections can be for a writer. 'One reaps the glittering top of the field, but there are no sheaves to bind', adding, 'I think the only way to live as a writer is to draw upon one's real familiar life'.[63] Mansfield also intended her unpublished work to be destroyed, leaving an ambiguous request in her last letter to Murry which he, fortunately for posterity, decided to interpret in a way that allowed everything, even the smallest fragments, to be preserved. Larkin, too, decided, as he lay dying, to erase the record of a life. He asked Monica Jones to destroy his journals. Betty Mackereth, his secretary and occasionally also his lover, who carried out the request, resisted the temptation to read them as she fed them into the shredder, but later said that the 'little bits and pieces' she had glimpsed as she tore them apart, were 'very unhappy. Desperate, really'.[64] Li, glancing back at both Larkin and Mansfield, comments that 'one always knows best how to sabotage one's own life'.[65]

Larkin may well have blamed his upbringing for the decisions he made as an adult and his inability to make close personal relationships. The poem which begins: 'They fuck you up, your mum and dad. / They may not mean to, but they do',[66] certainly seems to suggest this. Mansfield blamed herself for her mistakes, laying them before the reader with forensic clarity, like a prosecuting counsel.

'Let me take the case of K.M. She has led, ever since she can remember, a very typically false life.'[67] Her notebooks are littered with rigorous self-examination and recrimination. 'Am I ever free from the sense of guilt even? Never.'[68] Terminally ill, desperate for better health and time to complete her work, she continued to travel incessantly, expending what little strength she had left. Her life, too, could be seen as a succession of little acts of self-sabotage. But Mansfield's gift was to create, from this flawed and difficult life, recorded in notebooks and letters, an extraordinary body of work, and to leave, for both readers and other writers, a glimpse of the creative process that produced it.

Notes

1 Philip Larkin, *Letters to Monica*, ed. Anthony Thwaite (London: Faber & Faber, 2010), p. 127n, 3 November 1954.

2 Larkin, *Letters to Monica*, p. 126, 6 November 1954.

3 Anne Sexton, 'An Obsessive Combination of Ontological Inscape, Trickery and Love', *No Evil Star: Selected Essays, Interviews, and Prose*, ed. Steven E. Colburn (Michigan: University of Michigan Press, 1985), frontispiece.

4 *Notebooks* 2, p. 282.

5 Yiyun Li, *Dear Friend, from My Life I Write to You in Your Life* (London: Penguin Random House, 2017), p. 149.

6 Ibid., p. 129.

7 *Letters* 1, p. 192, 17 May 1915.

8 Philip Larkin, *Selected Letters*, ed. Anthony Thwaite (London: Faber & Faber, 1993), Larkin to Sutton, p. 17.

9 Philip Larkin, '(from the back)\ We're Middleton Murry & Somerset Maugham', *The Complete Poems*, ed. Archie Burnett (London: Faber & Faber, 2012), p. 879.

10 Larkin, *Selected Letters*, Larkin to Sutton, p. 35.

11 Larkin, *Selected Letters*, p. 137, Larkin to Alan Pringle, 4 March 1947.

12 Philip Larkin, *Required Writing: Miscellaneous Pieces 1955–1982* (London: Farrar, Straus, Giroux, 1984), p. 63.

13 James Booth, *Philip Larkin: Life, Art and Love* (London: Bloomsbury, 2014), p. 96.

14 Philip Larkin, *Jill* (New York: The Overlook Press, 1984), p. 97.

15 Larkin, *Letters to Monica*, p. 126, 6 November 1954.

16 Larkin, *Letters to Monica*, p. 60, 6 October 1951.

17 Larkin, *Letters to Monica*, p. 57, 15 September 1951.

18 Larkin, *Letters to Monica*, p. 98, 24 June 1953.

19 Virginia Woolf, *A Passionate Apprentice*, ed. Mitchell A. Leaska (London: The Hogarth Press, 1990), p. 144.

20 Larkin, *Letters to Monica*, p. 127, 3 November 1954.
21 Li, p. 76.
22 Ibid., p. 75.
23 Ibid.
24 Ibid., p. 123.
25 Larkin, *Letters to Monica*, pp. 124–5, 30 October 1954.
26 Larkin, *Letters to Monica*, p. 62, 6 October 1951.
27 Ibid.
28 Larkin, *Letters to Monica*, p. 124, 30 October 1954.
29 Larkin, *Letters to Monica*, p. 125, 30 October 1954.
30 *Letters* 4, p. 170, late January 1921.
31 Larkin, *Letters to Monica*, p. 126, 6 November 1954.
32 Larkin, *Required Writing*, p. 66.
33 Larkin, *Letters to Monica*, p. 125, 30 October 1954.
34 Larkin, 'An Arundel Tomb', *The Complete Poems*, p. 101.
35 *Letters* 5, p. 235, 7 August 1922.
36 Larkin, *Letters to Monica*, p. 125, 30 October 1954.
37 Larkin, 'On Being Twenty-Six', *The Complete Poems*, p. 405.
38 Larkin, *Letters to Monica*, p. 58, 15 September 1951.
39 Larkin, *Required Writing*, p. 63.
40 Philip Larkin, 'Not the Place's Fault', (essay) *Umbrella Magazine*, 1, no. 3 (1959): pp. 107–12.
41 Li, p. 149.
42 Ibid., p. 100.
43 Ibid., p. 149.
44 *Notebooks* 1, p. 222.
45 Li, p. 24.
46 Ibid., p. 140.
47 Ibid., p. 50.
48 Ibid., p. 82.
49 Janet Frame, *The Envoy from Mirror City* (London: Harper Collins, 1993), p. 166.
50 Kirsty Gunn, *My Katherine Mansfield Project* (Devon: Notting Hill Editions, 2015), p. 57.
51 Philip Larkin, 'I Remember, I Remember', *The Less Deceived* (London: Marvell Press, 1956).
52 Larkin, 'Not the Place's Fault', pp. 107–12.
53 'Phillip [*sic*] Larkin in Umbrella Magazine', Coventry Arts Umbrella Club Archive, 13 June 2011, https://coventryartsumbrella.blogspot.com/2011/06/not-places-fault-phillip-larkin-in.html (accessed 4 May 2019).

54 Andrew Motion, *A Writer's Life – Philip Larkin* (London: Faber & Faber, 1993), pp. 500–1.
55 Li, p. 27.
56 Ibid., p. 75.
57 Ibid.
58 Ibid., p. 133.
59 Ibid.
60 Ibid., p. 20.
61 Ibid., p. 143.
62 Ibid., p. 25.
63 *Letters* 5, p. 80, March 1922.
64 John Banville, 'Homage to Philip Larkin', *New York Review of Books*, 23 February 2006.
65 Li, p. 25.
66 Philip Larkin, 'This Be the Verse', *Collected Poems* (New York: Farrar, Straus and Giroux, 2001).
67 *Notebooks* 2, p. 288.
68 *Notebooks* 2, p. 238.

11

'An intellectual comradeship'

A reassessment of the relationship between George Bowden and Katherine Mansfield

Gerri Kimber

Biographies of Katherine Mansfield have not always been kind to her first husband, George Bowden (1877–1975). In some he is almost portrayed as a figure of ridicule, and his – admittedly brief – walk-on part in her life is seen as more of a footnote to an otherwise salacious story of unwanted pregnancies, double-crossings and shady Polish émigrés.

Bowden's full account of his relationship with Mansfield, written in the 1940s, some thirty years after the events it describes, and following a request by American researcher Lucy O'Brien, offers more or less the only evidence for what occurred between them, since Mansfield herself left almost no trace of her 'camping ground',[1] as she termed it, for the years 1909–10. All recent biographies have made use of Bowden's written account, but not the fascinating correspondence surrounding his writing of it. Mostly held in Texas, these documents offer a wealth of further information which enables us to revise our understanding of Mansfield's life during this period, as well as offering an opportunity to reappraise Bowden's own character. His candid responses to a series of questions presented to him over a number of letters and over several decades reveal a man who perhaps deserves more attention in biographies of Mansfield than he has previously received, and more credit for telling the truth, as he saw it. As he himself wrote in a letter in 1947: 'K.M. and I enjoyed a happy if short intellectual comradeship.'[2] It is just this sense of comradeship that is the focus of this chapter.

Born in 1877, Bowden was admitted as a choral scholar to King's College, Cambridge, in 1899, at the age of twenty-two, receiving his BA degree in 1902. After leaving Cambridge he became a lecturer on voice production and a teacher of singing, first in England and later in America. Bowden's second wife (after Mansfield) was Annie Frances Moore (known as Dina) and they were married on 22 March 1919 in Berkeley, California. She was twenty-five, and Bowden forty-one at the time of their marriage. He had gone to the United States in 1915 and taught music at the University of California in Berkeley from 1915 to 1918. He then moved to New York in 1918 and met Dina, who was studying music there. They spent nearly all of their married life in Mallorca, Spain, moving to the Isle of Man during the war, as there was a general fear that Mussolini would take over Mallorca. They would go on to have one son and three grandchildren.

First-hand accounts of Bowden in America given to O'Brien reveal that when he taught music appreciation at Berkeley all the students 'thought he was sort of peculiar. [... They] would come late to class and then get up in the middle of his lecture and walk out. [...] He was dressed like an Englishman of that period. He wore spats and carried a cane, had pink cheeks, and was rather short.'[3] His wife had first been introduced to him in California, but it was only on meeting him again in New York that their relationship took off. Dina's wealthy parents were initially opposed to the marriage because of the age gap, the fact that he had been previously married, that he was a music teacher and didn't earn much, plus his being a foreigner. Nevertheless, the objections were overcome, and the couple would go on to live on Dina's inheritance.

On 17 November 1947, George Bowden wrote a letter to John Middleton Murry, explaining that an American woman (O'Brien) had recently been in contact with him, in preparation for a new biography of Katherine Mansfield. Writing from his home in Mallorca, he explained that he had

> tried to describe our meeting and the milieu which for a brief period K. M. shared with me.
>
> I hope I have succeeded in giving an objective and dispassionate account of her and our relations as these appeared to me at the time, up to the break 'with the realisation of an incompatibility which made married life between us impossible'.[4]

However, Bowden was concerned when he discovered that O'Brien had sent him a series of questions, basing her knowledge on the depiction of himself as portrayed in Ruth Elvish Mantz's early biography of Mansfield from 1933, which she had co-written with Murry. Following its publication, Bowden had written to Murry expressing his disquiet, and Murry had agreed that the offending passage should be withdrawn. As with most promises Murry made, however, nothing actually happened. Bowden makes only the briefest of appearances in the volume and indeed is described in unflattering and derogatory terms. Given the importance Bowden attached to the offending section of the book, it is worth quoting in full:

> [Katherine] would become calm and cool and calculating. She would marry somebody who would respect her right to be an artist, who would stand between her and life, and secure to her the calm which she now believed to be necessary for creation. After all, that was what other women seemed to her to have done, or had had done for them; was not such a calm established – she did not guess with what toil and long-suffering – around a famous woman-poet with whom, and with whose family, she now came slightly into contact? And she came into contact with it by means of a man she had met in the musical circles of St. John's Wood. He was eminently fitted to be the link between the genuine Bohemianism of the professionals of Carlton Hill and the decorous combination of art and complete respectability which had been achieved in the famous family to which he introduced her. He was, indeed, a professional musician; a singer and a teacher of singing – but he had advanced into the profession by the flowery path of a choral scholarship at Cambridge. He had education and refinement; he was the gentleman-artist with the bedside manner, of the type afterwards depicted with subtle understanding in Mr. Reginald Peacock's Day. And he was, indubitably, like Mr. Peacock, an idealist, and, in particular, as it was almost an article of faith in the famous family, an idealist about women.
>
> He had, no doubt, a genuine respect for Katherine's talent; and perhaps he may have dreamed that he, with her, might found another such illustrious family, with another such centre of art and adoration in its midst. At any rate he offered Katherine homage – he spoke lavishly of 'laying himself at the feet of her genius' – and apparent security. In her weariness and disillusion, her desire to escape the exhaustions of Beauchamp Lodge, she suddenly accepted the offer, and married him in the spring of 1909. She was dressed all in black, with Ida Baker for her only attendant. Within a few days she had left him. Idealism about women at close quarters was not at all the refuge she had allowed herself to dream.[5]

It rightly irked Bowden that O'Brien was still using this unflattering, uninformed and at times erroneous paragraph as the basis for her understanding of his relationship with Mansfield, and as a result was prompted to write his own definitive account of his relationship with Mansfield.

In a letter to O'Brien dated 14 November 1947, Bowden wrote:

> The story of K. M.'s private life at the time as told in the Mantz-Murry book came as a complete surprise to me. And its version of our relations was such a travesty that I wrote to both publisher and author protesting against its highly imaginative imputations regarding myself. The reply was to the effect that it

> would be withdrawn, but the Spanish and World wars intervening I have never followed it up.
>
> K. M and I enjoyed a happy if short intellectual comradeship, but the marriage was not given a chance. She did not live at the flat at all and why she accepted an offer made in good faith was a mystery to me. I knew so little of her friends that except for the account I have already given you I should have to rely largely on conjecture, and that has no place in your biography.
>
> As to the divorce, though I asked her if she wanted it and the necessary arrangements were made before I left for America in '12, she appeared to be indifferent, and I imagine the unconventional way of life was in keeping with her ideas at that time. The fact that it was not completed for several years was due solely to this seeming indifference, my own preoccupation with life in the States and the war of '14-18.[6]

Bowden also enclosed copies of all his correspondence with Constable and Murry over his objection to the Mantz-Murry volume.

Indeed, Murry's initial response to Bowden, written on 29 November 1933, had certainly been conciliatory, offering to withdraw the offending passage immediately, admitting that he 'had no first-hand knowledge of these matters'.[7] Bowden wrote back on 5 December 1933, thanking Murry and repeating that 'it is not merely the implied reflection on myself, but the lack of accuracy both actual and tacit, which is my title to objection'. He then went on to admit:

> For a masculine figure in her foreground, with such security as might go with it, (more apparent than real in my case, I fear, and her allowance was almost worse for her than nothing), she found in me a congenial and sympathetic response to her literary enthusiasm and ambitions.[8]

Murry himself had also been corresponding with O'Brien since early 1946 and had sold her some precious Mansfield manuscripts to fund his acquisition of some farming equipment. On 19 February 1947, in response to a letter of O'Brien's requesting more information on Bowden, he had replied thus: 'I know extremely little about the man to whom Katherine Mansfield was married. The few facts I do know are these: His name was Bowden, he had been a choral scholar of King's College Cambridge [...] and he was a professional teacher of singing when Katherine met him'. He then tantalizingly added: 'I do in fact know a little more about him, but that I must not divulge to anybody. However, it is quite immaterial.'[9]

In fourteen typed pages called 'A Biographical Note on Katherine Mansfield' and sent to O'Brien, Bowden supplied, for the first time, an account of his entire relationship with Mansfield.[10] The process took two months and seems to have been quite a cathartic experience for him. Bowden wrote to O'Brien once he had posted it: 'I found the stimulus to put on paper events of forty years ago more interesting than I at first expected.'[11] In a handwritten note which O'Brien appended to Bowden's account when she deposited her materials at the Harry Ransom Center in Texas, she wrote: 'When I gave up K. M. work after [the] arrival of 2 miraculous babies, Bowden showed [the] MS to Alpers [...] who more or less ignored [it] in his book which is written from [the] viewpoint of Ida Baker – a needed one but still one overriding Bowden as a human being.'[12] And thus, the denigratory perception of Bowden became even more embedded.

Bowden recounted his initial meeting with Mansfield at the home of Dr C. W. Saleeby, a music enthusiast, whose wife was a daughter of the poet Alice Meynell. On introducing himself to Mansfield, Bowden found 'her wit was instantaneous and we had some rapid exchanges. Like others, I was to learn that the low chair and the demure air cloaked a very observant and critical eye' (p. 1). They discovered that they lived within walking distance of each other, for Mansfield was residing at Beauchamp Lodge in Paddington, and Bowden in a nearby bachelor flat, which he shared with his friend, Lamont Shand (a great friend of the Saleebys), together with a manservant called Charles, 'our Admirable Crichton', who had once worked for the Marchioness of Aylesbury: 'Only a P. G. Wodehouse could do full justice to Charles and his imperturbable mien' (p. 3).

The two men invited Mansfield to their flat, but before she took up their invitation, she and Bowden met again at a tea party given by a young continental soprano, newly arrived in London. Bowden was surprised to see her dress

> more or less in Maori fashion. [...] There was something almost eerie about it, as though of a psychic transformation rather than a mere impersonation. At such times even her facial lineaments might seem altered, and in trying to understand her complex personality this is a factor to be reckoned with. (p. 2)

Mansfield soon became a regular visitor to the flat, particularly for lunch: 'We chatted or made music as the spirit prompted and for love only' (p. 3). She ate very little, having 'the appetite of a bird, and would peck daintily at her food, not so much with palatial savour as with an air of detachment' (4). She would eventually 'have the free run of the flat' (p. 5).

After Bowden had his tonsils removed, it was Mansfield who came to collect him in a taxi and took him back to the flat. It was at this time that the pair became engaged,

> the occasion being marked by a festive celebration at the next Saleeby dinner party. K. dutifully did her share of the honours, introducing me to those of her relatives living in London, among them her guardian uncle and the novelist, 'Elizabeth' [...] her cousin. But she was impatient with this side of her existence [...]. Nor did they on their part appear to be familiar with her way of life or her friends, few of whom were even known to me. (p. 6)

Bowden recounted that Mansfield's guardian in London (Henry Beauchamp) had written to inform her parents of the engagement, but that she found the idea of having to wait for their consent – or worse, their arrival in London – 'repugnant', since 'it carried the unbearable suggestion that of suffering again the domination from which she had only just escaped' (p. 6). Bowden noted that he was very sympathetic with the aims of women at that time, and their struggle for enfranchisement, revealing himself to be both modern and enlightened in his political views. He was also complimentary about Mansfield's personal talents as a raconteur:

> Both in the little work she did with me and in the public recital of some of her own sketches given at one or two of my concerts, the use of her voice was quite unselfconscious. Its charm lay in its clear embodiment of her subject lit up by the delicate prism of her mind. The effect was a unity which maintained her integrity intact. (p. 9)

He also commented on the magnetic nature of her personality, remarking how, during the period when he knew her before their marriage,

> she normally exercised a definitely positive attitude socially, and must have found it easy to gain dominion if not domination in the intimate circle of her admirers. I fancy she knew on the instant where this power of hers was likely to be possible. But she also had a remarkable capacity in the opposite direction. [...] K. M. could make herself passively receptive to literary and other influences so completely as to be deeply affected by them. (p. 10)

Bowden remembered how she was an intense and 'even ecstatic lover of nature. Mother Earth was no mere figure of speech for her, and I've heard her speak of lying on the grass as though as though it meant direct contact with a live being' (10). He continued:

> Flowers were of course, living things to her. Mimosa came into the shops of London at the time, and its scent was an intoxication to her, though it inevitably must have reminded her of what she still regarded as an almost prison-like existence of her island home. Her constant talk of the 'open road'

> and of gypsy life generally was, I gathered, symbolic rather than literal in its admiration. (p. 10)

Mansfield was no rambler, however, and as it was winter, 'our excursions were such urban ones as going to a concert, to Rumpelmayer's for tea, or to a club of mine to write letters' (p. 10). Above all, Bowden recalls her determination to maintain her freedom and agency, after their marriage:

> It was freedom in life itself that K. M. stood for so passionately. And no doubt it was this in the individual and batchelor character of life at the flat which attracted her. Immediately on our engagement I received a long letter warning me not to expect too much of her. We would meet at the casual roadside camp fire of an evening rather than share the life of the open road together. This was another of her frequent figures of speech, but only the sense of urgency or strain in the letter surprised me. [...] But I was to recall later the note of foreboding in this letter. (pp. 10–11)

Talking of Mansfield's 'dark humours', Bowden noted that on such occasions she became 'unapproachable', and 'she appeared rather to dramatise herself and to enjoy the ill-health of the soul' (p. 11). One such mood produced the poem 'Loneliness', which she showed to Bowden, and who, on returning the manuscript, had suggested changing the title to 'Solitude', which as he now admitted, was outrageous, for it completely changed the tone of the poem: 'What followed was as near indignation as anything I ever saw in her' (p. 11).[13] Such sensitivity to criticism, which Murry would come to know only too well, manifested itself on another occasion regarding a piece of prose she had given Bowden to read. He made a suggestion about a comma:

> K. was standing at the other end of the room with her back to me facing a mirror. As I looked up I saw her head and neck rise as she slowly turned and said over her shoulder very distinctly indeed, 'You can't tell me anything about commas.' And there seemed no doubt about it; I couldn't. (p. 11)

When the time came for Mansfield to move into the bachelor flat, Bowden sensed a certain reticence, 'for she had an extreme and almost masculine sense of independence, and it might prove irksome to have it threatened'. He went on to note that in Mansfield's future relationship with Murry, 'it was [initially] she who owned the flat in the first place, and the other who was invited to share it' (p. 12).

In this initial long account, Bowden was particularly shy of discussing what passed between them on that fateful marriage night, stating only that 'there came an abrupt end, for the time being at any rate, to the care-free comradeship of the flat with the realisation of an incompatibility which made married life between us impossible' (p. 12). He said he felt 'bewildered' by events, and that details of Mansfield's flight abroad to Bavaria (though not the reason why) came at a personal time of crisis for himself with the death of his father, which took up all his time. He noted meeting Annie Beauchamp (who by then had arrived in London), at the offices of the Bank of New Zealand, and says there was 'constraint on both sides' and that the conversation had chiefly turned on the 'state of K's health. I gave my opinion that her manner of living had not conduced to a reasonable care of herself' (p. 12).

Bowden finally recounted how Mansfield came back into his life early in 1910. While staying at a country house in Lincolnshire he received two telegrams one evening in quick succession, saying she was back in London 'and urging me to see her' (p. 12). As soon as he arrived back in London it was arranged that Mansfield would move back in with him. 'But though we were the best of friends as ever, the venture proved short-lived, and only on the surface a success' (p. 12). Mansfield accompanied Bowden to his studio in Bond Street and sang on a few occasions, as well as reciting some of her sketches at a concert at a London college, which was a huge success, and where the Principal, Dr P. T. Forsyth 'was particularly enthusiastic both with her writing and the literary quality of her subjects' (pp. 12–13). Following an illness – officially peritonitis, but in fact, as Kathleen Jones reveals,[14] almost certainly an ectopic pregnancy following her relationship with Floryan Sobieniowski in Bavaria – Mansfield left Bowden for a nursing home and then recuperated in Rottingdean with Ida Baker, where Bowden went to see her, and 'where we had tea followed by a friendly talk in the cottage garden. Though she was far from well it was plain she had lost nothing [...] of her psychic fascination' (p. 13).

Before she left London, Mansfield had given Bowden her German Pension sketches to read, and at breakfast one morning he suggested sending them to the *New Age*, a weekly arts and literature paper. Never one to let the grass grow under her feet, by dinner Mansfield had taken them to the editor, A. R. Orage in person: 'She was full of the interview with Orage and the favourable impression her writing had made on him' (13). Bowden concludes his account by quoting from Aldous Huxley's book *The Perennial Philosophy*,[15] noting that Mansfield made of her art 'a matter of life and death practice [... in] her pilgrimage from self to authentic identity' (p. 14).

O'Brien wrote to Bowden after he had sent her his long account, asking further questions, 'not as maudlin curiosity on my part, but a desperate endeavor to get a whole story for the sake of the ultimate good I hope for'.[16] In clarifying his position to O'Brien in a letter of 21 November 1947, and his continued slight that the general public should perceive him as Reginald Peacock, as implied by the Mantz-Murry biography, he replied that 'I felt it was due to her memory to give a true picture of a relationship which for a while had a touch of enchantment and was not without dignity'.[17]

O'Brien sent Bowden a list of questions concerning Mansfield, which he responded to in the same letter. There were basic questions such as her height, weight and colour of hair. He confirmed that she was always spoken of as K. M.: 'Her intimates would use K., and her women friends Katie or Kathy.'[18] He also explained his own career at the time, and his reputation in musical circles in London, stressing his connection to the important composer Henry Wood, and noting that 'I gave the first public performance in London of Debussy's "L'Enfant Prodigue" with his orchestra at the Promenade Concerts, Queen's Hall.'[19]

Of their wedding day, he provided further information:

> Ida Baker, whom I had not met up to this time, was K. M.'s witness. [...] We were to spend the day about town and K. wore the best street clothes she had, of which there was not much choice. If the dress itself was black, I remember her as becomingly and suitably clothed, for ordinarily she took little or no pains about her appearance. Certainly the impression on me was not a funereal one.
>
> The passage leading to 'Within a few days she had left him' is perhaps the most misleading. The marriage was not consummated. For reasons of her own which she never confided to me, she could not go through with it, and never came to live at the flat.
>
> [...] As already stated, she had her own reasons; possibly she had too much inner integrity to be able to go on with what she realised did not possess her heart. The marriage proved [...] an illogical conclusion. The second attempt may have been made – it was a complete surprise to me – because as a marriage it must either go on or end in a more regular or legal manner. This is conjecture. The attempt only lasted two or three weeks.[20]

Of the papers apparently left behind at Gloucester Place after she left him for the second time, he discovered 'references to a child which were unintelligible to me at the time. But when I read the LIFE in 1933, I realised that they referred to the adopted child.' He went on to say: 'It seems incredible even to me now that there should have been all these complications in K's life and I remain totally unaware of them. I can only say that there was nothing in her bearing in either period which could have suggested them.' He also states that both periods when he knew Mansfield were 'around February-March, 1909–10'.[21]

On being pressed for more details about the references to a child, he replied to O'Brien in a letter of 10 March 1948 stating, 'This was a card from Miss Baker, I believe, and if my recollection is correct, referred to the child's health and the purchase of clothing.'[22] The child in question was a poor, undernourished little boy from the East End of London sent to Mansfield in Bavaria by Ida Baker, to help her get over the stillbirth of her own baby. He was sent back to London a few weeks later.[23]

Bowden also gave more details about the wedding day:

> You must bear in mind what I have described as the 'bachelor' character of our relationship from the beginning, in which we never questioned each other's coming and going. There was a festive lunch after the ceremony, and I recall two items which K. M. would choose when out with me. It was a partiality influenced, no doubt, by nomenclature, for they were Creamed Jerusalem Artichokes, and an Italian wine known as Lagrima Christi. When we parted it was with the understanding that she would join me at the flat. That she did not do so, and without any explanation, was a painful mystery to me. Her marriage made her no longer eligible for Beauchamp Lodge, and it was a week or ten days before I was given an address. I found her in a miserable room. But all she would say in response to my concern was, 'I can't come.'
>
> Years afterwards when the LIFE was published, I drew the conclusion that she felt the nature of our relations would not stand the stress of a complete confidence on her part – had she been disposed to give it – while on the other hand she refused to face the duplicity which withholding it must have entailed.
>
> At the second attempt a year later, when her immediate trouble of which I was ignorant was over, she may have thought a return to our former footing possible. But though we could renew our mutual interests in music and literature, and again enjoy such things as Jerusalem artichokes and Lagrima Christi wine, the break had been too complete. There was a sense of lack of the confidence essential to real comradeship.[24]

Learning that New Zealand author Antony Alpers was writing a new biography of Mansfield, Bowden wrote to him on 16 November 1949, once again condemning the earlier portrayal of himself in the Mantz-Murry volume:

> The second husband of a woman of literary genius is hardly the most likely or fitting authority for an unbiased critical appraisal of her first, and the relationship involved. Credits easily became debits, those given with the right hand being taken back by the left. Thus, he was a musician but . . . he was an idealist about women but . . . And he had a bedside manner but his wife fled his bed . . And so on.

> But possibly nothing indicates the incompleteness and shallow character of Mr Murry's story so much as the fact that the second half of the episode, in which for her own reasons K. M. urgently insisted on our living together normally as man and wife, is referred to with the simple remark, 'Katherine was in England in Feb. '10, and had apparently returned to her then husband' […] and this is not a fact, but an untruth.[25]

He goes on to provide new details about the marriage day, prompting the question, why did he not expand on this in his original full account to O'Brien? The material seems to have been drip-fed over a number of years:

> The marriage was rushed lest her parents delay it.
>
> Miss Baker's message in the dressing case, of which I now learn from your letter, may account for K. M.'s sudden and complete frigidity after we had reached the hotel suite where we were to spend the night. She had of her entirely free will entered into the marriage, we had had dinner and 'done a show' on our usual good terms, so that this anti-climactic denouement came as a complete surprise – not to say shock – to me.
>
> We left the hotel together the next morning, but instead of bringing her things from Beauchamp Lodge to the flat as arranged, she failed to appear, and it was something like a week before I could obtain an address.[26]

Some two years after the second attempt at living together, Bowden called on Mansfield and Murry at 69 Clovelly Mansions, Gray's Inn Road, in mid-1912, to find out what her intentions were:

> She did not seem to be concerned about any proceedings that would make remarriage possible for her […]. For on leaving I asked her in his presence – half jokingly – if they wanted to marry, and she looked quizzically at him and said something like, 'Do we, J. M.?' Incidentally […] it had happened that K. M., with the easy manner of a good hostess asked me if I would not sing something for them. And on finding a volume of Schumann's songs – for low voice, however – I went to the piano and played and sang one or two.[27]

These actions are not those of a Reginald Peacock – quite the opposite. Indeed, for the rest of his life, he would confirm to all who wrote to him that all initiatives at a divorce came from him and that at no time did Mansfield or Murry ever suggest expediting it. Regarding the divorce, 'Bowden against Bowden and Murry', the decree nisi was eventually formalized on 17 October 1917, citing that the respondent Kathleen Bowden had been guilty of adultery with the correspondent John Middleton Murry. The decree absolute came through on 29 April 1918.

What is less clear is why Bowden chose to ignore the facts he gave in his dealings with his wife's father, when in a letter dated 27 February 1919, he focused on Mansfield being 'sexually unbalanced': 'While her people in New Zealand were aware of this, her guardian in London was not, and as we married after a short acquaintance, it was only then conditions became known to me.'[28] Almost certainly he was trying to explain how he had been very much the innocent party in his first disastrous marriage, and over-egged his pudding by encouraging his future father-in-law to believe Mansfield was a lesbian, thereby rendering the marriage useless.

According to notes written by Mantz in the years following her biography, the reason Mansfield went back to George Bowden was given to her by Ida Baker: 'After K.M. returned from Bavaria, her father decreed that "since she was married" to George Bowden, she must return to him under threat of cancellation of her allowance of £100.'[29] Furthermore, Baker informed Mantz that Bowden 'had been lonely and had gone about',[30] that is had had multiple sexual partners since Mansfield had left him. As a result, she suffered 'piercing pains' and was never well afterwards. Baker of course only knew what Mansfield had told her, and it was far more likely that any venereal disease had been contracted as a result of her relationship with Florian Sobieniowski in Poland. It is also almost certain that Mansfield was pregnant on her return to England in January 1910, carrying Sobieniowski's child, thus precipitating her return to her legal husband. Bowden shies away from any mention of sexual relations with Mansfield, though given the information above, it seems likely these did occur.

In conversation with Orage, Mantz learnt even more information which never made it into her first biography of Mansfield. Bowden and his second wife, Dina, had introduced themselves to Orage when he was lecturing in New York in 1925: 'Orage was incredulous [about the second Mrs Bowden] – the same build, the way of holding the head, the cut of the hair, the kind of clothes – they were Katherine's.'[31] Bowden then reminded Orage of the first time Mansfield had visited him at the offices of the *New Age* in February 1910:

> 'I was with her that day, pacing up and down before the stairway of 38 Cursitor Street.' Though Orage had completely forgotten his first meeting with Katherine, or how it came about, the details in Bowden's mind were vivid with insistent distinctness.
>
> 'She dashed up with her manuscript, and she was back so quickly that I thought she hadn't managed to see you; but she cried, all in one breath, "I gave him THE-CHILD-WHO-WAS-TIRED. He said 'I'll read it.' I said, 'When'? 'He

> said, 'Now.' Then he glanced through it and said, 'I'll print it.' I said 'When?'. He said, 'Next week – if you'll make these corrections.'"
>
> Then she added in a childish voice: "I could kneel right here on this pavement!"'[32]

Alpers's first biography of Mansfield, which was published in 1953, prompted Bowden to write to O'Brien on 28 January 1954, upset once more, this time at Alpers's reliance on the memory of Ida Baker rather than his own recollections for his section on the Mansfield/Bowden relationship:

> My own part in it disappointed me because the author omitted [...] almost everything that lent the episode the slight dignity and good fellowship I had claimed for it. He met Ida Baker some time after beginning to write to me, and it is clear that she influenced him mightily. And as naturally she had resented K. M.'s marriage, Alpers was affected by her account as opposed to my own. In place he caricatures the episode so that it becomes unrecognisable to me, and when I taxed him with this, he replied that he was 'interpreting'! To my mind it is [...] determined to make a 'ridiculous affair' of it. At another point he makes the false statement that Ida Baker 'conveyed to me K. M.'s decision not to live with me anymore.' She would not have dared, as by that time I had discovered too much to make further connection possible. Yet Alpers says he must rely on Ida Baker's work despite my asseverations! Well, enough of all that. I'm sorry I ever lent my name to it.[33]

On 11 December 1963, Bowden's wife Dina replied to a letter from Lucy O'Brien, who had clearly decided to resurrect some part of her Mansfield project once more, and had more questions for her husband, with a desire to vindicate his reputation once and for all. Dina declined on his behalf; Bowden was now eighty-six, she explained, 'and the thought of returning to that brief episode in his life once again [...] does seem too much to ask.'[34]

What Bowden made of Ida Baker's volume of reminiscences on Mansfield, published in 1971, four years before his death in 1975, is not recorded.[35] By the time Baker had set down her recollections she too was old – eighty-three – and her memory of events that had taken place when she and Mansfield were in their early twenties, was, to say the least, unreliable. The discrepancies between her account and Bowden's are marked. She claimed that Bowden and Mansfield had in fact met in the autumn of 1908 (at the height of her romantic liaison with Garnet Trowell), having been introduced by her Beauchamp Lodge friend Margaret Wishart. According to Baker, Mansfield soon became the recipient of long letters from Bowden. Initially sympathetic, Baker recalls how

> Bowden was a kindly person, and, I believe, very much in love with Katherine. His letters were full of humble devotion and understanding, really beautifully expressed. I think he knew she did not love him, but he seemed to understand her and her needs, and offered security and a place where she would be sheltered and be able to work without anxiety. (pp. 45-6)

Baker claimed that Mansfield initially had no interest in marrying Bowden, but that once she realized she was pregnant with Garnet Trowell's baby, she knew she had to act. On the day after the wedding, 'Katherine was in a great state of despair and anxiety and neither of us had much money' (p. 47). Baker states that neither Bowden nor Mansfield's mother knew she was pregnant, her behaviour explained away by her 'lesbian' tendencies, hence her trip to Bavaria, where, as her mother put it, she could 'recover from all her adventures' (49). In her naivety, Baker believed Mansfield when she said, having returned from Bavaria in early 1910, that 'partly for the sake of the family, she would go back to her husband and try to make it work' (p. 54). According to Baker, 'Katherine was with Bowden in Gloucester Place for several weeks, meaning to work when he was out singing or teaching, but she was not happy and was much distressed by his lack of delicacy' (p. 54). A serious 'illness' now brought an end to this second period with Bowden. Officially, Baker was told it was peritonitis, but, as noted earlier, Jones claims in her own biography of Mansfield that it was almost certainly the result of an ectopic pregnancy, the result of her affair with Sobieniowski.[36]

Where Baker's account differs so markedly from Bowden's is with regard to the issue of divorce proceedings. As noted above, Bowden was insistent that at no time was Mansfield interested in a divorce and that, on the contrary, she almost seemed to relish her and Murry's irregular lifestyle. Not so, according to Baker, who claims that 'at the end of April 1912, they had written to Katherine's husband, George Bowden, to ask him to divorce her. He arrived one day to see her and there was much talk; but in the end he did nothing. So Murry and Katherine decided to live as man and wife without legal consent' (p. 75). However, Baker was not present at this meeting, and only had Mansfield's account of what happened to refer to. For all sorts of reasons Mansfield might have glossed over the truth of what happened, so as not to offend Baker's sensibilities.

It is true that in Mansfield's story 'A Little Episode' (1909), written within a few weeks of her marriage, she conveys all her bitterness and disillusion with life, following musician Garnet Trowell's abandoning her when pregnant, and her brief relationship with Bowden, her husband of convenience. Alpers suggested the story offers direct evidence of Mansfield's own circumstances at the time, concluding that it seems 'related to the marriage and the events that preceded it'.[37] Indeed, its unflattering portrayal of 'Lord Mandeville', the Bowden character, with the 'large bottle of Eucalyptus and two clean handkerchiefs' by his pillow, offers more than a hint of her distaste.[38] But the depiction of the music teacher in 'Mr Reginald Peacock's Day', from everything we have learnt above, seems far removed from the gentle, sensitive man who emerges from the correspondence and other documents, and whom Mansfield duped not once, but twice. One can only speculate as to whether, later in life, she felt any shame for the way she had treated the kind and very gentlemanly George Bowden.

Notes

1 *Letters* 5, p. 235, n. 1. Transcript of Mansfield's official will.

2 George Bowden letter to Lucy O'Brien, 14 November 1947. Katherine Mansfield collection, container 2.7, Harry Ransom Center, University of Texas at Austin (hereafter HRC).

3 Mrs Franklin M. Brown to Lucy O'Brien, 28 May 1947. HRC, KM collection, container 2.7.

4 George Bowden to John Middleton Murry, 17 November 1947. MS-Papers-11326-073. Alexander Turnbull Library, Wellington, New Zealand (hereafter ATL).

5 Ruth Elvish Mantz and John Middleton Murry, *The Life of Katherine Mansfield* (London: Constable, 1933), pp. 318–20.

6 George Bowden to Lucy O'Brien, 14 November 1947. HRC, KM collection, container 2.7.

7 John Middleton Murry to George Bowden, 29 November 1933. HRC, KM collection, container 2.7.

8 Ibid.

9 MS-Papers-11326-081, ATL.

10 HRC, KM collection, container 2.6. Hereafter all references to this account are placed parenthetically following each quotation.

11 George Bowden to Lucy O'Brien, 17 September 1947. HRC, KM collection, container 2.7.

12 HRC, KM collection, container 2.6.

13 'Loneliness', in *The Collected Poems of Katherine Mansfield*, eds Gerri Kimber and Claire Davison (Edinburgh: Edinburgh University Press, 2016), pp. 73–4.

> Now it is Loneliness who comes at night
> Instead of Sleep, to sit beside my bed.

Like a tired child I lie and wait her tread,
I watch her softly blowing out the light.
Motionless sitting, neither left nor right
She turns, and weary, weary droops her head.
She, too, is old; she, too, has fought the fight.
So! with the laurel she is garlanded.

Through the sad dark the slowly ebbing tide
Breaks on a barren shore, unsatisfied.
A strange wind flows . . . then silence. I am fain
To turn to Loneliness, to take her hand,
Cling to her, waiting, till the barren land
Fills with the dreadful monotone of rain.

14 Kathleen Jones, *Katherine Mansfield: The Story-Teller* (Edinburgh: Edinburgh University Press, 2010), p. 125.
15 Aldous Huxley, *The Perennial Philosophy* (New York: Harper & Brothers, 1945).
16 Lucy O'Brien to George Bowden, 12 October 1947. HRC, KM collection, container 4.8.
17 George Bowden to Lucy O'Brien, 21 November 1947. HRC, KM collection, container 2.7.
18 Ibid.
19 Ibid.
20 Ibid.
21 Ibid.
22 Ibid.
23 See Jones, p. 114.
24 Ibid.
25 Letter from George Bowden to Antony Alpers, 16 November 1949. ATL, qms-0263.
26 Ibid.
27 Ibid.
28 Letter from George Bowden to Andrew Moore, 27 February 1919. ATL, MS-Papers-3886.
29 Ruth Elvish Mantz collection. HRC, 'Swing on the Garsington Gate', miscellaneous box, n.p.
30 Ibid.
31 Ibid.
32 Ibid.
33 George Bowden to Lucy O'Brien, 28 January 1954. HRC, KM collection, container 2.7.

34 Dina Moore Bowden to Lucy O'Brien, 11 December 1963. HRC, KM collection, container 2.1.

35 Ida Baker, *Katherine Mansfield: The Memories of LM* (London: Michael Joseph, 1971). All page references to the volume are placed parenthetically in the text.

36 Jones, p. 125.

37 Antony Alpers, *The Life of Katherine Mansfield* (London: Viking, 1980), p. 90.

38 CW1, p. 543.

Social and domestic transactions

12

Economic women

Money and (im)mobility in selected stories by Katherine Mansfield

Janet M. Wilson

Mansfield and the economic woman

Regenia Gagnier's comment that late Victorian literature 'represents the everyday economic life between the genders' as 'refracted through the discourses of technology, machinery and economic operations' applies equally to modernist writing of the early twentieth century, especially before England's social structure was ruptured by the devastation of the Great War.[1] In Katherine Mansfield's stories the effects of modernity in the forms of 'economic events that shaped the contemporary world',[2] then, are crucial touchstones for the changing subjectivities and self–other relations of her characters. To read her work through an economic lens informed by twenty-first-century consumer discourses and the ideology of global capitalism is to become aware of the marketplace as a powerful, animating force that intersects with and destabilizes her characters in unpredictable ways, shaping her modernist response to money conceived as the basis of economic and social power.

The activities of financial transaction and management – expenditure, savings and cash flow – in domestic and public commercial marketplaces help define the various economic women of Mansfield's cosmopolitan stories. The term 'economic woman' points to a liminal, multiply defined figure as Lana L. Dalley and Jill Rappoport argue, who, in contrast to the singular dominance of 'economic man' in the new spaces of production and trade in the late nineteenth and early twentieth centuries, has been overlooked and ignored by economists and cultural historians of that era, or else confined to the private, domestic sphere by fiction writers such as Dickens.[3] In Mansfield's writing the concept applies to women represented in terms of motherhood, childrearing and domesticity but more specifically to types like the consumer, worker, the idle rich, unemployed or vagrant, who reveal uncertain structures of selfhood and fluctuating perceptions of others when engaged in financial transactions. The multidimensionality of the term 'economic woman' these proliferating images of women and the availability of new economic roles under early-twentieth-century capitalism.

The individualism of Mansfield's economic women, however, is usually at odds with the demands of the market economy: they are challenged or compromised by trading forces which arouse unexpected intimacies or divisions, financial dilemmas and moral confusions. Whether enjoying the privileges of wealth or, at the other extreme, being financially disadvantaged due to penury, insolvency or debt, they find that monetary interactions disrupt their expectations, test their identities or trigger a desire for the new. Responding with transitions of consciousness, imagined alternative identities and expansive dreams, they tell new narratives about themselves: stories or fantasies that often seem to be substitutes for developing self-knowledge or willingness to change. Inevitably, though, traditional distinctions of class are reinforced and despite the possibilities of social mobility that the modern world seemingly promises, Mansfield's heroines usually remain trapped in existing class structures.

On the other hand, new types of female economic independence were emerging in the early twentieth century, as women began to produce wealth and take financial control, seeing this as 'key to a new kind of freedom'. As Virginia Woolf commented: 'Of the two – the vote and the money – the money I own, seemed infinitely more important.'[4] Such economic expansion began to undermine patriarchy and unsettle class distinctions, and Mansfield's stories also hint at the levelling effects of modernization with its promise of social change. They confirm what Fredric Jameson claims is crucial about modernity, that artists were concerned with 'how modern people feel about themselves with the producers and consumers, and how they feel either producing the products or living among them'.[5] Although she was not an explicitly political writer, as Sydney Janet Kaplan points out, and did not subscribe directly to any feminist agenda, Mansfield was concerned with female victimization and discrimination in the marketplace and indirectly advocated social change.[6]

Mansfield's own financial vicissitudes were a vital source of writing that sharply observed the different impacts of insolvency or wealth on character. This is particularly true of her early time in London from September 1908 when she struggled to live within her means and was adjusting to a more frugal existence; her father's annual allowance covered her rent and subsistence but did not allow for the luxuries and extravagant gestures that she had been brought up to consider normal. During this period she was finding her way in the London literary marketplace, eking out her income by taking up professional invitations to perform and entertain, raiding her talent for impersonation and acting by telling stories, verse recitations, playing bit parts as a walk-on actor or performing in the touring Moody-Manners Opera Company; indeed, as Katie Jones points out, discovering the market's potential, and especially the fashion for live recital performance, helped shape her literary production.[7] As a colonial outsider, Mansfield's social mobility and professional fluidity, both in London and while travelling on the Continent, are features of this turbulent phase of her life. These undoubtedly gave her insights into the types of economic dependency that caused women's feelings of frustration and entrapment and encouraged her critique of class and gender, evident in her 1908 notebook comment about women, that 'we are firmly held in the self fashioned chains of slavery'.[8]

Mansfield's problems with and management of her financial resources at a time when she was positioning herself artistically in a cosmopolitan milieu frames the reading that follows of five stories in terms of the marketplace, its consumer culture, employment practices and the mechanisms of trade. I argue that, rather than showing the 'deep and fundamental hostility' to the market when treated as a site that facilitates, promotes and profits from modernization,[9] Mansfield draws on this milieu to explore the conscious and unconscious drives of her characters who are caught up in its values and ideology. The trading place is a locale of self-reference and identity as they undertake everyday work or seek new horizons through dream or fantasy without any prospect of material improvement or social change. Although this was an era when women began to take control of capital and acquire purchasing power, the problematic encounters of her heroines with systems of trade, debt and financial exchange expose their helplessness, economic dependence, susceptibility to exploitation and self-delusion.

All financial transactions occur as a product of human interaction, exchange and relationships. On the other hand, as David Graeber explains – as state and market are intertwined, not opposed – it is possible to reduce all human relationships to exchange, as if our ties to society can be imagined in terms of a business deal.[10] This interchangeability between the individual and the business world emerges in Mansfield's depictions of transactions involving labour, buying and selling, and non-payment or debt, in ways that emphasize female vulnerability. The capitalist market (and its ideology) is a disempowering overarching structure often associated with 'economic man', a 'conscious, knowing, unified, and rational subject' who 'desires to possess wealth';[11] it privileges profit and accumulation and is indifferent to human feelings. As Jameson observes, critiquing the market:

> Market ideology assures us that human beings make a mess of it when they try and control their destinies [...] and that we are fortunate in possessing an interpersonal mechanism – the market – which can substitute for human hubris and planning and replace human decisions altogether.[12]

To read Mansfield's stories through the optic of this 'interpersonal mechanism' that reduces decision-making and self-agency is to see financial operations functioning as both a catalyst of feelings, motivations and aspirations and a check on them.

Financial and class inequalities are filtered through the prism of work and the labour contract in 'Life of Ma Parker' (1921), through consumerism and seller/buyer relations in 'The Tiredness of Rosabel' (1908) and 'A Cup of Tea' (1922), and through the burden of debt as catalyst of fluctuating sexual mores in 'The Swing of the Pendulum' (1911) and 'Pictures' (1921). Mansfield draws on a range of literary models for these different types of individualism: the conventions of nineteenth-century realism and tropes from the romantics and aesthetes for working-class characters in 'Life of Ma Parker' and 'A Cup of Tea',[13] and the popular romance plot and modes of consumer fantasy[14] for lower-middle or upper-class characters in 'The Tiredness of Rosabel' and 'A Cup of Tea'. By contrast, echoes from T. S. Eliot's poems in *Prufrock and Other Observations* (1917) and the use of the techniques of silent cinema appear in 'Pictures' which, like 'The Swing of the Pendulum', draws on the practices of acting and impersonation for the various improvisations of its destitute heroine. All five stories address the dilemmas of women operating as consumers, sellers or traders in various domestic and public marketplaces, who suddenly find themselves in disorienting, destabilizing situations.

'Life of Ma Parker' and domestic labour

Mansfield's most radical attack on the discriminations of gender and class as enacted in the realm of domestic labour can be found in 'Life of Ma Parker', a story in which existing inequalities appear in the female worker's personal suffering due to a life of misery and victimization, and her employer's patronizing attitude towards her. Unlike the feudal servant whose duty and labour implied relations of loyalty and trust with their owner, Ma Parker's relationship with the middle-class 'literary gentleman' is based on the 'cash nexus'.[15] Financial exchange means that their relationship resembles that of master and slave, because, according to Graeber, it is in principle impersonal: 'Whether you've been sold or you have simply rented yourself out, the moment money changes hands, who you are supposed to be is unimportant.'[16] This is made painfully clear in the story's conclusion after Ma Parker has been paid by her employer: the imprisoning mismatch between her role, her individual subjectivity and even who she could be is reflected in her traumatized feelings of meaninglessness when she dares to question her place in the world.

Ma Parker is a rare study in modernist fiction of the interiority of the working-class labourer,[17] and Mansfield exposes the discrepancy between the stereotyped expectations of the workplace and Ma Parker's subjectivity by juxtaposing discourses of education and social privilege, associated with her employer, with those of her personal sacrifice and suffering.[18] Mother of thirteen children, she is a working-class contrast to the upper-middle-class householders of Mansfield's fiction, such as the grandmothers – Mrs Fairfield in 'Prelude' and the 'old woman' in 'New Dresses' – who are associated with mothering roles and household management within the home, and whose contribution to society is in the form of 'modes of service' that prioritize the needs of others, especially the girl child.[19] The literary gentleman (ironically named because his actions undermine the behaviour implied by this title) treats his charlady as a dispensable servant appropriate to his privileged bachelor lifestyle: 'You simply dirty everything you've got, get a hag in once a week to clean up, and the thing's done.'[20]

Ma Parker contradicts such stereotyping in her concern that her employer has 'no-one to look after him',[21] and in her overwhelming grief at the death of her grandson, Lennie, who with his mother Ethel are the only family members she has left. Mansfield represents her state of mind at this ultimate loss through an embedded first-person narrative, her *bildung*. This is a sub-category of the life story in its detailing of 'the injuries of industrialisation'[22] and is marked by the recurring phrase, 'I've had a hard life.'[23] She dwells on the cruelty she has suffered at the hands of past employers, her husband's death-inducing job as a baker, the disease which carried off seven of her children while those who survived all left home, apart from Ethel. The implication of this narrative act is reinforced by the final image of Ma Parker as alienated and isolated now that she has lost almost all those she loved. She is defined primarily by her role in the workplace, and so sees herself as no more than an object whose labour power – her only commodity or selling point – is part of a socialized system into which she has been inscribed and to which she is dispensable.

Mansfield's critique draws on Edwardian stereotypes of the working class which emphasize its marginality and high mortality by associating their lives with death and mourning. The literary gentleman looks upon Ma Parker as one of 'these people [who] set such store by funerals [...]. "I hope the funeral went off all right."'[24] By contrast, Ma Parker's desolation at the loss of her beloved grandson interrupts her work as memories flood back, distracting her from her present tasks and diminishing her capacity to make decisions. Characteristically defining herself through the needs of others, and now left only with memories of him, she is even more exposed than previously to the indifference and impersonality of the class system.

Mansfield reinforces these class disparities by introducing two financial transactions, represented as contrasting dialogues in tone, diction and voice, that stress the differences between Ma Parker's domestic and working relationships. Her formal exchange with the literary gentleman marked by 'Sir'[25] emphasizes the master/servant hierarchy, according to Graeber: 'You are capable of understanding orders and doing what you are told.'[26] Her employer's half-crown payment left in the tray of the inkstand symbolizes their social distance, while any hint of mutual trust in their business arrangement is undermined by his insinuation that Ma Parker has pilfered the last teaspoon of cocoa in the tin. By contrast, the flashback between Ma Parker and Lennie, 'Gran's boy', is a dramatic recreation in a working-class accent of intimacy and playful barter: she readily gives him money as a token of her unconditional love, with only the gift of himself in exchange:

> 'Gran, gi' us a penny!' he coaxed.
> 'Be off with you; Gran ain't got no pennies.'
> 'Yes, you 'ave.'
> 'No, I ain't.'
> 'Yes you 'ave. Gi' us one!'
> Already she was feeling for the old, squashed, black leather purse.
> 'Well, what'll you give your gran?'
> He gave a shy little laugh and pressed closer. She felt his eyelid quivering against her cheek.
> 'I ain't got nothing,' he murmured. . . . [27]

Here Mansfield exploits the symbolic parallels between money and love as forms of exchange and stresses the mutuality of affection in the 'unequal' negotiation. The shock of losing Lennie, her emotional touchstone, is repeated in Ma Parker's second shock, encapsulated in the story's ending after her housework is completed and payment received. Mansfield implies that the two exchanges are inextricably linked in implying abandonment, for Ma Parker now has no sense of a place in the world, either literally or psychically, 'where she could have her cry out – at last?'[28]

This failed catharsis reflects Ma Parker's entrapment in her role and the overlap between the expectations of servitude and her selfless prioritizing of others, magnified by her misery at her grandson's death. Her essential aloneness suggests that this doubling of finality, by death and payment, is experienced as a form of individual annihilation. Once she leaves the house she is like a social outcast, isolated and anonymous: 'What have I done?' is her cry of futility.[29] The mechanical repetition of routine has suppressed her emotions and denied the release she craves; furthermore, crying 'after all these years' would only reinforce the imprisoning status quo, for she fears 'she'd find herself in the lockup, like as not'.[30] Ma Parker's negative epiphany and placelessness underline her alienation and radical objectification as a result of being commodified in the economy of work – a 'cipher' in a bigger system of exchange.[31]

Consumer fantasies: 'The Tiredness of Rosabel' and 'A Cup of Tea'

In contrast to Ma Parker's cry of existential despair, representing the betrayal of all her class, is the lower-middle-class economic woman, the shop girl, in 'The Tiredness of Rosabel', who uses fantasy to overcome the ignominy of her class. Mansfield dwells on the buyer/seller relationship as enacted in the gilded, class-conscious milieu of an upper-class milliner's establishment in central London. Working in a genteel trade, her heroine is somewhere between working-class and lower-middle-class and 'subject to [the] unarticulated possibility of social transformation'.[32] The story consists of Rosabel's reflection in the private space of her lodgings in Richmond Road on the day's events: her encounter with her customers – a wealthy young couple, culminating in an erotic fantasy about herself and the young man.[33]

Masculine preference, taste and financial control set in motion a transfer of identity from customer to salesgirl. The rich husband, Harry, tells his wife she must have 'a black hat with a feather that goes right round it', and then when Rosabel at her client's request models the hat he has selected for her, the wife says, 'It suits you, beautifully.'[34] This codes Rosabel as romantically desirable;

yet class sensitivities militate against any easy acceptance of this compliment, and her anger and then studied indifference to Harry's 'tinge of insolence, of familiarity', 'as he leant over her as she made out the bill', indicate her resistance to being co-opted and commodified into their systems of value and aesthetics. But in her later recreation of the event, this very moment of commodification, 'as he counted the money into her hand – "Ever been painted?" he said',[35] is transformed into a new narrative with Rosabel at the centre. The intimate act of money changing hands is the springboard for romantic longing, and Rosabel's desire for the touch of those hands opens up a realm of fantasy and romance:

> Rosabel suddenly pushed the hair back from her face; her forehead was hot . . . if those slim hands could rest one moment! The luck of that girl!
>
> Suppose they changed places. Rosabel would drive home with him. Of course they were in love with each other, but not engaged – very nearly, and she would say – 'I won't be one moment.'[36]

Mansfield's focus on the subjective, interior world of the shop girl also involves a retreat from the capitalist ideology of finance and marketing, represented by the hoarding which she sees on her bus journey from Oxford Circus to Richmond Road. Advertising proclaims the message of modernization, of new efficiencies to replace human labour as the commercial world calls its mass consumers indiscriminately. Rosabel's distaste for technology and marketing is associated with the stark realities of her journey home: her 'horribly wet' feet and the 'black, greasy mud' on the hem of her skirt and petticoat both connotations of the daily grind of the poor.[37] New inventions appeal only when they might lift her above this, as in her wish for an elevator or escalator – 'a lift' or 'an electric staircase like the one at Earl's Court' – to save the walk up four flights of stairs to her room.[38] But seen from the Atlas bus, advertisements for new labour-saving devices are dismissed as worn out and irrelevant: 'How many times had she read [...] "Sapolio Saves Time, Saves Labour"'?[39]

Rosabel's criticism of her surroundings extends to the working-class practices of reading as she disdainfully observes her neighbour on the bus reading *Anna Lombard*, a popular sensational novel by a New Woman writer, 'mouthing the words in a way that Rosabel detested, licking her first finger and thumb each time that she turned the page'. But the phrases of seduction that she vicariously glimpses, a 'hot, voluptuous night, a band playing, and a girl with lovely, white shoulders',[40] are appropriated to her daydream of a whirlwind romance and happy-ever-after marriage to 'Prince' Harry. Kate Fullbrook comments on the contagious power of such images from popular romance in controlling the female consciousness as if an opiate of the masses.[41] But in the everyday world of commerce, finance and the retail markets of Oxford Street, popular romance is derided by the modern, elitist Rosabel as an inferior form of diversion in contrast to her invented fantasia. In literary terms Mansfield develops such images away from the provenance of mass fiction through the superior gaze of Rosabel, as she overcomes her claustrophobia due to the surrounding afflictions of poverty, squalor and damp weather, by redeploying them in her own romantic plot.

'A Cup of Tea' involves similar transformations catalysed by class and gender inequalities, but which in contrast focuses on the impulsive fantasy of an upper-class, idle, wealthy heroine whose anxieties about her looks and confusion over beauty and desire compromise her apparent freedom of action. The action begins in an antique shop in Curzon Street in central London, where Rosemary, a surrogate consumer, is intent on spending her husband's money. Her hesitation over purchasing an expensive 'exquisite little enamel box'[42] the antique dealer wishes to sell her, leads her to channel her desire for possession into her own power game, a seemingly altruistic gesture that offers a more gratifying self-image and the chance to re-narrativize her life for her friends: she bestows her munificence upon a young street woman, a vagrant, who solicits her for a cup of tea. But this 'thrilling' act of taking a beggar into her home and the fantasy of herself as a 'fairy godmother'[43] ultimately results in a challenge to her self-esteem.

Mansfield here might be satirizing written accounts of female philanthropy, women's efforts to articulate forms of mutually beneficial, ethical exchange that involve female solidarity, for her aptly-named heroine, Rosemary Fell, thought 'she would do one of those things that she was always reading about or seeing on the stage' so proving that 'rich people had hearts, and that women *were* sisters';[44] her fanciful invocation of a Dostoevsky novel as precedent for her 'adventure' only adds to the satire. For the beggar, a starving girl with the nondescript, non-threatening name of Miss Smith, the familiar romantic tropes of enchantment are used. She magically metamorphoses from the classical 'femme fragile' invoking frailty and vulnerability – 'thin dark, shadowy […] with enormous eyes'[45] – into a seductive femme fatale after consuming tea, cakes and sandwiches, luring to her Rosemary's husband who finds her 'so astonishingly pretty' with her 'tangled hair, dark lips, deep, lighted eyes'.[46] Unlike 'The Tiredness of Rosabel', fantasy implodes in 'A Cup of Tea', and when her husband seemingly implies that he prefers Miss Smith's looks to her own, Rosemary returns the vagrant to the streets with a gift of three pounds to salve her conscience.

Rosemary's rejection of her consumer role when the highly priced exquisite enamel box seems beyond her means, instead enhancing her self-image by dispensing charity, can only ever be temporary. The marketplace functions as part of a capitalist system that sustains her wealthy lifestyle, and the familiar wheels that guarantee her prosperity and marital security keep turning. The 'adventure' culminates in the reinforcement of her economic dependence and the restoration of marital equilibrium at a price: her husband agrees to pay for the jewel box that earlier she had considered too expensive. Miss Smith, like Ma Parker and her disposability in the labour system, is no more than a pawn in this renegotiation of the monetary stakes in the marriage by which patriarchal ownership is re-established.

Debt, doubt and identity: 'The Swing of the Pendulum' and 'Pictures'

The third type of marketplace encounter concerns the obligations incurred by the non-existent transaction: one that entails a debt. This is usually due to non-payment of rent in Mansfield's stories, as in the plight of the destitute heroines of 'The Swing of the Pendulum' and 'Pictures', stories with some autobiographical content.[47] Economists and moral philosophers who write on debt, often a modernist byword for living irresponsibly, point out how morally corrupting and damaging it is;[48] according to Pierre Bourdieu the power asymmetries that characterize the creditor–debtor relationship tend to be viewed from the perspective of creditors so that debtors are exposed to the moral obligations and corollary emotional attachments that inflict 'symbolic violence'.[49] Yet the reciprocity of debt and the moral case against creditors are also espoused: Doctor Johnson, for example, points out that the 'creditor always shares the act and more often shares the guilt of improper trust' in contracting a debt in the first place 'in the hope of self-advantage'.[50]

Mansfield shows affinities with Victorian and other modernist literary interpretations of the moral dynamics of debt that view such financial disasters tolerantly as 'misfortunes' rather than assigning 'personal culpability'. The 'disequilibrium of symbolic and emotional investments' typical of failed contractual relations appears in her heroines' self-alienation and confusion, psychological collapse and urgent reassessment.[51] For both the impoverished writer Viola in 'The Swing of the Pendulum' and the elderly, out-of-work contralto singer Ada Moss in 'Pictures', debt incurs initial self-righteous indignation, violent passion and primitive urges; their economic helplessness casts them into a moral limbo of sexual self-commodification as they make themselves available in the heterosexual marketplace.

The stories convey the symbolic degradation imposed by debt through the demeaning language of parasitic vermin and beasts that marks toxic exchanges with their landladies who demand payment of the rent: Ada Moss calls hers, Miss Pine, 'a bad, wicked woman' and 'a cockroach'; Viola's landlady implies her debtor is like lice, 'sneaking their way into furniture and eating up everything', while Viola privately condemns her as 'a dirty pigeon' and 'a filthy old beast'.[52] Both heroines challenge their creditors' imperious demands and attempt to exert power by rejecting accusations of culpability, so blurring the moral boundaries. But in private their emotional turbulence shows judgement yielding to impulse, a process of self-commodification that involves self-interrogation in the mirror. Destitute, Viola finds poverty is 'like a huge dream mountain on which her feet were fast rooted' as she speaks to her 'tragic reflection: "Money, money, money!"'[53] In a series of melodramatic self-reinventions she considers suicide and sudden rescue, then fantasizes about living not just debt free but beyond her means by marketing her personal assets and charms as 'a great courtesan'.[54] Mansfield introduces an allegory into these emotional dramatizations of an unknown, handsome stranger appearing at Viola's door, whom she invites into her room. The episode proves that such desire is illusory; the stranger's proposed exchange of sexual favours for money ends in a violently physical contretemps where Viola bites his hand in a vicious rebuff; despite his offer to pay off her debt she forces him out, and awaits the return of her impecunious, absent lover, Casimir, like her a writer, who cannot keep her in the expensive manner she desires.

The life-like vignette 'Pictures', by contrast, points to the enactment of the very contract that Viola so strenuously rejects, so that the rent can be paid. Ada Moss overcomes a similar psychological collapse, transforming her desperation and misery by acting out different roles in public spaces. Recovering from Miss Pine's attack, she comforts her tearful image in the mirror and with a dose of Dutch courage sallies forth, 'a stout woman in blue serge with a bunch of artificial "parmas" at her bosom'.[55] But her fruitless quest for employment as an actor or singer, doing the rounds of the various casting agencies and studios, indicating her availability to anyone who will hire her, only results in dismissive insults or off-hand disparagement. Miss Moss's vain hopes for recognition of her talents, and of gaining any professional work are finally demolished as she yields to masculine predatory desires in the shape of a little man with a very small hat whom she meets in the Café de Madrid.

Both stories suggest that such acts of self-transformation are ultimately circular, and that the status quo will continue. There is no obvious long-term answer to their dilemmas as Viola recognizes in considering that if she left Casimir: '"Where should I go to?" There was nowhere.'[56] Kate Fullbrook comments that Mansfield's ironic prose is 'a reflection of, and a commentary on, the kinds of false consciousness she diagnoses as classically working in her characters'.[57] In her appraisal of common responses to poverty and debt, showing women unconsciously clinging to prevailing ideologies and stereotypes that compromise their sense of self, Mansfield points to the lack of easily available alternatives to the financial protection offered by men; her social critique anticipates the work in this genre of later writers like Jean Rhys, Colette, Francis Carco and others.[58]

Conclusion: Trading the self

Mansfield's stories illustrate Jameson's dictum that the market's 'function is not to encourage and perpetuate freedom [...] but rather to suppress it'.[59] The perspective of the marketplace reveals the various constraints that disempower Mansfield's economic women. Those who are employed live precariously on subsistence wages, suffering class discrimination that reinforces their subservient status in the workplace; those who lack employment or need not work come to recognize their absolute dependence on male relationships and protection for survival. Symptomatic of their precarity and marginality to the contemporary world of business and finance are their consumerist preferences for goods and products that are either decorative or minimal, either surplus to need or falling below it: Rosabel's extravagant purchase of a bunch of violets though she desires 'something hot and strong and filling',[60] Rosemary Fell's exquisite antique box, Ada Moss's wistful hope for a cup of tea while starving for a 'Good Hot Dinner' or a 'Sensible Substantial Breakfast'.[61]

All five stories written between 1908 and 1922 offer snapshots of economic women trapped in the class structures into which they have been born. Unaccustomed to financial independence they are unable to make money work for long-term benefits, and their response is to trade some part of themselves or swap their unpalatable circumstances for dreams and fantasies, exchanges as potentially destabilizing psychologically as they seem inspiring. Mansfield focuses on how the machinery of the capitalist marketplace with its promise of modernity catalyses paradigmatic moments of suffering, fear and hope. It challenges women's identities and intimate desires, whether as consumers, labourers, sellers or debtors, exposing the constraints of class and gender, while intimating a world beyond them.

Nevertheless, Mansfield's semi-buried discourse of the marketplace is marked by a vital new animation of space where transactions are initiated, enacted and reflected upon. These may be public venues such as the railway station in 'The Little Governess' or the antique shop in 'A Cup of Tea', or private spaces such as the lodging-house bedroom, a site for dream and self-transformation in 'The Tiredness of Rosabel', and subject to invasion and imprisonment in 'The Swing of the Pendulum' and 'Pictures'. Liminal spaces such as doorways, windows and stairwells all assume symbolic significance as locales for transitions of consciousness, as female protagonists question themselves, exhibiting confusion, desperation and moral ambivalence in pondering the alternatives of greater freedoms or continued entrapment due to the entrenched forces of class and gender. Either inspired, hopeful or desperate, her subjects centre themselves in life narratives or fantasies located in these spaces. Even though, as Dominic Head points out, these stories are usually constructed as a defence against personal loss or lack and so need dismantling, they suggest new realms or alternative possibilities.[62] In these ways Mansfield exploits the potential of the impersonal marketplace for rethinking and reconfiguring the self while nevertheless acknowledging the cultural constraints that hold women in place.

Mansfield was able to look ahead to a vision where women determined their own destinies, saying 'I feel that I do now realise, dimly, what women in the future will be capable of achieving. They truly, as yet, have never had their chance'– adding that the chains of slavery are 'self fashioned, and must be self removed'.[63] Yet her female subjects, caught up in the processes of the marketplace but lacking the skills and self-knowledge to carve out a more independent path in society, spin out their dreams and hopes just at the point when they regress and collapse into the known and familiar.

Notes

1 Regenia Gagnier, 'Economic Women in Their Time, Our Time and the Future', in *Economic Women: Essays on Desire and Dispossession*, eds Lana L. Dalley and Jill Rappoport (Columbus: Ohio State University Press, 2013), pp. 219–24 (p. 220).

2 Adam Trexler, 'Economic Ideas and British Literature 1900–1930: The Fabian Society, Bloomsbury and *The New Age*', *Literature Compass* 4, no. 3 (2007): 862–7 (pp. 862–3). They include labour unrest and calls for economic reform.
3 Lana L. Dalley and Jill Rappaport, 'Introducing Economic Women', in *Economic Women*, pp. 1–21 (pp. 1–2).
4 Virginia Woolf, qtd in John Xiros Cooper, *Modernism and the Culture of Market Society* (Cambridge: Cambridge University Press, 2004), p. 16.
5 Fredric Jameson, *Postmodernism, or the Cultural Logic of Late Capitalism* (London: Verso, 1999), p. 310.
6 Sydney Janet Kaplan, *Katherine Mansfield and the Origins of Modernist Fiction* (Ithaca and London: Cornell University Press), p. 17. Kate Fullbrook's essay, 'Katherine Mansfield: Subjection and Authority', in *The Fine Instrument: Essays on Katherine Mansfield*, eds Paulette Michel and Michel Dupuis (Sydney: Dangaroo Press, 1989), pp. 51–60 (p. 53), argues she was 'looking for a revolution in social consciousness'.
7 See Katie Jones's chapter in this volume on Mansfield's early engagement with the London literary marketplace.
8 CW4, p. 91.
9 Jameson, p. 304.
10 David Graeber, *Debt: The First 500 Years* (London: Melville House, 2011), p. 19.
11 Ronald Schleifer, *A Political Economy of Modernism: Literature, Post-Classical Economics, and the Lower Middle-Class* (Cambridge: Cambridge University Press, 2018), p. 4; Susan Feiner, qtd in Dalley and Rappaport, p. 2.
12 Jameson, p. 273.
13 Charles Ferrall, 'Katherine Mansfield and the Working Classes,' in Special Issue, *Katherine Mansfield: Masked and Unmasked, Journal of New Zealand Literature*, 32, no. 2 (2014): 106–20 (p. 117).
14 Lisa Shapiro Sanders, *Consuming Fantasies: Labor, Leisure and the London Shopgirl 1880–1920* (Columbus: Ohio State University Press, 2006); she defines these as '*absorption* or immersion in a particular narrative trajectory' (as in popular romance) and 'the nonnarrative experience of *distraction*' (as in 'variety entertainments'), p. 4.
15 See Maurizia Boscagli, citing Eric Hobsbawm, 'The Art of Work: Katherine Mansfield's Servant and Perception', in *Re-forming World Literature: Katherine Mansfield and the Modernist Short Story*, eds Gerri Kimber and Janet Wilson (Stuttgart: Ibidem-Verlag, 2018), pp. 71–92 (p. 72).
16 Graeber, p. 352.
17 Ferrall, pp. 107–8, points out the dearth of literary representations of the working class, implying Mansfield is something of an exception.
18 See Alex Moffett's chapter in this volume discussing the relationship between labour and narrative.

19 Dalley and Rappoport, p. 2.
20 CW2, p. 293.
21 Ibid.
22 Jeremy Seabrook, *Pauperland: Poverty and the Poor in Britain* (London: Hurst & Co, 2013), p. 157.
23 CW2, p. 293.
24 CW2, p. 292.
25 CW2, p. 295.
26 Graeber, p. 352.
27 CW2, p. 293.
28 CW2, p. 297.
29 CW2, p. 296.
30 Ibid.
31 John Fordham, *James Hanley: Modernism and the Working Class* (Cardiff: University of Wales Press, 2002), p. 4.
32 Sanders, p. 29.
33 Kate Fullbrook, in *Katherine Mansfield* (Brighton: Harvester Press, 1986), p. 37, notes the brilliant placing of Mansfield's parenthetical aside 'at the moment of sexual surrender': ('The real Rosabel, the girl crouched on the floor in the dark, laughed aloud and put her hand up to her hot mouth'). CW1, p. 137.
34 CW1, p. 135.
35 Ibid.
36 CW1, pp. 135–6.
37 CW1, p. 133.
38 CW1, p. 134.
39 CW1, p. 133.
40 Ibid.
41 Fullbrook, *Katherine Mansfield*, pp. 37–8.
42 CW2, p. 462.
43 CW2, p. 463.
44 CW2, pp. 463–4.
45 CW2, p. 465; Barbara Korte, 'The Femme Fragile: Decline and Fall of a Literary Topos', *Anglia*, 105, no. 3/4 (1987): 366–89.
46 CW2, p. 466.
47 Viola in 'Swing of the Pendulum' has parallels with Mansfield's situation in 1909: the absent lover is possibly a prototype of her lover Garnet Trowell; Ida Baker in *Katherine Mansfield: The Memories of LM* (London: Virago, 1985), p. 53, says the stranger is modelled on 'a rough bully from whom she wished to escape', someone Mansfield met in Badworishofen later that year. 'Pictures' may draw on her experience as bit actor for the movies. See Jane Stafford, 'The Boyfriends', in *Katherine Mansfield's Men*, eds Charles Ferrall and Jane Stafford

(Wellington: Katherine Mansfield House and Steele Roberts, 2004), pp. 27–46 (pp. 36–7).

48 Nigel Dodd, *The Social Life of Money* (New Haven: Princeton University Press, 2014), p. 91.

49 Pierre Bourdieu, *Language and Symbolic Power*, ed. John B. Thompson, trans. Gino Raymond and Matthew Adamson (Cambridge: Polity Press, 1991), pp. 139–40.

50 Samuel Johnson, qtd in Margaret Atwood, *Payback: Debt and the Shadow Side of Wealth* (Bloomsbury, 2008), p. 128.

51 Franco Moretti, qtd in Margot C. Finn, *The Character of Credit: Personal Debt in English Culture, 1740–1914* (Cambridge: Cambridge University Press, 2003), pp. 62–3.

52 CW1, p. 179; CW2, p. 243.

53 CW1, p. 243.

54 CW1, p. 246.

55 CW2, p. 180.

56 CW2, p. 246.

57 Fullbrook, 'Katherine Mansfield: Subjection and Authority', p. 55.

58 See Ann Herndon Marshall's chapter on the character of Miss Moss in this volume.

59 Jameson, p. 273.

60 CW1, p. 133.

61 CW2, p. 243.

62 Dominic Head, *The Modernist Short Story: A Study in Theory and Practice* (Cambridge: Cambridge University Press, 1992), p. 123.

63 CW4, p. 91.

13

Labour, idleness and life narrative in *The Garden Party and Other Stories*

Alex Moffett

Introduction

A society's tastes change over time and the aesthetic judgements of one generation can seem quite baffling to the generation that follows it. However even with that said, contemporary readers who learn the titles of the first Katherine Mansfield stories to be adapted to radio might be rather surprised by the choices. Most twenty-first-century Mansfield critics hold stories such as 'The Garden Party' or 'Daughters of the Late Colonel' or 'Bliss' to be among the first rank.[1] However, when the BBC first adapted Mansfield's work for radio in 1932, they selected neither of these stories. Rather, they chose 'Life of Ma Parker', which was broadcast on the compilation show 'A Miscellany' on 1 April 1932.[2] A year later, the BBC broadcast two more Mansfield stories: 'The Lady's Maid' and 'Pictures' (retitled, after its protagonist, 'Miss Moss'). On 18 April 1937, these three stories were reperformed for the BBC under the umbrella title 'Three Women: Portraits from stories by Katherine Mansfield' (see Figure 2).

It's fair to say that today 'Life of Ma Parker' would not be everyone's first choice for a Mansfield story to adapt; indeed the sentimental tone of the story has sometimes been criticized in recent years.[3] And while 'Pictures' is often admired, 'The Lady's Maid' has attracted a comparatively minor degree of scholarly attention. The discrepancy between these three stories and what twenty-first-century scholars would recognize as the essential Mansfield canon tells us something about her reputation in Britain in the two decades following her death. It's clear that, for the 1930s programmers at the BBC National Programme, the formally innovative aspects of Mansfield's work were less important than the theme that unites that particular trio of stories. 'Life of Ma Parker', 'Pictures' and 'The Lady's Maid' each represent the toll of human labour specifically upon

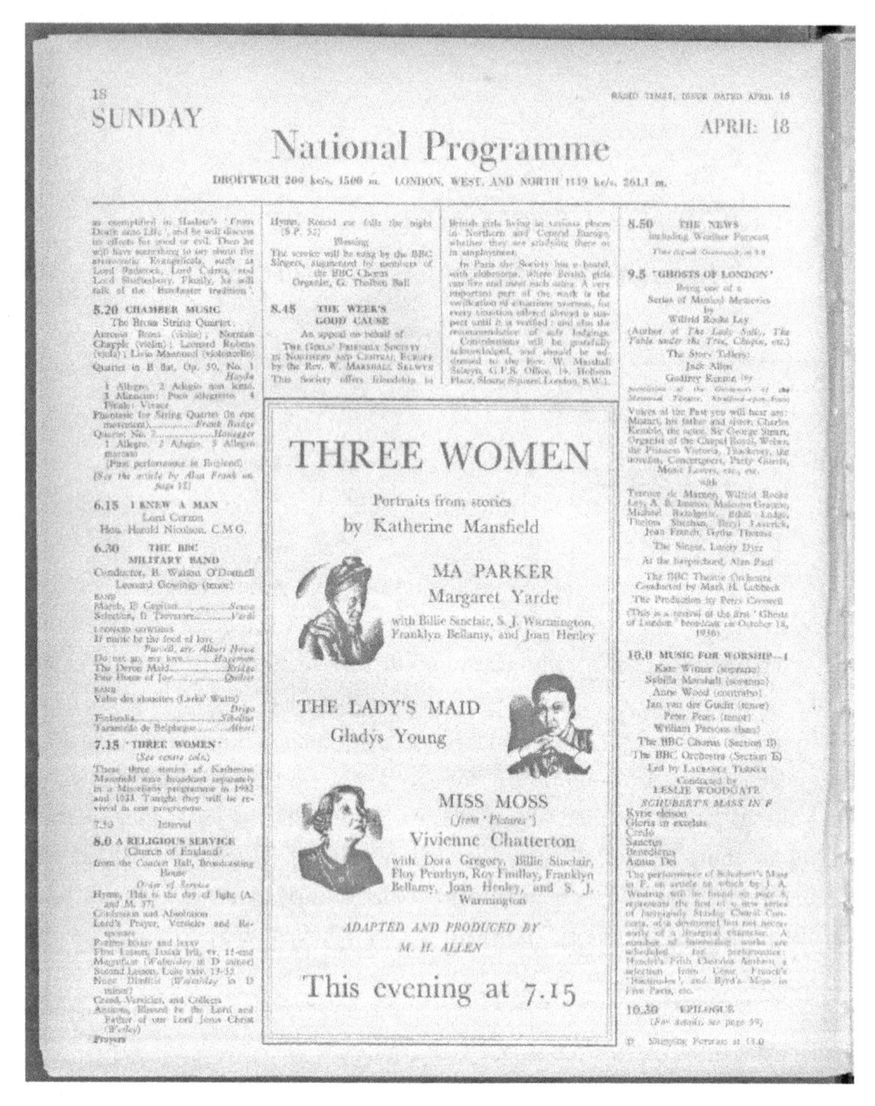
18
SUNDAY
APRIL 18

National Programme

THREE WOMEN

Portraits from stories
by Katherine Mansfield

MA PARKER
Margaret Yarde
with Billie Sinclair, S. J. Warmington, Franklyn Bellamy, and Joan Henley

THE LADY'S MAID
Gladys Young

MISS MOSS
(from 'Pictures')
Vivienne Chatterton
with Dora Gregory, Billie Sinclair, Floy Penrhyn, Roy Findlay, Franklyn Bellamy, Joan Henley, and S. J. Warmington

ADAPTED AND PRODUCED BY
M. H. ALLEN

This evening at 7.15

Figure 2 Page from *Radio Times*, 18–24 April 1937.

women. The power of each of these stories lies in their demonstration of the cumulative effects, both physical and psychological, of many years of labour upon the lives of their female protagonists.

Two of these three stories – 'Life of Ma Parker' and 'The Lady's Maid' – were written in the last few years of Mansfield's life, and were included in the last short story collection published in her lifetime, *The Garden Party and Other Stories* (1922). These two stories are not the only representations of labour in that anthology. There is also Old Mr. Neave, the family patriarch of 'An Ideal Family', whose industrious habits have not been inherited by his son Harold. There is the domestic work of the Burnell women in 'At the Bay'. The recurrence of this theme of labour in *The Garden Party and Other Stories* suggests strongly that Mansfield harboured a burgeoning interest in the issue, and it perhaps points to a direction that she might have continued to follow in her fiction had she lived. In the rest of this chapter, I want to examine such representations of work in three stories in particular: 'Life of Ma Parker', 'An Ideal Family' and 'The Lady's Maid'. I choose these stories because they all have a distinctive element above and beyond merely presenting scenes in which people work: they each place that labour in the context of a biographical narrative, one whose scope exists in a tension with the short story form in which Mansfield inscribes it. The narrative technique of each of these stories is slightly different from the others, and I propose Mansfield is, in a nascent way, reaching for new narrative models to represent different kinds of lives from that typically presented in the Western *Bildungsroman*, that is, lives characterized by relentless toil.

Labour and Mansfield's narrative technique

To conceive of Mansfield as being a writer of labour requires us to adjust slightly our usual view of her. The current popular narrative of Mansfield imagines her as a modernist trailblazer, an image that is intertwined with her unconventional and bohemian lifestyle. Such an image can sometimes obscure her commitment to social issues and how they might be represented in fiction. We can see an instance of such a commitment in Mansfield's *other* negative review of a Virginia Woolf book. Mansfield scholars are very familiar with the unenthusiastic assessment of *Night and Day* published in the *Athenaeum* in 1919, as well as her accompanying letters to John Middleton Murry on the topic of the novel. However, Mansfield would deliver a similar, albeit entirely private, verdict on *Monday or Tuesday*, Woolf's collection of short stories published by the Hogarth Press in 1921. Writing to the author Sylvia Lynd in September of that year, Mansfield records the following opinion of the book:

> I've only just read Virginia Woolf's Monday or Tuesday stories. I didn't care for them. They're detached from life – it won't do – will it? Nothing grows. It's not even cut flowers, but flower heads in flat dishes. I don't think one can 'scrap' form like that. In fact I suspect novelty *as* novelty – don't you.[4]

Mansfield had ceased writing her regular book reviews for the *Athenaeum* at this point so this assessment never entered the public sphere, and this section on *Monday or Tuesday* is not a major portion of the letter – it is merely a passing comment. Nonetheless, it is an intriguing observation when compared to those earlier remarks on *Night and Day*. These two bodies of commentary have some similarities: both raise objections that concern the formal qualities of the texts, and both agree that the book in question is 'dead' when it should really be alive. These similarities are particularly surprising in light of the radical differences between these two texts. For all its virtues, *Night and Day* possesses a fairly conventional narrative structure, and it accords with our sense both of the development of British literary modernism and of the temperament of Mansfield that she should have found it wanting. However, the stories compiled in *Monday or Tuesday* are very different; they demonstrate Woolf's commitment to experimenting with the possibilities of narrative prose discourse, and to testing techniques that would become instrumental to her subsequent masterpieces of the 1920s. Such a work might seem far more likely to be Mansfield's cup of tea than was *Night and Day*, especially since she had very favourably reviewed the *Monday or Tuesday* story 'Kew Gardens' when it first appeared in 1918.[5] However, her specific objection to the forms of the stories is in some ways the opposite of her opinion of *Night and Day*; rather than being straitjacketed by the form, as Mansfield felt the earlier novel was, the stories of *Monday or Tuesday* altogether go too far in the other direction.

The letter is a revealing document for Mansfield scholars, because we learn here that her commitment to modernist experimentation was qualified by competing concerns. Innovation *qua* innovation meant nothing to her if it was too 'detached from life'. Such Mansfieldian pronouncements are always a little opaque, since in the epistolary form she is arguably not developing a set of programmatic theories of literature. However, it is probable that she means that the *Monday or Tuesday* stories, as a whole, do too little to represent actual moments in the lived lives of human beings, in spite of Woolf's commitment to that end in her famous essay 'Modern Fiction'.[6] In the absence of such representations, the experimentation is empty and maybe even solipsistic.[7]

I raise these issues of form and content because they provide an interesting context to Mansfield's literary work at the time. She was steadily writing fiction in late 1921 when she composed this letter to Lynd, and she had already produced many of the works that would be included in her last collection. These stories are, of course, very much not 'detached from life', and even the most experimental story of the lot – the plotless, impressionistic 'Bank Holiday' – is replete with minute observations of human interaction. While the *Monday or Tuesday* stories were concerned with modelling the lived experience of human consciousness (as articulated in Woolf's 'Modern Fiction' essay), Mansfield's work was much more likely to also include a representation of the material conditions of that existence. And for her working-class characters, that commitment means an honest consideration of the effect of human labour.

Mansfield's earlier stories were already scrupulous in their depiction of those individuals who must labour for a living. For instance, as Morag Shiach has observed, there are thematically significant representations of laundry and washing in stories such as 'Pictures' and 'The Man Without a Temperament'.[8] Many of these representations are of domestic servants or of individuals in the working class, but one of Mansfield's most notable labourers is not from these social spheres at all. In 'Prelude' and 'At the Bay' Mrs. Fairfield essentially acts as the primary housekeeper for the Burnell household. In the former story, Mansfield emphasizes the work Mrs. Fairfield performs in setting up the household. Her daughter Beryl draws Stanley Burnell's attention to this labour when he returns from work to his new home for the first time, stating: 'The servant girl and I have simply slaved all day, and ever since mother came she has worked like a horse, too. We have never sat down for a moment. We have had a day.'[9] Beryl's statement, which evokes a defensive response from Stanley, emphasizes the critical role of womens' labour to keep this household functional, even while it simultaneously reinforces class distinctions by denying a name to the servant Alice. In keeping with Beryl's equine analogy, Mrs. Fairfield's relationship to Stanley in this section is entirely instrumental: he gives a couple of commands and she replies: 'Yes, Stanley.'[10] However, when the narration brings us within Mrs. Fairfield's consciousness in the sixth section, we perceive her relationship to labour as being considerably less dehumanizing. With her arms 'bare to the elbow and stained a bright pink' as she washes dishes, Mrs. Fairfield's labour becomes the primary agent of order in the household: 'It was hard to believe that she had not been in that kitchen for years; she was so much a part of it. She put the crocks away with a sure, precise touch, moving leisurely and ample from the stove to the dresser, looking into the pantry and the larder as though there were not an unfamiliar corner.'[11] Here is a more tonally positive vision of Mrs. Fairfield's work. Mansfield generates it by having the narrative perspective move to Mrs. Fairfield in this section; for the first time in 'Prelude', she becomes the focalizing character. Her labour becomes a source of personal pride, and the order she provides comes across as being a magical product of her touch alone. The duality of this portrayal of Mrs. Fairfield's work is of course intentional. By portraying Mrs. Fairfield's labour as being both dehumanizing and yet a source of personal satisfaction, Mansfield encourages the reader to value women's work while at the same time decrying the social conditions that render it as an imperative.

'At the Bay' provides more descriptions of Mrs. Fairfield at work. For instance, she helps Stanley get ready for the morning commute, and once again takes orders from him.[12] She also apparently helps to look after the baby overnight, while also being the primary caregiver for the other children. Such depictions have implications for the issue of literary form. Sydney Janet Kaplan has read 'Prelude' in particular as a reconceptualization of the *Bildungsroman*, one in which the phases of a woman's life are represented simultaneously, rather than consecutively.[13] Bearing this observation in mind, the period of old age and widowhood exemplified by Mrs. Fairfield is revealed to be a time of labour, one in which women must continue to toil in order to make themselves useful to the household and in exchange for continued safety and lodging.

Writing the labouring life in *The Garden Party and Other Stories*

There are many other problematic episodes of labour, in every sense of the word, in the 'Prelude'/'At the Bay' sequence: Beryl's labour in service to the household, the servant Alice, Linda's difficult pregnancies, Jonathan Trout's feelings of entrapment in his own job and so on.

However, I rush through these familiar instances of the Burnell stories in order to talk in more detail about the less acclaimed stories 'Life of Ma Parker', 'An Ideal Family' and 'The Lady's Maid'. I group these three as a sort of triptych because I think they have a couple of significant elements in common with each other. First, they do not depict labour so much as they depict a labouring *life* and the effect that that labour has had upon the life narrative of a character. For instance, in 'An Ideal Family', we do not actually see Old Mr Neave doing any of the work that has enabled his family to live a life of upper-middle-class comfort, but we do see the consequences of that labour upon both him and his family. Secondly, in each of these three stories, Mansfield juxtaposes representations of labour with images of extreme idleness. The labourers are in close contact with characters whose lives of languor are facilitated by the toiling subjects of the stories: the literary gentleman in 'Life of Ma Parker', the son Harold in 'An Ideal Family' and the lady whom the 'The Lady's Maid' serves. The contrast between these pairs of characters helps to set these labouring lives in stark relief; Mansfield heightens the tragedy of these life stories by reminding us of the trivialities that these years of work have enabled.

We might add another, extra-textual commonality between the three stories, which is that each of the three has generally been dismissed in the critical discourse on Mansfield, in no small part, I think, because of the close proximity in *The Garden Party* collection of such familiar Mansfield masterpieces as 'Daughters of the Late Colonel', 'Miss Brill', 'At the Bay' and the title story. Mansfield was working at great speed on many of the stories written in that 1921 period. Indeed, one might describe them as being workmanlike, and such an appellation might not have displeased her. In her letters of the period, she often discusses her work ethic and occasionally fantasizes about living arrangements that would maximize it. '[John Middleton Murry] and I live like two small timetables', Mansfield wrote to Ottoline Morrell on 24 July 1921. 'We work all the morning and from tea to supper.'[14] There are many people for whom living like timetables would not feel like a satisfactory state of affairs, but Mansfield clearly means it in an approbative sense. The most palpable explanation for her focus on her own work ethic is her declining health, and the feeling that she had to make the most of the time that remained to her.[15] I would not challenge such an explanation, but I would append to it one perhaps unprovable speculation: that this foreknowledge that her death might be soon and its consequent effect on her work habits led Mansfield to become more interested in exploring the relationship between labour and life narrative. The composition of these three similarly themed stories within eight months of each other in the period 1920–1 suggests that such issues were much on her mind; indeed, 'An Ideal Family' was completed only two days before the aforementioned letter to Morrell.

Of these three stories, it is 'Life of Ma Parker' that most obviously announces that close relationship between labour and narrative, through its title of course, but also through the circumstances of its narrative in which the title character reflects upon her life after the funeral of her grandson. As the narrative indicates, that life has been filled with both spiritual and physical agony, agony that has been the product of her labouring, both as a mother – seven of her thirteen children have died and most of the others have left her – and as a charwoman. Mansfield does not diminish that physical dimension of Ma Parker's pain: 'To take off her boots or to put them on was an agony to her, but it had been an agony for years. In fact, she was so accustomed to the pain that her face was drawn and screwed up ready for the twinge before she'd so much as untied the laces.'[16] The deteriorated state of her physical body is a palpable product of the life she has led, which is revealed through a series of short narrative flashbacks that, in Joanna Kokot's words, 'disturb the border between the real and imagined, the actual and remembered, the present and the past'.[17] This disturbance is not just an avant-garde literary effect; it is also connected to the regularity of Ma Parker's labour; she does the same work every week at the literary gentleman's house (and presumably every day at the house of others). Under such monotonous labouring conditions, time collapses.[18]

In the narrative present, the movement of the story is in three phases. First, there is Ma Parker's apprehension of her life of labour. While she performs her chores at the literary gentleman's house, she reflects upon the vicissitudes of her working life: '"Yes", she thought as the broom knocked, "what with one thing and another, I've had my share, I've had a hard life"'.[19] In this passage, the disassociation of the sound of the broom from any sort of agency – the broom seems to be knocking by itself rather than because she is sweeping with it – is not accidental. Mansfield achieves a similar effect later in the story, where she interrupts Ma Parker's mournful contemplation of her life with a catalogue of the various chores she is performing:

> Then young Maudie went wrong and took her sister Alice with her; the two boys emigrimated, and young Jim went to India with the army, and Ethel, the youngest, married a good-for-nothing little waiter who died of ulcers the year little Lennie was born. And now little Lennie – my grandson. . . .
>
> The piles of dirty cups, dirty dishes, were washed and dried. The ink-black knives were cleaned with a piece of potato and finished off with a piece of cork. The table was scrubbed, and the dresser and the sink that had sardine tails swimming in it. . . .
>
> He'd never been a strong child – never from the first.[20]

Mansfield's narrative voice shifts from the free indirect discourse of the biographical paragraph to the passive voice to describe Ma Parker's chores, and then back again to free indirect discourse for the subsequent paragraph about the fate of Lennie. The shift in voice models the unconscious way in which Ma Parker performs her tasks, and in doing so achieves a literary representation of something like Marx's theory of alienated labour.[21] Her disassociation from her work is so complete that her narrative grammatically detaches her from its completion.

Ma Parker's contemplation of her biography is followed by the second phase of the story: a search for some meaning in her suffering and that of her grandson Lennie: 'Why must it all have happened to me? she wondered. "What have

I done?" said old Ma Parker, "What have I done?"' (296). The search for meaning in human suffering is of course an ancient literary trope, but the answers given by other writers, whether positive (such as in Dostoevsky) or negative (such as in the Book of Job), are absent in this story. There is not only no rational answer to this question in 'Life of Ma Parker' but also no value in even asking the question; it doesn't lead to any kind of self-awareness as it does, say, in Thomas Hardy's poem 'Hap'. The only response Ma Parker can muster is pure affect: she feels the horror of it all, and wants to have a good cry. This then is the third phase of the story, the need for pathos. But it's a need that's unmet, for there is no place she can go to for that good cry. The final line of the story is a statement of existential despair: 'There was nowhere.'[22]

Mansfield identifies the gentleman whose life of ease has been facilitated by Ma Parker's housekeeping as being a literary gentleman. Why such specificity when none is needed? As Lorna Sage says, the literary gentleman is disengaged from life, when Ma Parker's story should be the sort of thing he should be narrating.[23] And Susan Lohafer suggests that the gentleman may well be a stand-in for Mansfield's deficient husband, John Middleton Murry.[24] Perhaps, but I propose that Mansfield's indictment is focused less upon the individual and more upon the modes of literary expression he embodies. The narrator tells us that 'occasionally he laid aside his tomes and lent an ear, at least, to this product called Life'.[25] The word 'tomes' suggests books that are both lengthy and archaic, two adjectives that are antithetical to Mansfield's fiction. And the logic of the sentence juxtaposes 'tomes' to 'Life', a logic that is furthered by the sound of the word 'tomes', which is almost homonymic to 'tombs'. This identification of the literary man with the sort of literature that Mansfield most definitely does not write suggests that 'Life of Ma Parker' seeks to criticize outmoded literary forms and their ability to represent human lives. Part of the work of the conventional biography or *Bildungsroman* is to present some sort of structure to the sort of questions Ma Parker is asking. And if it fails to answer those questions or lead readers to some sort of self-awareness, it at least provides them an opportunity to have a good cry about it and get it out of their system. But such cold comforts are unavailable to Ma Parker whose life of labour can generate neither meaning nor pathos for her. She is denied the cathartic solace of her own story. For Charles Ferrall, 'Life of Ma Parker' is an example of Mansfield's inability 'to represent [the working] class except in ways that largely reproduce popular genres or the conventions of nineteenth-century realism'.[26] However, I would argue that Mansfield's innovation is principally formal rather than generic: she makes the case for the modernist short story as a more promising vehicle for representing a life narrative than lengthy prose fiction. The story itself might operate as a bit of a tearjerker, but in doing so it knowingly emphasizes the artificiality of those narratives that jerk our tears in such a way and reveal their inattention to the material conditions of the suffering subject.

'Life of Ma Parker' then is a life narrative that undermines the formal conventions of life narrative. Another story of labour in *The Garden Party*, 'The Lady's Maid' is similarly resistant to such conventions. It is also an experimental story, told by a first-person narrator, Ellen, in such a way that it implies a dialogue between her and a guest at the lady's house. Mansfield omits the other half of the dialogue, which achieves two effects: it implicitly places the reader within the story by having Ellen respond to the usual silent questions we bring to any new text, and secondly it reverses the conventional situation of social literary fiction in which servants are silent. Here, Ellen gets the chance to speak. Her story is very similar to Ma Parker's inasmuch as she has performed a lifetime of labour supporting the comfortable lifestyle of a person of a higher social class, a lifestyle whose easiness starkly contrasts with her own. And as with 'Life of Ma Parker', Mansfield once again undoes the expectations of a *Bildungsroman* narrative. This deconstruction is particularly present in her description of her courtship by Harry, a courtship that ends when she realizes she cannot leave her lady to manage without her. The moment is very similar to that which takes place at the conclusion of Joyce's 'Eveline'. Both stories construct a conventional romantic life narrative – a courtship from a handsome lad offering an escape from a restrictive domestic situation – only to demolish it when the protagonist refuses to take the romantic option. Just as 'Eveline' leaves the title character suspended and motionless, so too in 'The Lady's Maid' we get this moment of separation:

> 'Take them all back,' I said, 'it's all over. I'm not going to marry you,' I said, 'I can't leave my lady'. [...] I had to slam the door, and there I stood, all of a tremble, till I knew he had gone. When I opened the door – believe me or not, madam – that man *was* gone! I ran out into the road just as I was, in my apron and my house-shoes, and there I stayed in the middle of the road . . . staring. People must have laughed if they saw me. . . .[27]

Standing in the middle of the road in her house shoes staring, Ellen becomes a Joycean image of paralysis. And, just as 'Life of Ma Parker' keeps from its protagonist any hope of intellectual or emotional closure, so too does 'The Lady's Maid'. The concluding paragraph of the story presents this heartbreaking admission:

> . . . Oh dear, I sometimes think . . . whatever should I do if anything were to . . . But, there, thinking's no good to any one – is it, madam? Thinking won't help. Not that I do it often. And if ever I do I pull myself up sharp, 'Now, then, Ellen. At it again – you silly girl! If you can't find anything better to do than to start thinking! . . .'[28]

Ellen denies herself even the ability that Ma Parker has to at least contemplate her fate. And as in 'Life of Ma Parker', the narrative voice of this story has implications for this life of labour. The first-person narration allows Ellen to articulate her own voice, but it also reminds us that she can never stop inhabiting her professional role. The reader never gets to perceive Ellen's actual thoughts, only what she tells to her unnamed interlocutor. And so Ellen's concluding confession of her self-denial of thought within the story has a complement within the narrative discourse itself, which also denies her the ability to think. It is significant, then, that the title of the story is 'The Lady's Maid' and not 'Ellen' or something similar. The very title of the story demonstrates her inability to escape her professional role.

'An Ideal Family' differs from the previous two stories in that its protagonist, Old Mr. Neave, is not a domestic servant; his labour has propelled him firmly into the bourgeoisie. However, as with the other two stories, that labour facilitates the leisure of others, his family and specifically his handsome and indolent son Harold, to whom Mansfield has rather impishly given the name of her own father. Old Mr. Neave's labour has apparently been unrelenting, and has not left him time for anything other than his office work. His family entreats him to take more time off or to take up hobbies, but he is dismissive of the idea:

> Where would Lola and her sisters and Charlotte be if he'd gone in for hobbies, he'd like to know? Hobbies couldn't pay for the town house and the seaside bungalow, and their horses, and their gold, and the sixty-guinea gramophone in the music-room for them to dance to.[29]

Old Mr. Neave has characteristics both of Mrs. Fairfield (they share the appellation 'old') and of Stanley Burnell; indeed, with his stick that he brandishes, his compulsion to work and his distanced relationship with his female family, he seems to be what Stanley might be like in another twenty years.

Unlike Stanley, Old Mr. Neave seems distantly aware of an existential crisis about the meaning of his labouring life. This crisis is expressed through a dream in which he sees a version of a Sisyphean journey on an endless staircase. At first this figure is distinctly human and is ascending the staircase: 'And somewhere at the back of everything he was watching a little withered ancient man climbing up endless flights of stairs. Who was he?'[30] Falling asleep in his room later in the story, Old Mr. Neave returns to the dream:

> And now that little ancient fellow was climbing down endless flights that led to a glittering, gay dining-room. What legs he had! They were like a spider's – thin, withered. [...]
>
> Down, down went the little old spider, and then, to his horror, old Mr. Neave saw him slip past the dining-room and make for the porch, the dark drive, the carriage gates, the office. Stop him, stop him, somebody![31]

The increasingly arachnoidal figure that appears in Old Mr. Neave's dream is now descending rather than ascending, a journey that culminates in a return to the office where he has presumably spent most of his life. Unlike Ma Parker's consideration of her own life, Old Mr. Neave's biographical narrative is completely allegorical. However, as with those of Ma Parker and of Ellen, the story resists finding any kind of meaning for Old Mr. Neave. He is left with a sense of disassociation from his own life: 'What had all this to do with him – [...] Life had passed him by.'[32] In spite of the class differences between him and Ma Parker and the discrepancy between their degrees of autonomy, their lives of labour have caused them to experience a similar sense of dislocation.

Mansfield's depictions of labour in *The Garden Party and Other Stories* are characterized by sympathy and sensitivity. They are aware of the dignity of work, but also the tragedy of human lives that are wasted by it. It is little wonder then that in the worldwide economic depression and subsequent slow recovery of the 1930s that the BBC might look to Mansfield's stories and their sympathetic portrayals of working-class lives. These explorations of the relationship between labour and life narrative in *The Garden Party and Other Stories* anticipate directions in British culture of the 1920s and 1930s, which moves away from a Copperfieldian model of a *Bildungsroman*, and towards more realistic portrayals of working-class lives such as those in Walter Greenwood's *Love on the Dole*. But if Mansfield's explorations of the relationship between labour and life narrative demonstrate a burgeoning awareness of social inequity and exploitation, they also evince something altogether more personal. We can see in them what she expressed in letters to Murry in late 1922 as she joined the Gurdijeff community at Fontainebleau. Mansfield's 10 November letter to her husband asserts her belief that 'one can, through work, escape from falsity & be true to ones own self – not to what anyone else on earth thinks one is.'[33] Here, she expresses the same awareness she relates in *The Garden Party* stories: a cognizance of the ontological importance of labour for one's self, a knowledge that work is an essential constituent element of a life well-lived.

Notes

1 The most recent version of the *Norton Anthology of English Literature* selects 'The Garden Party' and 'The Daughters of the Late Colonel' as the representative Katherine Mansfield stories.

2 I am indebted to Professor Janet Wilson of the University of Northampton for drawing these broadcasts to my attention.

3 For instance, in his essay 'Katherine Mansfield and the Fictions of Continental Europe', in *Katherine Mansfield and Continental Europe*, eds Janka Kascakova and Gerri Kimber (Basingstoke: Palgrave Macmillan, 2015), pp. 236–49, C. K. Stead writes that 'Life of Ma Parker' is 'worthy in intent but artistically inauthentic' (p. 236). Likewise, in *Reading for Storyness: Preclosure Theory, Empirical Poetics and Culture in the Short Story* (Baltimore: Johns Hopkins University Press, 2003), Susan Lohafer writes that '"Life of Ma Parker" is an unabashed tearjerker. [… T]he emotional bribery is so patent, the assault on pity so bald, it's hard not to dismiss this story as an embarrassing lapse, one of quite a number of stories in which Mansfield's tougher insights and cooler ironies fail to control her sentimentality. The story is dissipated in the emotive response, which is triggered too simply and spent too quickly' (p. 72).

4 *Letters* 4, p. 285.

5 In the *Athenaeum*, 13 June 1919. Collected in *Katherine Mansfield: Novels and Novelists*, ed. John Middleton Murry (New York: Knopf, 1930), pp. 36–7.

6 Published in *The Common Reader* (New York: Harcourt, 1984), pp. 146–54.

7 This observation helps explain the exception of 'Kew Gardens' which, setting aside the question of influence, is the most Mansfieldian story in the collection with its sequence of human interactions.

8 Morag Shiach, *Modernism, Labour and Selfhood in British Literature and Culture, 1890–1930* (Cambridge: Cambridge University Press, 2004), pp. 89–91. Shiach also cites Mansfield's later story 'The Doll's House' (1922) as an example of this commitment.

9 CW2, p. 63.

10 CW2, pp. 62–3.

11 CW2, p. 69.

12 CW2, p. 347.

13 Sydney Janet Kaplan, *Katherine Mansfield and the Origins of Modernist Fiction* (Ithaca: Cornell University Press, 1991), p. 117.

14 *Letters* 4, p. 252.

15 Mansfield had this sense of her mortality at a very young age. For instance, in an early 1909 letter to an unknown recipient, she writes that 'I do not think that I shall live a long time – Heaven knows I *look* well enough […] but I am not at all well – my heart is all wrong. […] So that is the reason I want to get so much into a

short time' (*Letters* 1, p. 94). Gerri Kimber argues in '"That Pole outside our door": Floryan Sobieniowski and Katherine Mansfield' that the addressee of this letter was Ida Baker. In *Katherine Mansfield and Continental Europe*, eds Janka Kascakova and Gerri Kimber (Basingstoke: Palgrave Macmillan, 2015), pp. 59–83 (p. 72).

16 CW2, p. 292.

17 Joanna Kokot, 'The Elusiveness of Reality: The Limits of Cognition in Katherine Mansfield's Short Stories', in *Katherine Mansfield and Literary Modernism*, eds Janet Wilson, Gerri Kimber and Susan Reid (London: Bloomsbury, 2011), pp. 67–77 (p. 76).

18 In 'The Art of Work: Katherine Mansfield's Servant and Perception', Maurizia Boscagli observes that 'Mansfield's simultaneously "objective" and "subjective" impressionistic style is undercut by the excess of Ma Parker's suffering, paradoxically amplified by the protagonist's inability to express it'. In *Re-forming World Literature: Katherine Mansfield and the Modernist Short Story*, eds Gerri Kimber and Janet Wilson (Stuttgart: Ibidem-Verlag, 2018), pp. 71–92 (p. 84).

19 CW2, p. 293.

20 CW2, p. 295.

21 Karl Marx, 'Estranged Labor', in *The Economic and Philosophic Manuscripts of 1844*, ed. Dirk J. Struik (New York: International Publishers, 1964), pp. 106–19.

22 CW2, p. 297.

23 Katherine Mansfield, *The Garden Party and Other Stories*, ed. Lorna Sage (London: Penguin, 1997), p. 157n.

24 Susan Lohafer, 'Why the "Life of Ma Parker" Is Not So Simple: Preclosure in Issue-Bound Stories', *Studies in Short Fiction*, 33, no. 4 (Fall 1996): 475–86 (p. 477).

25 CW2, p. 294.

26 Charles Ferrall, 'Katherine Mansfield and the Working Classes', *Journal of New Zealand Literature*, 32, no. 2 (2014): 106–20 (p. 117). Maurizia Boscagli responds to this critique by compellingly arguing that the infusion of sentimentality in this story allows Mansfield to establish a narrative technique that resists the aloofness and distance that typifies modernist praxis (p. 81).

27 CW2, p. 265.

28 Ibid.

29 CW2, p. 318.

30 CW2, p. 320.

31 CW2, p. 321.

32 CW2, p. 321–2.

33 *Letters* 5, p. 320.

14

Here's to you, Miss Moss

Katherine Mansfield's prostitute

Ann Herndon Marshall

Katherine Mansfield's worldliness made an impression on Virginia Woolf who wrote about her 'sharpness and reality – her having knocked about with prostitutes and so on'.[1] Mansfield's wide experience supported her presentation of a woman on the margin of the sex trade in the story 'Pictures'. Her clever, unsentimental treatment of Ada Moss works in counterpoint to portraits of prostitutes by her earnest contemporaries who follow the Victorian tradition of reducing prostitutes to victims of sensational exploitation. An example well known to Mansfield was the work of feminist and socialist W. L. George, who portrayed a prostitute as a valiant heroine overcoming exploitation through hard-won economic independence in *A Bed of Roses* (1911). George made a career of writing and speaking about women as victims of the patriarchal system; the individuality and plausibility of his central characters are consistently sacrificed to his ideological aims. Another friend of Mansfield, Francis Carco, specialized in the demi-monde, but his central aim, revealing the dehumanizing psychology and violence of the Paris underworld, did not include such a well-rounded character as we find in Mansfield's contradictory Miss Moss. Ada Moss is a classically trained singer who seeks work as a film extra, but she never gives up her sense of her superiority, even as she faces the demeaning compromise of prostitution. Carco's Irma, in the novel *Perversity*, is a more familiar type, a doomed victim completely under the sway of a ruthless pimp. Like George, Carco made larger-than-life villains of men who cause the suffering of women in their orbit. It is not the maleness of these writers per se but their political and literary aims that undercut convincing portraits of female prostitutes. Against the background of George's and Carco's prostitutes, it is easier to see Mansfield's success in humanizing hers by avoiding sentimentality and sensationalism.

Her Miss Moss reveals a profound, undervalued feminist truth: all women, prostitutes included, are complex human beings.

Like her contemporaries, Mansfield inherited a long history of literature in which prostitutes were rendered as stylized characters. The prostitute provides comic relief in Restoration drama and displays the wiliness of a picaresque hero in early modern texts like John Cleland's *Fanny Hill*.[2] By the nineteenth century, the 'fallen woman' was often used as a mechanism to expose social ills, especially the unfair limits on female employment. In Elizabeth Gaskell's *Mary Barton* (1848), the fall of Aunt Esther draws attention to an economic system which allowed women few jobs and poor wages if employed in 'respectable' positions. It is probably not until Émile Zola's *Nana* (1880) that a modern writer elevates the prostitute beyond social victimhood. Treated as a window onto sexual psychology, Nana may not be endowed with great depth, but she does show an agency lacking in the stock character of the frail woman of the street.[3]

Mansfield is not alone among twentieth-century authors who aimed for a fresh and complex portrait of a prostitute. Colette and Jean Rhys are two contemporaries of Mansfield who allow agency to their prostitute characters.[4] In *Chéri*, Colette focuses on the courtesan Léa who overcomes a painful separation from her young lover Chéri and retires plump and contented, defying the romantic stereotype of the consumptive, self-sacrificing courtesan.[5] Jean Rhys often portrays women hovering between social classes, and her heroines show an unexpected excitement as they tentatively enter the sex trade. Mansfield's portrayal of Ada Moss, like Jean Rhys's portrait of Anna Morgan in *Voyage in the Dark* (1938), avoids both the reformist agenda and the sensationalism that had served feminist politics since the Victorian era.

Rhys, Mansfield and the excitement of prostitution

Rhys dramatizes the liminal position of prostitutes detached from respectable society or 'unclassed'.[6] She describes her complex feelings towards her first lover and his support of her: 'The whole business of money and sex is mixed up with something very primitive and deep. […] It is once humiliating and exciting.'[7] Rhys expresses an ambivalence startling for readers trained to regard prostitutes simply as victims. Conventional writing about sex workers relies on the sentimentality of which she was wary. In Rhys's early short story 'In a Café', the narrator encounters the lyrics of 'Les Grues de Paris!' The singer praises the prostitute's 'charity, her warm-heartedness, her practical sympathy' and challenges the 'ingratitude that was her requital'.[8] Rhys's narrator examines this conventional image of *grues* (literally 'cranes'): 'The grues are the sellers of illusion of Paris, the frail and sometimes pretty ladies, and Paris is sentimental and indulgent towards them. That, in the mass and theoretically of course, not always practically or to individuals.'[9] The song promotes indulgence without acknowledging individual personhood.

Rhys challenges the *grue* stereotype in another story, 'Tea with an Artist'. The narrator visits a reclusive artist who believes he has found the ideal mate in an ex-prostitute, saying: 'The Fallen are the only women with souls. They will walk on the necks of all the others in Heaven.'[10] When the narrator visits the artist's studio, she is startled by the woman depicted in the paintings: 'Heavy-faced, with big, sturdy peasant's limbs, she was entirely destitute of lightness and grace'.[11] The narrator's assumptions about prostitutes are overturned as she watches 'the big hands' of the woman touch the artist's cheek.[12] The story strives to undo the frail stereotype and celebrates a not entirely new alternative, the tough and capable prostitute, muse to the modern artist.

In *Voyage in the Dark* (1934), a mature novel based on her own early diaries, Rhys undermines assumptions about call girls with her depiction of Anna Morgan, an unusually refined chorus girl adrift in London. When it dawns on Anna she has entered the category of kept woman, she is startled by the unmarked transition, asking 'How did this happen?'[13] She is poised on a threshold she finds exhilarating: 'I am hopeless, resigned, utterly happy. Is that me? I am bad, not good any longer, bad. That has no meaning, absolutely none. Just words. But something about the darkness of the streets has a meaning.'[14] Drawn to the life of the streets, Anna is also a student of prostitute literature. She reads Zola's *Nana*, while her friend, the sexually experienced Maudie, rejects the novel as inauthentic: 'I bet you a man writing about a tart tells a lot of lies one way and another.'[15] Maudie encourages reluctant Anna to 'go off' with a man and introduces her to prospective lovers, but Anna, unlike her practical friend, bases her choices on a need for privacy. She is alienated from an English stepmother, who despises her Caribbean origins, and from other chorus girls who mock her drawling accent. At first sceptical of arrangements with a stockbroker, she capitulates to his sly manoeuvring. He sends his physician to her bedside when she is ill. He even poses as a concerned relative for the benefit of the suspicious landlady. Still, Anna's late-night returns make her too obviously a 'tart', and her dislike of disapproval makes her eager to move into a private apartment supplied by her lover. *Voyage in the Dark* also dramatizes the fear among women of losing respectability by association. For Anna's landlady, a 'tart' threatens her status, and once the landlady assumes Anna is disreputable, there is no hope of altering that perception.

Judith Walkowitz has described the roots of such ostracism in Victorian social policy.[16] Under the Contagious Disease Acts, suspected prostitutes were arrested and forcibly examined for venereal diseases. If found to be infected, they were isolated in 'lock hospitals', disrupting their networks of community support. Despite the rhetoric of inclusion voiced by feminist crusaders, the 'increased social marginality' of prostitutes continued in the twentieth century, long after the repeal of the Acts.[17] Josephine Butler and her cohort stressed 'the casual nature of prostitution as a temporary occupation for women down on their luck'.[18] In campaigning against the Acts, they also publicized heinous cases like that of thirteen-year-old 'Nancy' who made deliveries of washing to a navy garrison for her mother. The innocent child was arrested, roughly examined and left with spinal injuries.[19] Publicity surrounding such narratives hastened the repeal of the Acts but also fuelled a culture of paranoia among working-class women. In the writing of both Rhys and Mansfield, it is the landladies who police the behaviour of unmarried tenants. In the case of Miss Moss from Mansfield's story 'Pictures', the landlady, Mrs. Pine, focuses on tell-tale signs. Details are observed by the chambermaid and conveyed to Mrs. Pine's sister, who regards Ada's laundry habits as handwriting on the wall for a respectable establishment: '[If] she's washing her own wovens and drying them on the towel rail, it's easy to see where the finger's pointing.'[20]

Mansfield examines a privileged woman's charity towards the marginalized woman in 'A Cup of Tea'. Unlike Miss Moss's landlady, the wealthy, upper-class Rosemary Fell attempts to overcome the division between respectable and marginal women by befriending the vagrant Miss Smith: 'After all, why shouldn't you come back with me? We're both women. If I'm the more fortunate, you ought to expect…'.[21] Her rhetoric of sisterhood echoes that of nineteenth-century reformers, but Rosemary is undone in her outreach by her husband's attraction to Miss Smith. The story draws attention to the complexity of sisterhood for haves and have-nots, the first group sheltered by patriarchy, the other a threat to the status quo.

Like Rhys, Mansfield was engaged in the lives of women on the margins. Unlike Rhys, she had not been supported by a wealthy lover, but she did experience the financial benefit of an allowance, her patriarchal lifeline, a dependence that may have lent her insight into the precarious position of women artists who were less fortunate. Furthermore, she had had experience of the Fell/Smith divide as recipient of patronage from Ottoline Morrell. As far as we know,

Mansfield's knowledge of prostitution per se came vicariously, perhaps gathered during her time with Garnet Trowell and the troupe of travelling entertainers known as the Moody-Manners Opera Company, or during her brief stint as a film extra, or as part of her experience of London and Paris life. Virginia Woolf appears envious of Mansfield's worldliness, and Beatrice Campbell recalls her unashamed identification with prostitutes when Mansfield suggested to her they might experience Ottoline Morrell's Bloomsbury home as though they were prostitutes 'in a decent house'.[22] This playful slipping into the role, in this case for amusement, finds a consequential parallel in Mansfield's ironic treatment of Miss Moss in 'Pictures', where Miss Moss, convinced of her own aesthetic superiority, embraces the indignity of sex with a stranger.

In contrast to some literary contemporaries, Mansfield is neither celebrative nor activist nor overtly sympathetic in portraying the situation of Miss Moss. However, she is intimate. By focusing dispassionately on details of her body, she makes Ada Moss feel close at hand, not the distant inhabitant of the demi-monde. Ada's body odour is implied, a signal that makes it, as Gerri Kimber has said, difficult 'to hide her true predicament'.[23] Miss Moss's self-image as an accomplished, college-trained contralto contrasts with her abject 'othering' by the fed-up landlady who snatches her letter when Ada fibs that it contains news of a possible job. Later, she is insulted by a rude taxi driver, ignored by tea-shop employees, put in her place by the 'baby', who questions her attractiveness for 'fill-ums' and finally in the evening of the story's one day, she is enlisted by a John or pimp who desires a 'firm and well-covered' body.[24]

Maurizio Ascari labels 'The Common Round' (1917), the earliest version of 'Pictures', as 'first and foremost a study in the dynamics of capitalist exploitation',[25] but Mansfield's earlier sketch, like her later revisions, has too much playful satire of Miss Moss's predicament to be reduced to a stern critique of capitalism. Like the later versions, the original dialogue sketch begins by satirizing the technique of film flashbacks. Miss Moss considers her uncharacteristic chill: '"It's because I don't have a good hot dinner in the evenings." (Pageant of Good Hot Dinners passes across the ceiling, all of them accompanied by a bottle of Nourishing Stout.)'[26] Mansfield preserves this zany tableau in 'Pictures' making Miss Moss's hunger suggest a movie cliché. The early title, 'The Common Round', injects more irony: Miss Moss does not consider herself common, and that is her *hubris*, a dedication to artistic excellence which we admire, laugh at, and finally cringe at, as we see her being picked up by a stranger.

Miss Moss does not appear a 'natural wanderer' of the sort Deborah Parsons dubs the modern 'flâneuse'.[27] However, she does behave as a typical city-dweller coaxed by the stream of city life and mobilized by her need for employment. Urbanist Richard Sennett explains how street planning and architecture spur modern city dwellers into motion.[28] Ada Moss makes her way in pursuit of work, stopping briefly at the ABC tea shop with 'one and thrippence' in her vanity bag.[29] She walks unfed through a patriarchal world, clinging to the hope that one of the phantom impresarios who hide behind unsympathetic clerks will cast her, but like her name, Ada Moss, she is old-fashioned and ill-suited to the new industry that features the gamine. Poverty pushes her to make a transition from singer to actress or film extra and finally lady of the evening, yet it is important to highlight Mansfield's wry and knowing approach to her artist character. At a time when other writers are championing fallen women without irony to convey a social message, or to put forth a new and daring urban realism, Mansfield follows neither course. In fact, she seems to react against ideas of both the prostitute heroine and the anti-heroine associated with two male writers who were her friends, W. L. George and Francis Carco.

W. L. George's feminist treatment of a prostitute

W. L. George began his career as an activist and journalist publishing *Labour and Housing at Port Sunlight* (1909), a favourable critique of the Lever brothers' planned community. Established in London before Katherine Mansfield and Middleton Murry made their mark, George frequently invited young writers to his 'at-homes' in St. John's Wood. At one of those, he introduced Murry to Mansfield. At the time of that gathering, George was already well known for his bestselling novel *A Bed of Roses* (1911), a defence of an alluring young widow who tries to find respectable work, but who must ultimately resort to prostitution. Unlike Mansfield's 'Pictures', George's tale of a prostitute is partly a pretext to examine contemporary labour issues. The novel's success with a general audience, including men, probably stemmed from its attention to the exploited heroine's physical charm. He defends the prostitute, as do his nineteenth-century reformist predecessors, but with a difference – George's heroine is indomitable, her raven-haired beauty only marred by too strong a chin, perhaps the outward sign of a feminist soul. When beautiful Victoria Fulton returns from India as a poor army widow, she determines her own course through innate intelligence, toughness and the patronage of a lover who dies, conveniently leaving her a house in St. John's Wood.

Victoria is not attracted to men, a detail suggesting George knew something of the performative aspect of prostitution, but men are frequently attracted to her. When she takes a job as housekeeper, the young man of the family is so smitten that his parents feel they must sack her. She finds employment as a waitress, ending up at 'the PRR', a low-end version of the ABC tea shops.[30] Victoria's intelligence attracts a mentor there who has her read Marx and Nietzsche, so she acquires his socialist world view. In the spirit of reform, she even makes an attempt to organize three sex workers, having them to lunch at her house.[31] As she moves from waitress to prostitute to householder, Victoria loses touch with her confidante Betty; theirs is the novel's only sentimental love story. They had spent Sundays in parks and visiting picture galleries: 'When they parted in the evening, Victoria kissed her affectionately. Betty would then hold the older woman in her arms, hungrily almost, and softly kiss her again.'[32] Though never a prostitute, Betty falls lower than one when she becomes the house-slave of an abusive husband.[33]

George's novel exposes the exploitation of women from tea-shop waitresses to streetwalkers to wives, and in that respect aligns itself with feminist projects of the past. *A Bed of Roses* takes its title from a passage in *Mrs. Warren's Profession* (1893), but unlike Shaw's 'New Woman' drama, George's novel shows its heroine triumph over society.[34] As her first employer's son pines away, Victoria makes a speech at his deathbed to his mother: 'Your Society waved before my eyes the lily-white banner of purity, while it fed me and treated me like a dog', a 'Society of men, crushing, grinding down women, sweating their labour, starving their brains'.[35] This feminist warrior eventually leaves London, buys a home in the country and gains the notice of the 'Squire of Cumberleigh'.

Mansfield certainly knew George and probably this triumphal novel that launched his career as a popular novelist and flamboyant speaker. Though its scenes of sexual arousal are subdued in comparison to those of *Lady Chatterley's Lover* (1928), *A Bed of Roses* received praise for both daring and seriousness. The Modern Library printed it in faux-leather binding while cheap editions were stocked in shops next to men's sexual-performance-enhancing damaroids.[36] By 1915, Mansfield's respect for George had faded. She once enjoyed his impudence but grew to resent his audacity when it played out as 'pro-Germanics' during the First World War.[37] Meanwhile, George gained fame for his much-publicized talks on feminism. One detail that suggests Mansfield may actually have read *A Bed of Roses* is the varicose veins that afflict both Victoria and Mansfield's Miss Moss: '[Victoria Fulton's legs] were covered with a network of veins, some narrow and pale blue in colour, others darker, protruding and swollen.'[38]

Mansfield includes a similar description in 'Pictures': 'Sitting on the side of the bed, furious and shivering, [Ada Moss] stared at her fat white legs with their great knots of greeny-blue veins.'[39] The more telling point, however, is how different the characters are. While George focuses on Victoria's forceful character and her triumph, Mansfield focuses on the indignities suffered by a destitute artist.

Francis Carco's sensational prostitute

Among the Paris stories of Jean Rhys is a satirical portrait of an American who considers herself sophisticated because she has read the novels of Francis Carco, 'which tell of the apaches of to-day'.[40] At the other extreme from George's *A Bed of Roses* with its uber-woman is Carco's novel *Perversité* (1925). His sensational story of Irma exposes 'the beastly backside of the world'.[41] Carco focuses on cruelty, not heroism. *Perversité* was published after Mansfield's death, but Carco's interest in the psychology of prostitutes appears to have been life long, dominating his screenplays as well. Carco and his fascination with the Parisian underworld, as Mansfield revealed, was one inspiration for the character of Duquette, the 'friend' and gigolo who narrates Mansfield's story 'Je ne parle pas français'. Duquette's Iago-like acuity shows the extent to which Mansfield could enter the imaginative space of seasoned prostitutes and pimps. Carco's friendship with Mansfield goes back to her time in France when she followed him to the army zone in Gray in 1915 and later made use of his Paris apartment, on the Quai aux Fleurs, near Notre Dame.

In *Perversité*, the prostitute Irma has a live-in pimp – Bébert – who takes a plausible dislike to her passive brother Emile. Bébert sets about disciplining Emile with a knife, sadistically cutting him but holding back from killing him. Emile does not consider leaving the house where he lives with Irma nor does Irma. Emile is given to perversity himself: 'It was a long time since he had heard Irma cry, and in spite of himself he was filled with pleasure and excitement'; he 'told himself that now he was not the only one to be ill-treated by Bébert'.[42] Throughout his trials, Irma is perversely attached to her pimp, the 'abject, hard-hearted, insensible' man.[43]

In her story 'Pictures', Mansfield does not feature the gritty content of Carco any more than the romantic feminism of George; however, there is a Carco-like touch in the appearance of the 'stout gentleman' who picks up Miss Moss at the Café de Madrid.[44] Miss Moss's stout man is distinguished by 'a very small hat that floated on the top of his head like a little yacht',[45] and in Mansfield's earlier dramatic sketch, it is 'a very small felt hat'.[46] This man is a Parisian type as much as a London one. In Carco's novel, Bébert has a stout friend and fellow-pimp, Bouboule (French for 'Butterball'), who sports a felt Cronstadt hat and, unlike the thuggish Bébert, is capable of politeness: '[Emile] considered Bouboule's pink silk shirt, his cuffs with metal studs, his ridiculous Cronstadt hat with great annoyance, and thought him a self-satisfied and most unpleasant person.'[47] Because Emile has been reluctant to have sex at a bordello, Bébert punishes him with a 'violent kick'.[48] Bouboule defends Bébert's bad temper: 'He concluded with formal ceremony, his Cronstadt hat in his hand: "We others, Madame, we have savoir-vivre."'[49]

Urban thresholds: The transition of Miss Moss

It is the self-satisfied *savoir-vivre* of a similar stout, be-hatted gentleman in 'Pictures' that intervenes in the life of Miss Moss. His directness comes across as comic irony: 'Miss Moss, to her surprise, gave a loud snigger.'[50] His proposition followed by her reaction may surprise readers lulled by Miss Moss's ladylike persona. Her distaste at the obvious assaults on her dignity by 'Cheeky' girls and a noisy taxi driver, 'Look out, Fattie; don't go to sleep!',[51] may not prepare us for the man's eventual success: 'The stout gentleman considered her, drumming with his fingers on the table. "I like 'em firm and well covered," said he.'[52] That sentence was added to the dialogue when Mansfield turned her dramatic sketch into a story in *Arts and Letters* in 1919.[53] Previously, Ada's 'snigger' followed on the discussion of her 'tempting' pink ribbon, a juxtaposition that leaves her some coy modesty. In the revision, Mansfield grants her greater participation in the encounter to which she consents:

> Five minutes later the stout gentleman heaved himself up.
> 'Well, am I goin' your way, or are you comin' mine?' he asked.
> 'I'll come with you, if it's all the same,' said Miss Moss. And she sailed after the little yacht out of the café.[54]

The story's ironic arc depends on the imagery of Ada's uncovered and covered body. The stout gentleman's preference for a 'firm and well covered' body takes the reader back to Ada's initial shame over a compromised nightdress, which kept her from getting out of bed and grabbing the contested letter. The nightdress 'slit down the back' contrasts with the 'buttoned bodice' of her antagonist, the landlady. At the end, clothing is again revealing. The nautical metonymy of the stout man's hat, or 'little yacht', rescues Miss Moss from her earlier 'sinking', the hunger she experiences in the morning when she walks the city with her nightdress under respectable dress, and shakily observes an image of her own desperation, 'an old brown cat without a tail' lapping up spilt milk.[55]

Ada's flamboyant rescue fantasy before the stout man enters the café reveals a remarkable confidence in her talent given her unemployment:

> 'A dark handsome gentleman in a fur coat comes in with a friend, and sits at my table, perhaps. "No, old chap, I've searched London for a contralto and I can't find a soul. You see, the music is difficult; have a look at it."' And Miss Moss heard herself saying: 'Excuse me, I happen to be a contralto, and I have sung that part many times . . . .' Extraordinary! "Come back to my studio and I'll try your voice now."'[56]

The man in the small hat is quite a comedown from the imagined 'handsome gentleman in a fur coat'. The fantasy rescuer recalls the portrait of Oscar Wilde dressed in similar fashion. The fin-de-siècle imagery is consistent with a woman decked out with 'artificial "parmas" at her bosom, a black hat covered with purple pansies',[57] whose ancient powder puff turns her nose mauve. Ironically, opportunity lies instead with a very different sort of 'gentleman', but Miss Moss maintains the poise of a veteran performer as she accepts the stout man's offer.

Although Miss Moss bends under pressure from her landlady and the repeated cattle calls, the capitalist system is not the obvious villain it is in George's novel, nor is Miss Moss a feisty feminist like Victoria Fulton. Her own stout body covered in sensible blue serge, she also lacks the *jolie laide* glamour of Carco's sexy Irma, sensational prey to a vicious pimp. The end of 'Pictures' is intentionally abrupt giving nothing away about the 'stout gentleman' except for his unceremonious proposition: 'Well, am I goin' your way, or are you comin' mine?' The match is made with the singsong rhythm of a reply that echoes the invitation, as though the pair were performing together a music-hall song: 'I'll come with you if it's all the same'.[58]

Both George and Carco had probably been *with* prostitutes, but they had never *been* prostitutes. Rhys, on the other hand, understood the complex experience of pairing money and sex. Likewise, Mansfield in 'Pictures' portrays the peculiar humiliation and excitement of a complicit woman. As she sails out of the café, Miss Moss has found not just a stay against hunger but also a temporary elegance implicit in the image of the 'little yacht' on a stout man's head.

When Freud describes 'famous symbols', he adds 'Why hats and cloaks should have been turned to the same use [as snakes] is certainly difficult to discover, but their symbolic meaning leaves no room for doubt.'[59] Whether phallic or not, the man's hat is an image Ada Moss finds reassuring, a daring aspect of the story that Mansfield accentuates with her revisions in the final version of 'Pictures'.

Readers may be surprised by how quickly Miss Moss complies with the man's invitation and then wonder if it is her first such encounter. Like Rhys's refined characters who 'tread a thin line between the status of friend, mistress, and prostitute in their dealings with men', Mansfield's Miss Moss complicates the idea of the 'streetwalker'.[60] Parsons explains that Sasha Jensen from Rhys's *Goodnight, Midnight* finds a 'new self-awareness [revealed in] mockery at the pathos of her position'.[61] There is a similar mocking tone in the narration of 'Pictures'. After a final rejection at the Bitter Orange Company, Miss Moss screws up her courage, 'I might just have a stroke of luck' in the Café de Madrid, but her residual optimism is contradicted by the pictures she sees in her mirror. Like the glass in her bedroom, her pocket mirror mocks her: 'But the person in the pocket mirror made a hideous face at her, and that was too much for Miss Moss; she had a good cry.'[62] The repeated mirror trick, like the initial food tableau, has the character of a silent movie special effect or even Dorian Gray's hidden portrait registering his grim decline.

Miss Moss is not laughing at herself but crying to herself. In the final scene her giggle may be only a reflexive accommodation to the man's aggression.[63] Miss Moss giggles as she is picked up by a stranger who reduces her to the qualities of furniture, 'firm and well-covered'. The scenario might be less disturbing if Miss Moss registered the statement as an insult, but instead she reacts to it as a benign transaction. The stranger's stated preference reflects the avoidance of intimate contact that urbanists ascribe to the modern city. Modern cities are designed to keep people in motion and discourage sociability,[64] so that 'the individual body lacks physical awareness of other human beings'.[65] Richard Sennett gives an account of the nineteenth-century innovation of easy chairs by the French upholsterer who called them '*confortables*'.[66] In highlighting Miss Moss's upholstered appearance, the stout man reflects the individualistic pursuit of comfort without contact.

Like Rhys's heroines, Mansfield's Miss Moss behaves in a way that defies expectations for someone of her class and education. As she frequently insists, she has the advantages of music college credentials. She does not resemble the romantic heroine of *La Dame aux Camélias* nor her operatic counterparts. As a contralto, the female equivalent of male counter-tenor, she occupies a different range more compatible with her tragicomedy. Readers begin by laughing at her hunger displayed in cinematic tableau.[67] They are not prepared to justify her as a wronged *grue*. Still, her landlady's ultimatum hangs over Miss Moss as she follows the man from the café. The man's desire for a 'covered' woman has particular irony as readers think back to the buttoned-up landlady, a representative of propriety, whom Miss Moss, in her snobbery, dehumanizes as a 'cockroach'. Ada enters the café still in imaginary conflict with Mrs. Pine: 'Why shouldn't I go to the Café de Madrid? I'm a respectable woman – I'm a contralto singer, And I'm only trembling because I've had nothing to eat today. . . .'. She echoes the voice of her landlady: 'A nice little piece of evidence, *my lady*.'[68] Her landlady's 'sepulchral' voice intoning 'my lady' still haunts her from the morning's struggle.[69] Ironically, Miss Moss's surrender is the fulfilment of Mrs. Pine's prophecy previously tied to laundry habits. If we join with a prophetic landlady in condemning Miss Moss's arrogance, we side against a woman whose artistic aspiration garners sympathy despite her class snobbery. Mansfield does not provide a simple cautionary tale for women who pursue careers in the arts. At the same time, the suggestion of that cautionary tale would have been funny to bohemian women like Mansfield and her peers at *The New Age* where Miss Moss made her debut. They too perhaps had wrangled with landladies.

Finally, Sydney Janet Kaplan's observation about Mansfield's 'feminist insights' is apt: that Mansfield 'did not articulate her social critique of human suffering in recognisably political terms'.[70] By not playing for sympathy nor overly dramatizing Ada Moss's troubles, 'Pictures' avoids reducing its character to a pitiable *grue* or her story to a Marxist-feminist commentary of the sort W. L. George made into a career. Miss Moss's independence from ideological colouring offers room for eccentricity. As a believer in her own artistic gifts, Ada Moss is a quixotic figure, more memorable than the militant Victoria Fulton in *A Bed of Roses*, or her glamorously doomed counterpart, Irma, in Carco's *Perversité*. Like Jean Rhys's Anna, excited on the threshold of prostitution, the case of Miss Moss does not advocate for reform. If there is a whiff of ideology about her, it is her old-fashioned faith in art. That belief comically underlies her compromise at the Café de Madrid. By attaching jaunty imagery and music-hall stylization to Miss Moss's prostitution, Mansfield continues the disturbance begun with the peculiar nightdress 'slit down the back' and reinforces the risky proposition that prostitution dwells just the other side of an artistic vocation which fails to provide a hot meal.

Notes

1. Letter 2418: to Vita Sackville-West, Saturday [8 August 1931], in *Congenial Spirits: The Selected Letters of Virginia Woolf*, ed. Joanne Trautmann Banks (New York: Harvest, 1989), p. 293. In this letter, Woolf admits to envy: 'I think her sharpness and reality – her having knocked about with prostitutes and so on, whereas I had always been respectable – was the thing I wanted then.'
2. John Cleland, *Memoirs of a Woman of Pleasure* (Oxford: Oxford University Press, 2008 [1748]).
3. Nana exemplifies scientific naturalism. Zola writes of her coy resistance: 'A pack of hounds after the bitch who is not even in heat and makes fun of the hounds following.' Quoted by Jill Warren in 'Zola's View of Prostitution in *Nana*', in *The Image of the Prostitute in Modern Literature*, eds Pierre L. Horn and Mary Beth Pringle (New York: Frederick Ungar Publishing Co., 1984), pp. 29–51 (p. 32).
4. Mary Lou Emery also sees in Rhys's work 'a reconceptualizing of the subject beyond victimization'. *Jean Rhys at 'World's End': Novels of Colonial and Sexual Exile* (Austin: University of Texas Press, 1990), p. 32.
5. Léa's outcome contrasts with the sentimental sacrifice of *La Dame aux Camélias* (1848) by Alexandre Dumas, *fils*.
6. George Gissing's writing on the 'unclassed' includes his idealistic male protagonists and the prostitute they befriend: they all 'dwell in a limbo external to society'. *The Unclassed* (London: Chapman and Hall, 1884), p. vi.
7. Rhys illustrates her conflict: a lawyer's letterhead infuriates her, yet an allowance, when delivered by her lover's nephew, brings the security of childhood, in *Smile Please: An Unfinished Autobiography* (New York: Harper and Row, 1975), pp. 97–8.
8. Jean Rhys, *The Collected Short Stories* (New York: Norton, 1987), p. 14.
9. Ibid., p. 14.
10. Ibid., p. 30.
11. Ibid., p. 32.
12. Ibid., p. 33.
13. Jean Rhys, *The Complete Novels* (New York: Norton, 1985), p. 24.
14. Ibid., p. 35.
15. Ibid., pp. 4–5.
16. Judith R. Walkowitz, *Prostitution and Victorian Society: Women, Class, and the State* (Cambridge: Cambridge University Press, 1980).
17. Despite Butler's activism, for the first time, English 'working-class prostitutes were transformed into a specially identified professional class' (Walkowitz, p. 210).
18. Walkowitz, p. 111.
19. Leigh Denton, 'Josephine Butler', in 'Dangerous Women Project', Institute of Advanced Studies in the Humanities, University of Edinburgh, http://dangerouswomenproject.org/2016/11/14/josephine-butler/ (accessed 29 April 2019).

20 CW2, p. 179.

21 CW2, p. 464.

22 'Katherine and I found ourselves wandering round the large drawing-room [...], and she said softly to me, "Do you feel that we are two prostitutes and that this is the first time we have ever been in a decent house?"' in Beatrice (Campbell) Lady Glenavy, *Today We Will Only Gossip* (London: Constable, 1964), p. 80.

23 Gerri Kimber, *Katherine Mansfield and the Art of the Short Story* (London: Palgrave Macmillan, 2015), p. 18.

24 CW2, p. 185.

25 Maurizio Ascari, *Cinema and the Imagination in Mansfield's Writing* (New York: Palgrave Macmillan, 2014), p. 47. He emphasizes a pro-labour thread in *The New Age*, 31 May 1917, in which Mansfield's sketch first appeared, p. 48.

26 CW2, p. 36.

27 Deborah L. Parsons, *Streetwalking the Metropolis* (Oxford: Oxford University Press, 2003), p. 131.

28 Richard Sennett, *Flesh and Stone: The Body and the City in Western Civilization* (New York: Norton, 1992), especially Chapter 8, 'Moving Bodies', and Chapter 9, 'The Body Set Free', pp. 256–316.

29 CW2, p. 18.

30 At the ABC Miss Moss gets the cold shoulder from a waitress who shows off a pin from her soldier son. Ada Moss is an outsider to the wartime pride of the working-class mother.

31 The youngest makes a claim for her pimp's good intentions, enraging two veteran prostitutes.

32 W. L. George, *A Bed of Roses* (London: Frank Palmer, 1911), p. 164.

33 One day, Victoria's train happens to pass Betty's tenement, and she bestows some of her fortune on her old friend.

34 George uses a quotation from Shaw's character Mrs. Warren as an epigraph: 'It's not work that any woman would do for pleasure, goodness knows; though to hear the pious people talk you would suppose it was a bed of roses.'

35 George, p. 376.

36 George's publisher Alec Waugh describes the novel's placement with damaroids on store shelves to illustrate the way the book's serious aims were undermined by its sensational subject matter. 'W. L. George', in *My Brother Evelyn, and Other Portraits* (New York: Farrar, Straus, and Giroux, 1968), pp. 105–14 (p. 106).

37 See my 'Turning the Table', in *Katherine Mansfield and the Bloomsbury Group*, ed. Todd Martin (New York: Bloomsbury Academic, 2017), pp. 125–41.

38 George, p. 185.

39 CW2, p. 179.

40 'Tout Montparnasse and a Lady', eventually published in *The Left Bank* (1927). See Rhys, pp. 16–19 (p. 17).

41 Angela Carter points to an irony: 'Those women who see most of the beastly backside of the world – prostitutes – are least in a position to utilise this invaluable experience as art.' 'Colette', *London Review of Books*, vol. 2, no. 19 (October 1980): 15–17 (p. 15).
42 Francis Carco, *Perversity*, trans. Jean Rhys (Berkeley: Creative Arts, 1987 [1928]), p. 60.
43 Ibid.
44 CW2, p. 184.
45 Ibid.
46 CW2, p. 41.
47 Carco, p. 33. Bouboule reveals a sinister history when he tells of Montreal where he married women in order to lure them across the US border and exploit them as prostitutes.
48 Carco, p. 49.
49 Ibid.
50 CW2, p. 185.
51 CW2, p. 181.
52 CW2, p. 185.
53 This second version was entitled 'The Pictures' and appeared in *Arts and Letters*, 2, no. 4 (Autumn 1919): 153–62.
54 Mansfield, p. 162.
55 CW2, p. 180.
56 CW2, p. 184.
57 CW2, p. 180.
58 CW2, p. 185.
59 Sigmund Freud, 'X. Symbolism in the Dream', Paragraph 17 in Part Two: 'The Dream', in *A General Introduction to Psychoanalysis*, trans. G. Stanley Hall (New York: Boni and Liveright, 1920), https://www.bartleby.com/283/10.html (accessed 28 April 2019).
60 Parsons, p. 146.
61 Parsons observes Sasha's self-awareness: 'She can assert some identity by being aware of her situation and mocking it'; see Parsons, pp. 132–3.
62 CW2, pp. 183–4.
63 Raymond W. Gibbs Jr., Patrawat Samermit and Christopher R. Karzmark summarize the 'benign violations theory of humor': 'Humor responses, including certain laughs or smiles [...] communicate that a potential threat is not a concern.' 'Humor, Irony, and the Body,' *Review of Cognitive Linguistics*, 16, no. 1 (May 2018): pp. 72–96 (p. 76).
64 Sennett, p. 343. He cites trains where rows of well-upholstered seats replaced sociable compartments.

65 Sennett, p. 23.

66 Sennett, p. 340.

67 There were popular stage productions of *Camille* and film adaptations of *La Dame aux Camélias* during the years when Mansfield conceived Miss Moss.

68 CW2, p. 184.

69 CW2, p. 179. In *Voyage in the Dark,* Rhys's Anna finds her stepmother's propriety irksome: 'A lady – some words have a long, thin neck that you'd like to strangle.' Rhys, *Complete Novels,* p. 86.

70 Sydney Janet Kaplan, *Katherine Mansfield and the Origins of Modernist Fiction* (Ithaca and London: Cornell University Press, 1991), p. 17.

Bibliography

Key works by Katherine Mansfield

The Edinburgh Edition of the Collected Works of Katherine Mansfield: Vols 1 and 2 – *The Collected Fiction*, eds Gerri Kimber and Vincent O'Sullivan (Edinburgh: Edinburgh University Press, 2012).

The Edinburgh Edition of the Collected Works of Katherine Mansfield: Vol. 3 – *The Poetry and Critical Writings*, eds Gerri Kimber and Angela Smith (Edinburgh: Edinburgh University Press, 2014).

The Edinburgh Edition of the Collected Works of Katherine Mansfield: Vol. 4 – *The Diaries of Katherine Mansfield, including Miscellaneous Works*, eds Gerri Kimber and Claire Davison (Edinburgh: Edinburgh University Press, 2016).

The Collected Letters of Katherine Mansfield, 5 vols, eds Vincent O'Sullivan and Margaret Scott (Oxford: Clarendon Press, 1984–2008).

The Collected Poems of Katherine Mansfield, eds Gerri Kimber and Claire Davison (Edinburgh: Edinburgh University Press, 2016).

The Katherine Mansfield Notebooks, 2 vols, ed. Margaret Scott (Minneapolis: University of Minnesota Press, 2002).

Selected bibliography

Addyman, Mary, '"All else is vain, but eating is real": Gustatory Bodies', in *Food, Drink and the Written Word in Britain, 1820–1945*, eds Mary Addyman, Laura Wood and Christopher Yiannitsaros (London: Routledge, 2017), pp. 207–20.

Alpers, Antony, *The Life of Katherine Mansfield* (Oxford: Oxford University Press, 1980).

Anderson, Sherwood, *Sherwood Anderson's Memoirs* (New York: Harcourt, Brace and Company, 1942).

Ascari, Maurizio, *Cinema and the Imagination in Mansfield's Writing* (New York: Palgrave Macmillan, 2014).

Auerbach, Erich, 'The Brown Stocking, on Woolf and Proust', in *Mimesis: The Representation of Reality in Western Literature*, trans. Willard R. Trask (Princeton: Princeton University Press, 1953), pp. 525–33.

Baker, Ida, *Katherine Mansfield: The Memories of LM* (London: Michael Joseph, 1971).

Beach, Sylvia, *Shakespeare and Company* (London: Faber and Faber, 1956).

Blavatsky, H. P., *The Secret Doctrine, Vol. Two: Anthropogenesis* (London: The Theosophical Publishing Company, 1888).

Boehmer, Elleke, *Postcolonial Poetics: 21st-Century Critical Readings* (Basingstoke: Palgrave Macmillan, 2018).

Bomberger, E. Douglas, *MacDowell* (Oxford: Oxford University Press, 2013).

Bongie, Chris, *Friends and Enemies: The Scribal Politics of Post/ Colonial Literature* (Liverpool: Liverpool University Press, 2008).

Boscagli, Maurizia, 'The Art of Work: Katherine Mansfield's Servant and Perception', in *Re-forming World Literature: Katherine Mansfield and the Modernist Short Story*, eds Gerri Kimber and Janet Wilson (Stuttgart: Ibidem-Verlag, 2018), pp. 71–92.

Bourdieu, Pierre, *Language and Symbolic Power*, ed. John B. Thompson, trans. Gino Raymond and Matthew Adamson (Cambridge: Polity Press, 1991).

Briganti, Chiara, 'Giving the Mundane Its Due: One (Fine) Day in the Life of the Everyday', *ESC: English Studies in Canada*, 39, no. 2–3 (June/September 2013): 161–80.

Buell, Lawrence, *The Future of Environmental Criticism: Environmental Crisis and Literary Imagination* (Oxford: Blackwell, 2005).

Campbell, Thomas, *Gertrude of Wyoming; a Pennsylvanian Tale* (London: Longman, Hurst, Rees, and Orme, 1809).

Cave, Terence, *Thinking with Literature: Towards a Cognitive Criticism* (Oxford: Oxford University Press, 2016).

Deleuze, Gilles, *Difference and Repetition*, trans. Paul Patton (New York: Columbia University Press, 1994).

Diment, Galya, Gerri Kimber and Todd Martin, eds, *Katherine Mansfield and Russia* (Edinburgh: Edinburgh University Press, 2017).

Dodd, Nigel, *The Social Life of Money* (New Haven: Princeton University Press, 2014).

Donaldson, Laura E., *Decolonizing Feminisms: Race, Gender and Empire-Building* (Chapel Hill: University of North Carolina Press, 1992).

Dupuis, Michel and Paulette Michel, eds, *The Fine Instrument: Essays on Katherine Mansfield*, eds Paulette Michel and Michel Dupuis (Sydney: Dangaroo Press, 1989).

Eagleton, Terry, Fredric Jameson and Edward Said, eds, *Nationalism, Colonialism, and Literature* (Minneapolis: University of Minnesota Press, 1990).

Emery, Mary Lou, *Jean Rhys at 'World's End': Novels of Colonial and Sexual Exile* (Austin: University of Texas Press, 1990).

Felski, Rita, *The Limits of Critique* (Chicago: University of Chicago Press, 2015).

Ferrall, Charles, 'Katherine Mansfield and the Working Classes', *Journal of New Zealand Literature*, 32, no. 2 (2014): 106–20.

Ferrall, Charles and Jane Stafford, eds, *Katherine Mansfield's Men* (Wellington: Katherine Mansfield Birthplace Society, 2004).

Finn, Margot C., *The Character of Credit: Personal Debt in English Culture, 1740–1914* (Cambridge: Cambridge University Press, 2003).

Fishkin, Shelley Fisher and Elaine Hodges, eds, *Listening to Silences: New Essays in Feminist Criticism* (Oxford: Oxford University Press, 1994).

Flint, F. S., 'Imagisme', *Poetry*, 1, no. 6 (March 1913).
Fordham, John, *James Hanley: Modernism and the Working Class* (Cardiff: University of Wales Press, 2002).
Forth, Aiden, *Barbed-Wire Imperialism: Britain's Empire of Camps, 1876–1903* (Berkeley: University of California Press, 2017).
Froula, Christine, Gerri Kimber and Todd Martin, eds, *Katherine Mansfield and Virginia Woolf* (Edinburgh: Edinburgh University Press, 2018).
Fullbrook, Kate, *Katherine Mansfield* (Brighton: Harvester Press, 1986).
Gagnier, Regenia, 'Economic Women in Their Time, Our Time and the Future', in *Economic Women: Essays on Desire and Dispossession*, eds Lana L. Dalley and Jill Rappoport (Columbus: Ohio State University Press, 2013), pp. 219–24.
Gibbons, Luke, *Joyce's Ghosts: Ireland, Modernism and Memory* (Chicago: University of Chicago Press, 2015).
Gillies, Mary Ann, *Henri Bergson and British Modernism* (Montreal: McGill-Queen's University Press, 1996).
Glenavy, Lady Beatrice (Campbell), *Today We Will Only Gossip* (London: Constable, 1964).
Glenn, Cheryl, *Unspoken: A Rhetoric of Silence* (Carbondale: Southern Illinois University Press, 2004).
Gordimer, Nadine, *Telling Times: Writing and Living 1950–2008* (London: Bloomsbury, 2011).
Graeber, David, *Debt: The First 500 Years* (London: Melville House, 2011).
Graf, Fritz and Sarah Iles Johnston, *Ritual Texts for the Afterlife: Orpheus and the Bacchic Gold Tablets*, 2nd edn (New York: Routledge, 2013).
Graves, Robert, *The Greek Myths: Complete and Unabridged Edition in One Volume* (Mt. Kisco: Moyer Bell Limited, 1960).
Gunn, Kirsty, *My Katherine Mansfield Project* (Devon: Notting Hill Editions, 2015).
Gurr, Andrew, 'Katherine Mansfield: The Question of Perspectives in Commonwealth Literature', *Kunapipi*, 6, no. 2 (1984): 67–80.
Hammond, Meghan Marie, *Empathy and the Psychology of Literary Modernism* (Edinburgh: Edinburgh University Press, 2014).
Hankin, Cherry, *Katherine Mansfield and Her Confessional Stories* (London: Macmillan, 1983).
Hanson, Clare, *Re-reading the Short Story* (Basingstoke: Macmillan, 1989).
Hanson, Clare, Gerri Kimber and Todd Martin, eds, *Katherine Mansfield and Psychology* (Edinburgh: Edinburgh University Press, 2016).
Harrison, Jane Ellen, *Prolegomena to the Study of Greek Religion*, 2nd edn (Cambridge: Cambridge University Press, 1908).
Hastings, Beatrice, *The Old New Age: Orage and Others* (London: Blue Moon Press, 1936).
Head, Dominic, *The Modernist Short Story: A Study in Theory and Practice* (Cambridge: Cambridge University Press, 1992).
Huxley, Aldous, *The Perennial Philosophy* (New York: Harper & Brothers, 1945).

Jameson, Fredric, *Postmodernism, or the Cultural Logic of Late Capitalism* (London: Verso, 1999).

Jones, Kathleen, *Katherine Mansfield: The Story-Teller* (Edinburgh: Edinburgh University Press, 2010).

Kaplan, Sydney Janet, *Katherine Mansfield and the Origins of Modernist Fiction* (Ithaca and London: Cornell University Press, 1991).

Kimber, Gerri, *Katherine Mansfield and the Art of the Short Story* (Basingstoke: Palgrave Macmillan, 2015).

Kimber, Gerri, '"That Pole outside our door": Floryan Sobieniowski and Katherine Mansfield', in *Katherine Mansfield and Continental Europe: Connections and Influences*, eds Janka Kascakova and Gerri Kimber (Basingstoke: Palgrave Macmillan, 2015), pp. 59–83.

Kokot, Joanna, 'The Elusiveness of Reality: The Limits of Cognition in Katherine Mansfield's Short Stories', in *Katherine Mansfield and Literary Modernism*, eds Janet Wilson, Gerri Kimber, and Susan Reid (London: Bloomsbury, 2011).

Korte, Barbara, 'The Femme Fragile: Decline and Fall of a Literary Topos', *Anglia*, 105, no. 3/4 (1987): 366–89.

Larkin, Philip, *Letters to Monica*, ed. Anthony Thwaite (London: Faber & Faber, 2010).

Li, Yiyun, *Dear Friend, from My Life I Write to You in Your Life* (London: Penguin Random House, 2017).

Lohafer, Susan, *Reading for Storyness: Preclosure Theory, Empirical Poetics and Culture in the Short Story* (Baltimore: Johns Hopkins University Press, 2003).

Mantz, Ruth Elvish and John Middleton Murry, *The Life of Katherine Mansfield* (London: Constable, 1933).

Martin, Todd, ed., *Katherine Mansfield and the Bloomsbury Group* (London and New York: Bloomsbury Academic, 2017).

Marx, Karl, *The Economic and Philosophic Manuscripts of 1844*, ed. Dirk J. Struik (New York: International Publishers, 1964).

McDonnell, Jenny, *Katherine Mansfield and the Modernist Marketplace: At the Mercy of the Public* (Basingstoke: Palgrave Macmillan, 2010).

Miller, Tyrus, *Late Modernism: Politics, Fiction, and the Arts between the World Wars* (Berkley: University of California Press, 1999).

Morrisson, Mark S., *The Public Face of Modernism: Little Magazines, Audiences and Reception, 1905–1920* (Wisconsin: University of Wisconsin Press, 2001).

Morrow, Patrick D., *Katherine Mansfield's Fiction* (Ohio: The Popular Press, 1993).

Olsen, Tillie, *Silences* (London: Virago, 1980).

Orage, A. R., 'Talks with Katherine Mansfield', *Century Magazine*, November 1924, pp. 36–40.

Orage, A. R., 'What Is Man?', *Theosophical Review*, 39, no. 231 (November 1906): 237–42.

Parsons, Deborah L., *Streetwalking the Metropolis* (Oxford: Oxford University Press, 2003).

Pilkington, Adrian, *Poetic Effects* (Amsterdam: John Benjamins, 2000).
Pratt, Anne, *Flowers and their Associations* (London: Charles Knight and Co., 1840).
Rault, Jasmine, *Eileen Gray and the Design of Sapphic Modernity: Staying In* (Abingdon: Routledge, 2016).
Rhys, Jean, *Smile Please: An Unfinished Autobiography* (New York: Harper and Row, 1975).
Rowe, Aimee Carrillo and Sheena Malhotra, eds, *Silence, Feminism, Power: Reflections at the Edges of Sound* (London: Palgrave Macmillan, 2013).
Sage, Lorna, *Moments of Truth: Twelve Twentieth-Century Women Writers* (London: Fourth Estate, 2002).
Sanders, Lisa Shapiro, *Consuming Fantasies: Labor, Leisure and the London Shopgirl 1880–1920* (Columbus: Ohio State University Press, 2006).
Schuchard, Ronald, *The Last Minstrels: Yeats and the Revival of the Bardic Arts* (Oxford: Oxford University Press, 2008).
Seabrook, Jeremy, *Pauperland: Poverty and the Poor in Britain* (London: Hurst & Co., 2013).
Selver, Paul, *Orage and the New Age Circle* (London: George Allen & Unwin, 1959).
Sennett, Richard, *Flesh and Stone: The Body and the City in Western Civilization* (New York: Norton, 1992).
Seshagiri, Urmila, *Race and the Modernist Imagination* (Cornell: Cornell University Press, 2010), pp. 127–39.
Shen, Dan, *Style and Rhetoric of Short Narrative Fiction: Covert Progressions Behind Overt Plots* (New York: Routledge, 2014).
Shiach, Morag, *Modernism, Labour and Selfhood in British Literature and Culture, 1890–1930* (Cambridge: Cambridge University Press, 2004).
Smith, Angela, *Katherine Mansfield: A Literary Life* (Basingstoke: Palgrave, 1991).
Spark, Muriel, *A Far Cry from Kensington* (London: Constable, 1988).
Sperber, Dan and Deirdre Wilson, *Relevance: Communication and Cognition*, 2nd edn (Oxford: Blackwell, 1995).
Stafford, Jane and Mark Williams, *Maoriland: New Zealand Literature 1872–1914* (Wellington: Victoria University Press, 2006).
Stead, C. K., *Answering to the Language: Essays on Modern Writers* (Auckland: University of Auckland Press, 1989).
Taylor, Paul Beekman, *Gurdjieff and Orage: Brothers in Elysium* (York Beach: Weiser Books, 2001).
Toner, Anne, *Ellipsis in English Literature* (Cambridge: Cambridge University Press, 2015).
Walkowitz, Judith R., *Prostitution and Victorian Society: Women, Class, and the State* (Cambridge: Cambridge University Press, 1980).
Warren, Jill, 'Zola's View of Prostitution in *Nana*', in *The Image of the Prostitute in Modern Literature*, eds Pierre L. Horn and Mary Beth Pringle (New York: Frederick Ungar Publishing Co., 1984), pp. 29–51.
Wenk, Arthur, *Claude Debussy and the Poets* (Berkeley: University of California Press, 1976).

Woolf, Virginia, *The Common Reader* (New York: Harcourt, Brace and Company, 1925).

Woolf, Virginia, *The Death of the Moth and Other Essays* (London: Hogarth Press, 1945).

Yeats, W. B., *Essays and Introductions* (London: Macmillan, 1961).

Zambreno, Kate, *Heroines* (South Pasadena: Semiotext(e), 2012).

Zupancic, Alenka, *Why Psychoanalysis?: Three Interventions* (Uppsala: Nordic Summer University Press, 2008).

Index

Lightning Source UK Ltd.
Milton Keynes UK
UKHW022009210720
366928UK00003B/105